R

AF718808

Predictive Sentencing

KF
9715
P7
1976

for L.C
7-6-76

Predictive Sentencing

An Empirical Evaluation

LAW LIBRARY
GOLDEN GATE UNIVERSITY

Leo H. Whinery
University of Oklahoma

Thomas J. Nagy
University of California, Berkeley

Gregory A. Sather
University of Oklahoma

Kaye D. Fisher
City of Norman, Oklahoma

Lexington Books
D.C. Heath and Company
Lexington, Massachusetts
Toronto

Library of Congress Cataloging in Publication Data

Main entry under title:

Predictive sentencing.

Bibliography: p.
Includes index.
1. Sentences (Criminal procedure)—United States. 2. Juvenile courts—United States. 3. Traffic violations—United States. I. Whinery, Leo H., 1926-
KF9715.P7 345'.73'077 75-3
ISBN 0-669-99333-6

Copyright © 1976 by D.C. Heath and Company.

All rights reserved. No part of this publication may be reproduced or transmitted in any form or by any means, electronic or mechanical, including photocopy, recording, or any information storage or retrieval system, without permission in writing from the publisher.

Published simultaneously in Canada.

Printed in the United States of America.

International Standard Book Number: 0-669-99333-6

Library of Congress Catalog Card Number: 75-3

77-1-290

Contents

List of Figures

List of Tables

Foreword

Predictive Sentencing: An Empirical Evaluation is of immediate practical value to the more effective sentencing of the repeated traffic offender. But its significance is larger than that, much larger. The book describes one of the few serious attempts at principled sentencing of any type of criminal and has many lessons for all who wish to deal rationally and effectively with crime.

The task would seem so simple: subject roughly similar groups of offenders—as similar as practicable—to diverse treatments or punishments. Measure carefully which sentences "work," in terms of later recidivism, assessed by the frequency and gravity of later crimes, with which subtypes of offenders. From these data make predictions that link offender types and types of punishments. Then, apply these predictions to another cohort of similar offenders so that the optimum sentence for each offender category will be tested, validated, and refined. And so we will move from speculation and prejudice to knowledge and effectiveness. This seven-year study does nothing to disprove the wisdom of that course. If anything, it supports it; but it does show, in the moving squalors of life, how difficult it is to realize that simple progression. The world does not stand still for the researcher; from research design to validated knowledge is no small step.

In the long run only by these hard and long empirical processes can we move to rational sentencing. That they prove difficult and protracted merely underlines both the need and its urgency. Professor Whinery and his group are pathfinders over a difficult and extensive terrain.

What is so impressive about this study is its utter and precise honesty, its meticulous accuracy in a field characterized too often by the unsubstantiated claims, and the simplistic remedy. Professor Whinery and his colleagues have not only shown us the path to principled sentencing, they have done so with a rigorous methodological integrity that is admirable.

For the time being, we are told, until our knowledge of effective sentencing with a due respect for human rights is much advanced, "the judge, in sentencing, should concern himself more with reinforcing society's moral condemnation of the conduct in which the offender has engaged than with more complicated preventative sentencing techniques." But within this over-arching limitation of the "deserved" punishment, this study gives some useful clues on how to achieve a more parsimonious and effective punishing system.

All who are interested in traffic offenses will find this a necessary book, as will all serious scholars of the criminal justice system.

Norval Morris
Dean and Professor of Law
and Criminology
University of Chicago
Law School

Preface

It is now seven years since I first went to the University of Oklahoma Research Institute (now the Office of Research Administration) to suggest a small project I had in mind for both the sentencing of youthful offenders and assessing the effects of the sentences on their subsequent behavior. I would also have (perhaps) left the Institute as quickly as I arrived if anyone had even hinted at that time that I would become involved in a sentencing and research effort that would extend over a seven-year period and ultimately involve eight Oklahoma communities. Neither I, nor my coauthors, had any idea of the magnitude of the project, the problems associated with its administration, or the difficulties inherent in engaging in social action research in the courts and their sentencing processes. Yet, even with these complexities, the project team has now concluded its work. We have completed an official report for our funding agencies, published by the University of Oklahoma Office of Research Administration, which contains a complete description of the project. This report, *Predictive Sentencing of 16-18 Year Old Male Habitual Traffic Offenders*, is in three volumes. Volume I, The Study, contains a detailed description of the methodology, results, conclusions, and implications of the research. Volume II, The Appendices, contains all supporting documentation for the research described in Volume I. Volume III, The Project Manual, contains a complete description of the probationary and research procedures followed.[a]

By contrast, the present work presents a detailed summary of the research and its results unencumbered by the more technical analysis of the official three volume report. Moreover, unlike the official report, this volume explores in more detail the implications of the research, not only for the offenders studied, but for research in the sentencing process throughout the field of criminology. While the official report is intended for researchers, the present volume is written for practitioners, students, and observers of the criminal justice system: judges, lawyers, court administrators, criminologists, probation systems personnel, social scientists, and interested citizens.

By no means have the conclusions derived from this research entirely met our expectations. We have found that predictive sentencing of youthful traffic offenders, while theoretically appealing, has limited practical utility, at least within the context of this experiment. At the same time, the project's controlled experimental design has enabled us to make conclusions concerning the behavior of youthful traffic offenders, the influences in society that significantly affect that behavior, and the conditions that must exist to optimize the value to society of rational sentencing in altering the behavior of these offenders. The research certainly suggests that exaggerated claims of the effectiveness of this or

[a]The three volume official report can be obtained from the Department of Continuing Legal Education, University of Oklahoma Law Center, Norman, Oklahoma 73019.

that treatment modality as a preventative cannot be supported without careful empirical testing and verification. As a correlate, this research demonstrates the need for further research efforts on the effects of sentencing if we are to approach the sentencing process as a preventative, rather than a process that simply reinforces, through the sentence, society's moral condemnation of the conduct in which the offender has engaged.

Moreover, the unexpected finding of the apparent influence-on-treatment effect of economic conditions, as measured by unemployment, suggests that in any future research on the effects of particular types of sentences on particular types of offenders, greater attention should be paid not only to those variables relating to the offender himself but also to variables reflecting the prevailing social conditions, such as unemployment level and confidence in government. Looking to the more immediate practical effects of the project findings on a sentencing judge, the observed result that the innovative treatment in the latter two years of the project was no better than the control group (traffic fine) may suggest that the judge, in sentencing, should concern himself more with reinforcing society's moral condemnation of the conduct in which the offender has engaged than with more complicated preventative sentencing techniques. This philosophical approach to sentencing is perhaps less appealing, but in the last analysis, this essentially retributive justification for punishment may be the only practical approach, given the cost to society of more elaborate sentencing schemes, if no better results can be achieved.

However, this pessimism must be weighed against the strongly demonstrated empirical finding that probationers counseled during times of normal unemployment did significantly better than the control group (traffic fine). This pessimism is further counteracted by the persistence, year after year, of the salutary effect of the innovative treatment.

Finally, accounting for the variables most critical in predicting outcome of particular types of treatment, such as the influence of unemployment, is a formidable enterprise. Nevertheless, the research still suggests that careful presentence screening of habitual misdemeanants appearing in the lower courts, using not only variables that describe the offender himself but also those that describe the social conditions in which he functions, such as economic status, might suggest a treatment most suited to his needs, which, in turn might also reduce the risk to society.

As indicated in the Acknowledgements, a project of the magnitude and duration as this one is dependent upon the talents and assistance of many people. We are especially grateful to John G. Bruhn and Richard E. Hilbert, coinvestigators, in the early stages of the project for their assistance in designing and implementing the sentencing program and, later, to W. Alan Nicewander, coinvestigator, for his expertise and assistance in coping with the multitude of statistical issues involved in designing and testing the sentencing scheme. Maurice K. Temerlin, who also served as a coinvestigator, was of assistance in the preparation of the project's early funding proposals. Saleem A. Shah, Chief of the Center for Studies of Crime and Delinquency of the National Institute of Mental Health and his associate, George H. Weber, now the Acting Deputy Director of the Division of Special Mental Health Programs, have provided welcome leadership and support for the project throughout its long duration, including giving us the opportunity on several occasions to bring project results to the attention of interested observers. The efforts of these loyal and dedicated people and the many others associated with the project have made it possible to complete the project and write this book.

Acknowledgments

A project of the size and duration involved in this study needs the dedicated support of many persons. All personnel, in both the probation and research divisions of the project have worked long hours, frequently under difficult conditions, to bring this project to a conclusion.

In Norman, the project had the assistance of the following counselors in the probation division: Roger Benham, Roy Don Bruner, Ronald Corly, Don M. Holyfield, Roger Housley, Glen Huff, Roy Isenberg, Arthur Marchessault, Earl W. Murphy, Michael L. Reeves, Robert Revenaugh, Gary Stoner, R. Daniel Webster, Bob White, and John B. Wimbish. The following persons assisted in the research division: Betty C. Chandler, James R. Curran, Lorna G. Curran, Linda Dobkins, Patricia Jenkins, Don L. McCombs, Jr., Virginia McCombs, Pierliugi Molajani, Jorge Mendoza, Larry Nicolai, Ron Phillips, Rebecca Smith, and Ron Starr. Secretarial personnel included: Kris Akey, Carol Bates, Pamela H. Berry, Pat J. Blackwood, Lee Douthitt, Jean M. Ezell, Eileen Goodman, Helen Kerr, Nina Meyer, June Moffitt, Becky Rao, Barbara Sears, and Maureen Wells. Judy Simpkins, Clerk of the Municipal Criminal Court of Norman also assisted in the project.

In the expansion of the project into four other Oklahoma regions, the project was supported by Larry H. Kirkland, former Governor's Representative, Oklahoma Highway Safety Programs, and Sandra M. Johnson, former Chief of the Traffic Court Division, Office of the Administrative Director of Oklahoma Courts, and Marian Opala, Administrative Director of Oklahoma Courts. We would also like to thank the following people for their assistance and work in the expansion areas: in Ardmore, Durant, and Madill, Judge James W. Bolt, Judge R.W. Fleak, and Judge Darrel McGuire, Prudence Little and Judy K. Simmons, Clerks, and James C. Brown, William M. Freeman, and Robert Donnel Gwin, Assistant Probation Officers; in Lawton, Judge Bill Hensley, Bill D. Howeth, Clerk, and Charles B. Davis, Ron Fitzpatrick, William J. May, and William Stowell, Assistant Probation Officers; in Ponca City and Blackwell, Judge David Denton, Judge David Garrison, Judge Daniel McClung, and Judge J.F. Raley, Catherine H. Horner, Clerk, and Raymond E. Ham, Glen D. Huff, and Larry Lahman, Assistant Probation Officers; and in Tulsa, Judge Tom Crewson and Judge Hayden Downie, Pam J. Hatcher, Clerk, and Steven J. Anthony, Clarence Gene Brown, Bobby Busby, Peyton James Cook, J. Patrick Cremin, Bruce D. Hiltibrand, Mike McDaniels, William R. Nichols, and Gary W. Wood, Assistant Probation Officers.

We also benefitted from the consultation of: Herbert Costner, University of Washington; Benjamin Fruchter, University of Texas at Austin; Don M. Gottfredson, Rutgers University; Frances Morse; Harvard University; Laura Nelson, Bayview Mental Health Center (San Francisco); Daniel Ogilvie, Rutgers University; Philip J. Stone, Harvard University; Ralph Switzgebel, Harvard University; Paul Takagi, University of California (Berkeley); and Don Tarver, Bayshore Mental Health and Mental Retardation Center.

The special assistance of the following persons who supplied us with needed exogenous data quickly is greatly appreciated: Neil J. Dikeman and Marjorie Earley, University of Oklahoma Center for Economic and Management Research; Billy R. Curry, United States National Weather Service; Don M. Holyfield, Norman, Oklahoma Police Department; and Wolfgang Huber, Mental Health Center, Griffin Memorial Hospital.

The data analyses were performed at the computation centers of the University of Texas at Austin, University of Oklahoma, University of California (Berkeley), and Harvard University. The tables and figures contained in this volume are reprinted from the Final Report, Predictive Sentencing of 16-18 Year Old Male Habitual Traffic Offenders, University of Oklahoma Office of Research Administration (1976), with the permission of the University of Oklahoma.

Finally, we would like to especially acknowledge Charles L. Goff and Ruth Boyd, University of Oklahoma, for their administrative support and assistance and Doris E. Whinery for preparing the manuscript for publication.

The study that forms the basis for this book has been funded by the following agencies, and their support of the study is gratefully acknowledged. However, the views expressed herein are those of the authors and should not be construed to represent the views of or the official position of any of these agencies: National Institute of Mental Health, Center for Studies of Crime and Delinquency (NIMH Grant Numbers 1 RO1 MH17946-01 to 03 and 2 RO1 MH7946-04 and 05); Oklahoma Highway Safety Program, Department of Transportation (DOT Grant Number 7B-74-01); Walter E. Meyer Research Institute of Law; University of Oklahoma Graduate College; University of Oklahoma College of Law; and The City of Norman, Oklahoma.

Part I
The Study

Introduction to Part I

In Part I the rationale of predictively sentencing habitual traffic offenders is examined. How was the study justified, what were its goals, and how were these goals implemented? The data gathering descriptive phase of the project is summarized, the generally favorable Group 2 counseling results are disclosed, and the statistical techniques employed to develop the regression equations are described. The regional cross-validation of the equations in the predictive phase is described, the failure of Group 2 counseling is reported, the anomalous results are disclosed, and the investigators trace the course of their inquiry in an attempt to reconcile and explain these anomalous findings. Their final assessment, that some exogenous factor, such as unemployment, attenuated the Group 2 treatment, is then explained and justified.

1 Rationale

Youthful Traffic Offenders, Major Crimes, and Lower Courts

The magnitude of the traffic problem in the United States today, in terms of personal injury, property damage, and law enforcement activity, suggests a need for a greater understanding of this problem in all of its various facets. One of the most significant variables related to the problem is the automobile driver. It is also significant that a substantial portion of the problem involves drivers under the age of 25 years. Studies involving the young driver, particularly the category of drivers involved in the present study, seem peculiarly important not only in relation to dealing with the traffic problem itself but in coping with some of the major problems involved in crime and delinquency in the United States today.[1]

It is an obvious fact that traffic offenses are more common than any other category of misdemeanor in the United States. It is also obvious that more young people are involved in the commission of traffic offenses than any other offense. Initially, the average "law-abiding" young citizen comes in contact with the traffic laws and their administration more readily than he does with other categories of offenses, both serious and not serious. And, at least among the middle class population, traffic offenses may constitute a prelude to more serious crimes or may frequently be involved in the commission of major crimes. Accordingly, the study of traffic offenses and the treatment of offenders to learn more about the correctional process in relation to youthful traffic offenders provides a useful framework through which the risk of personal injury and property damage created by these offenders might be minimized, graduation to felony crimes might be retarded, and constructive attitudes toward law and order generally might be developed.

An equally obvious fact is the importance of the lower courts in the prevention or deterrence of crime. Here the overwhelming majority of misdemeanants appear and are processed. More often than not the first crime is a traffic offense or involves other petty criminal activity over which the lower courts exercise jurisdiction. It is in these courts, therefore, that potential habitual offenders first come into contact with the law and its sentencing and correctional processes. As argued in the President's Commission on Law Enforcement and Administration of Justice:

> Studies made of the careers of adult offenders regularly show the importance of juvenile delinquency as a forerunner of adult crime. They support the conclu-

sions that the earlier a juvenile is arrested or brought to court for an offense, the more likely he is to carry on criminal activity into adult life; that the more serious the first offense for which a juvenile is arrested, the more likely he is to continue to commit serious crimes, especially in the case of major crimes against property; and that the more frequently and extensively a juvenile is processed by the police, court, and correctional system, the more likely he is to be arrested, charged, convicted, and imprisoned as an adult.

The earlier that attempts are made to prevent further criminal activity, the greater the likelihood of making progress in the prevention of adult crime; and as long as the lower court system is to be involved in the prevention of adult crime, that this process should begin at the lower court level seems almost axiomatic.

Of course, as in the administration of the criminal law generally, just as the fine and imprisonment so frequently fail in the objectives sought by their use, so one would expect to find difficulty in devising other treatment modalities that might be any more efficacious in the correctional process. As two authorities in criminal law have said:

> We can be reasonably certain that no methods of treatment can be devised which will deter all potential offenders or reform all actual offenders or, what is even more difficult, do both at once. We do know, of course, that death and life imprisonment are effective methods of incapacitation. We do not know and may never know with certainty what methods of treatment are most efficacious any method of treatment is.[2]

Yet, even within these obvious limitations, the development of viable correctional programs to deal with youthful offenders constitutes a continuing challenge for a rational system of sentencing.

The Sentencing Dilemma

Unfortunately, the quest for rationality in sentencing is stymied at the outset by the essentially discretionary role in which the judge functions when sentencing and, correspondingly, without the benefit of efficacious sentencing criteria. At most, the sentencing process, unlike the adjudicating process of determining innocence or guilt, largely involves unfettered discretion in the selection of specific sanctions within the predetermined range of legislatively authorized sanctions that can be imposed for the commission of an offense.

In adjudicating innocence or guilt, the judge at least begins with the rule of law—the predetermined major premise in the syllogism of trial containing the types of factual conditions from which legal consequences emanate. In the process of proof, the minor premise of the syllogism is established, namely, whether there has been an occurrence of specific instances of the conditionally relevant factual conditions of the rule of law from which the judge can conclude the innocence or guilt of the person charged. Assuming no dispute as to the substantive law, ideally at least, the problem is simply one of proving the occurrence of particular instances of the more general factual conditions embodied in the rule of law. It is true that there may be a dispute as to the existence, applicability, or interpretation of the rule of law. There may also be a dispute as to the existence of a specific occurrence of the factual conditions of the rule of law. In both cases, however, the decision-making process is guided by statutory and case law precedents and by rules of procedure and evidence. Moreover, the historical nature of the inquiry, even with all its attendant problems, is mainly one of resurrecting the past. Here the evidential processes for judicial decision-making are reasonably well established and, in spite of many limitations, probably produce defensible results. Moreover, the judge who is skilled in the legal process will find his role in adjudicating innocence or guilt generally compatible with his training and skills.

In sentencing, the average judge will find neither the comfort of a precise body of interpretable sentencing standards or a body of knowledge or methodology comparable to that in the law when adjudicating. No longer is he engaged in an essentially historical inquiry involving the behavior of the offender in the past. Nor does he have the comfort of evidence of what occurred in the past to support his adjudicative decision. His concern now is with the behavior of the offender in the future. And because the relation between past and future behavior is not straightforward, evidence of what has occurred in the past is of very little practical use in deciding what the offender might, or might not, do in the future, much less his reaction tomorrow to this or that fine or term of imprisonment the judge might impose today. Finally, the judge of today, perhaps moreso than the judge of a generation ago, surely finds himself far less comfortable in the sentencing process. Advances in psychology, together with the increasing awareness of the effect of changes in social and economic well being on the behavior of people, thrusts the contemporary judge in an alien sentencing environment, one in which he is far less sure of his decision-making role than when involved in adjudication.

Is it any wonder that we concern ourselves with the broad discretion vested in judges in the sentencing process? Why do legislators fail to give guidance to judges by addressing themselves in their legislation to the purpose and function of sentencing? And then, addressing themselves to this issue, why do they fail to develop adequate sentencing criteria and sanctions to implement this policy?[3] Is it any wonder that the sentence of a particular judge on a particular day will reflect his own, rather than society's perception of the justification for punishment? In the last analysis, is it really surprising that we find such large-scale disparity in sentencing, particularly in the lower courts where the range of penalties varies so greatly, not only from state to state but frequently within the confines of a single jurisdiction as well, and without any corresponding criteria for assisting judges in exercising their discretion within the range of authorized sanctions?[4]

Sentencing Policy and Prediction

Rational sentencing depends on sound sentencing policy. And in spite of the obvious difficulties, at least three requirements must be met. First, the sentence (punishment) must be justified. Public intervention, in the form of punishment, into the privacy of an individual through the sentence of a judge focuses attention on the conflict of rights between the right of society to interfere and the right of the individual to be free of interference. This conflict between society and the individual is a moral issue involving correlative rights and duties, and if the state is to exercise its pain-inflicting power over the individual for the welfare of society, it requires explication and justification. All agree on the necessity for the explication and justification of punishment. There is divergence on its rationale.

Of the four principal schools of thought—retribution, rehabilitation, deterrence, and social defense—social defense affords the most appealing rationale for a sentencing policy.[5] First, with social defense the focus is on society and its right to protect itself from those persons dangerous to society. In this respect, social defense is similar to deterrence, which focuses on society as a whole in the sense that by punishing one you deter others. Social defense differs in that it seeks to isolate *individual* potential wrongdoers and minimize their risk to society.

At the same time, social defense does not concern itself with the individual as does retribution and rehabilitation. In retribution, society punishes because the offender has broken the law, while with rehabilitation, the justification is in reforming the offender either through self-reform by the imposition of pain-inflicting measures or by imposing upon him a program of psychological and social therapy. In social defense, the individual is important only insofar as he presents a risk or is dangerous to society.

However, social defense is not exclusive of concern for the individual, since by its very nature it places limitations on the conditions under which interference with the privacy of an individual is justified, namely, to protect society. And by focusing on the individual who is a risk to society, social defense aims at a systematic resocialization of the offender under limited conditions, thereby maximizing the freedom of the individual without corresponding detriment to society. As stated by a leading exponent:

> The intention of social defense is to carry such social protection into effect, quite naturally, by means of a body of measures that . . . are designed to "neutralize" the offender, either by his removal or segregation, or by applying remedial or educational methods.[6]

Second, if punishment is to be justified through resort to social defense, it necessarily follows that intervention must be predicated on a scientific understanding of antisocial behavior and the personality of offenders in relation to that behavior. What are the personality, social, and economic characteristics relating to the offender, and what is the nature of the social milieu in which he functions? What types of risks, or threats, does he pose to the community? Is it in the nature of the social and economic cost involved in the enforcement of the traffic laws? Is it the threat of personal injury and property damage to others through accident involvement? Or, is it the real, or apparent, threat that the youthful traffic offender poses to the community in the commission of felony-grade crimes?

Wise sentencing involves more than simply an understanding of the personality of the offender and the behavior that is deemed undesirable to society as a whole. It also involves an understanding of treatment alternatives calculated to correct that behavior and, more particularly, how different offenders are likely to react to alternative correctional programs. Even then there is no assurance that the treatment will be successful in preventing the behavior deemed dangerous to society.

Third, prediction then becomes a key element in a rational sentencing policy. However, unlike the general prediction employed by the deterrent school, that unless the particular offender is deterred, others in society will commit similar antisocial acts, social defense theory predicts that a particular offender will recidivate unless he is somehow prevented from doing so. Prediction in sentencing involves an extension of this concept. Not only does it involve a prediction of the risk or threat to society by the particular individual involved, but also the judge is seeking to predict the reaction of different types of offenders to different types of treatment modalities posed by the different patterns of response one expects from the range of differences in psychology, knowledge, values, and social and economic status that sets offenders apart in a complex social order.

Ideally, then, prediction could deal effectively with the sentencing ills that beset the lower courts. The use of predictive sentencing models directly associating offender characteristics with treatment modality and with the minimization or prevention of harm would eliminate much of the irrational sentencing that exists in the judicial structure today. And while treatment would be individualized with the particular offender, the resultant disparity would be positive as opposed to the negative disparity derived from the discretionary sentence of the judge. And in many of the lower courts, as a result of burdensome caseloads or the lack of trained personnel, judges ordinarily do not have the luxury of comprehensive presentence reports. Here the use of regression equations or expectancy tables could facilitate a more rationale sentencing process.

The Research Challenge

Unfortunately, each year judges impose roughly two million sentences with little or no objective information on the effect of those sentences on subsequent behavior. Correlating behavior with the characteristics of youthful offenders and the type of treatment they receive seems essential in a rational correctional process, if we are to prevent behavior that is deemed socially undesirable. A prediction, as a sentence, requires an understanding of the type of risk or danger against which society desires to protect itself, the type of treatment or intervention most likely to minimize the risk or danger with the least interference in the life of the offender, and those characteristics of the offender related to treatment effectiveness. Unfortunately, precious little study has been done relative to predictive sentencing and the effects of the sentence on subsequent offender behavior.[7]

If the lower courts fill as important a role in the correctional process, as we contend, correlation of offender characteristics with recidivism is most needed in the lower courts where delinquency often first manifests itself, often in connection with the use of one of the most popular "vehicles" for the expression of antisocial behavior today—the automobile. Attempts at reducing traffic or nontraffic recidivism, or accident involvement, in a probation setting offer perhaps the best opportunity for careful experimental control in determining the effects of sentencing and treatment of youthful offenders. And individuals who appear to hold the potential for becoming habitual offenders present a significant challenge for developing programs that not only attempt to reduce future criminality through probation but at the same time make systematic inquiries into the factors characterizing such offenders and the type of treatment that works best with particular types of offenders in preventing that behavior deemed socially undesirable.

The report that follows represents an empirical evaluation of the concept of predictive sentencing to one type of sentencing strategy in the lower courts, together with its implications. By no means have the conclusions derived from the research entirely met our expectations. We have found that predictive sentencing of youthful traffic offenders, while theoretically appealing, has a practical utility limited by external economic circumstances, at least within the history of this particular experiment. At the same time, the project's controlled experimental design has enabled us to make some observations concerning the behavior of youthful traffic offenders, the influences in society that may have a significant effect on that behavior, and the kinds of conditions that conceivably must exist to optimize the value to society of a predictive sentencing counseling program in altering the behavior of these offenders. The conclusions derived from this work may evoke negative or positive reactions. They may suggest further combined probationary and research efforts with the concept of predictive sentencing. Or they may suggest that the ultimate pay-off is not worth the sentencing and research effort or the financial resources necessary to support that effort to develop effective predictive sentencing models.

Whatever the ultimate assessment may be, the research, or learning, goals of this work seem vitally important. In this sense, ultimately, the offender and his relationship to society is what this work has involved. Ultimately, the purpose is to help the offender understand his own individuality and express himself as he chooses but yet at the same time understand his relationship to society and his responsibility to the community in which he lives, so that others might have that same breadth of freedom he seeks without interference from him. Judges and probation officers can accomplish this only if they are knowledgeable concerning the offender, the treatment most suited to his needs, and the factors affecting the treatment process. We can become knowledgeable only if we are willing to quantify our work in such a way as to achieve measurable results. If it is said we have experimented, the answer is yes. Every sentence imposed on an offender is, in a sense, an experiment. And judges experiment every day in the sentencing process: too many experiment too often without adequate hypotheses based on reliable data. Hopefully, this effort has opened new doors of understanding to the correctional process and the lower court system will be better for the work.

Notes

1. Laurer, A.R., *The Psychology of Driving* (Springfield, Ill.: Charles C. Thomas, 1972); Parry, Meyer H., *Aggression on the Road* (London: Tavistock Publications, 1968), Pelz, Donald C., and Schuman, Stanley H., *Countermeasures for Young Drivers*, University of Michigan Press (1972); and Willett, T.C., *Criminal on the Road* (London: Tavistock Publications, 1964).

2. Michael, Jerome, and Wechsler, Herbert, *Criminal Law and Its Administration* (Chicago: The Foundation Press, 1940), p. 13.

3. An example of such an approach, though by no means intended as a model, will be found in the *Code of City of Norman*, Section 20-214 as follows:

Sec. 20-214. Deferred sentencing for minors.

(a) Persons under eighteen (18) years of age who are convicted of a third violation of this chapter within a twelve (12) month calendar period shall be immediately subject to a presentencing investigation and report prior to the imposition of any penalty.

(b) This presentencing investigation and report shall be conducted by the probation division of the Municipal Criminal Court, shall obtain information regarding the offender's personality, family, and socioeconomic conditions, and shall indicate whether, in the division's opinion, the offender could benefit from probationary counseling.

(c) Upon receipt of the presentencing report, the judge shall impose the applicable penalty, which shall be deferred as hereinafter provided.

(d) The execution of any imposed penalty shall be deferred conditioned upon:

(1) the presentencing report's conclusion that the offender could benefit from probationary counseling; and

(2) the offender participates in no less than twelve (12) nor more than

twenty-four (24) one-hour counseling sessions adapted to his rehabilitative needs, and so arranged that there be no more than one such counseling session per week.

(e) Persons under eighteen (18) years of age who are convicted of more than three (3) violations of this chapter and who have previously complied with the terms of a deferred sentence, may receive another deferred penalty by the judge, again conditioned upon the above subsection (d).

(f) All deferred penalties shall be in lieu of a monetary fine, only so long as the offender complies with the terms of deferred penalty. (Ord. No. 0-7273-67)

4. Frankel, Marvin E., *Criminal Sentences: Law without Order* (New York: Hill and Wang, 1973); Middendorff, Wold, *The Effectiveness of Punishment (Especially in Relation to Traffic Offenses)* (South Hackensack, N.J.: Fred B. Rothman & Co., 1968).

5. Gerber, Rudolph J., and McAnany, Patrick D., *Contemporary Punishment: Views, Explanations and Justifications* (University of Notre Dame Press, 1972).

6. Ancel, Marc, *Social Defense: A Modern Approach to Criminal Problems* (New York: Schocken Books, 1965).

7. Gottfredson, Don M., "Prosecution and Sentencing Decisions," *Decision Making in the Criminal Justice System.* Reviews and Essays (Rockville, Md.: National Institute of Mental Health, Center for Studies of Crime and Delinquency, 1975), p. 56.

2 Implementation

The Conceptual Scheme

Background

Initial efforts in dealing with the innovative sentencing of youthful offenders in the Municipal Criminal Court of Norman, Oklahoma began in 1965 through a cooperative effort of the court and the Institute of Group Relations of the University of Oklahoma. A graduate student from the institute served as a probation officer for the court and the program had as its primary objective the rehabilitation of habitual traffic offenders and other misdemeanants through counseling in cases where a fine was felt to be relatively ineffective. During the year in which the program was operative, the fine as a preventative was compared with a counseling approach utilizing both an individual and group counseling process.

The individual counseling process employed two guidance techniques as points of orientation. First, the probation officer explored and developed with the offender insight into various factors, such as the emotional climate of the family, adequate or inadequate parental supervision, or barriers to communication, that may have been instrumental in influencing the offender to exhibit the type of behavior that had characteristically brought him into contact with enforcement agencies. Second, if the probationer was a traffic offender, the probation officer would introduce information about various phases of traffic safety, such as automotive safety features, licensing regulations, driver attitudes, and law enforcement efforts to develop an awareness of, and stimulate interest in, the subject of traffic safety. It was hoped that these two guidance techniques might help the offender gain greater control over his behavior. The group counseling technique was directed largely toward the same two areas of inquiry as in individual counseling. Again the ultimate objective was to produce an active awareness of the importance of public safety, but with the added dimension of group discussion and interaction.

The program included 48 offenders between the ages of 14 and 30 who had committed three or more offenses within a period of six months to a year or who, for other reasons, had demonstrated a potential for the development of continuing antisocial behavior. The program was evaluated at 6 months and again at 12 months using recidivism as the criterion variable for comparing the effectiveness of the fine and counseling. The limited data accumulated suggested that probation, rather than the fine, was generally more effective in the case of these offenders. However, a valid assessment of the effectiveness of this program at its termination was difficult due to several limiting factors. First, the effectiveness of the program was evaluated after a lapse of only one year. Second, only a relatively small number of individuals were treated in the program. Third, the limited resources of the program prevented any sophisticated research effort. There was no systematic gathering of data concerning the characteristics of offenders and their infractions; hence only limited statistical analyses were possible. The general trends observed in the program were encouraging, and it was decided to develop plans for a more extensive program of treatment and research.

One tentative, but important, conclusion of the earlier program was that the probation technique was generally more effective than the fine in the case of the habitual offender, approximately 17-years-old, who had committed four to five violations within a period of one year. This could, of course, serve as one indicator to the sentencing judge of a class of offender needing the more innovative treatment.

The earlier program did not deal with the etiological factors involved in recidivism nor, more importantly, for the benefit of the sentencing judge, with the specific types of treatment that were most effective in relation to the etiological factors pertaining to particular offenders or classes of offenders. Similarly, knowledge concerning the characteristics related to high recidivism among youthful traffic offenders had not been systematically obtained with the objective of some form of treatment in mind, particularly with reference to those characteristics related to attitudes, behaviors, and sociodemographic factors of offenders as compared with nonoffenders. An expanded program for predictively sentencing youthful habitual traffic offenders resulted from this early effort.

Experience perhaps counted for more than anything else in the development of the conceptual scheme to implement the predictive sentencing concept for habitual traffic offenders appearing in the Municipal Criminal Court of Norman, Oklahoma. Youthful habitual traffic offenders observed in the court during the period 1965-1969 seemed to involve three specific groups. These were the offenders who seemed psychologically motivated to violate the traffic laws; offenders who lacked a knowledge of the law and therefore failed to comply; and offenders who simply disagreed with the value implicit in the law (or particular laws). Accordingly, the offender appeared to have an orientation that was causally relevant to an explanation of his action. This orientation could have one, or any combination, of three aspects. These were: (1) *deviant motivation*, that is, the investment of emotional or psychic energy in a person that motivates him to violate the law; (2) *cognitive knowledge*, or lack of knowledge, relevant to the violation of law; and (3) *values* relevant to a person's concern, or lack of concern, for compliance with the law. In any of these three aspects, the orientation was a variate of the offender that was related to traffic violations through the mediating factors of behavior. Therefore, change in any one of these three orientations would better come through the employment of an intervention strategy related to either the offender's deviant motivation, his knowledge, or his values. By designing intervention strategies to effect changes in any one of these aspects of the offender's orientation, it was hoped that changes in his behavior would follow. These strategies consisted of counseling on deviant motivation to violate the law, drivers education, and counseling on the consequences of illegal driving practices.

Offender of Interest

In the development of the predictive sentencing project, it was never felt that any elaborate sentencing program could be justified for the occasional teenage traffic offender. Such an offender did not constitute a significant threat to the community, either in requiring increased enforcement activity or court intervention, or in their posing a significant risk to the community in personal injury or property damage. The traditional fine, for whatever preventative value it might have, was deemed adequate for the occasional teenage traffic offender.

From experience, however, the fine demonstrated little, if any, effectiveness in the case of the offender who made repeated appearances before the court within reasonably short periods of time. He also appeared to constitute the greatest risk to society, either in enforcement problems, accident involvement, or other injurious nontraffic behavior. If innovation and experimentation were to be justified at all, it would be for this group of "dangerous teenage drivers," which for the purposes of the study was operationally defined as any 16-18 year-old male convicted of three traffic offenses within a period of twelve months. This became the target population for the study. By counseling these offenders in treatment modalities associated with the underlying reasons for their continuing violation of the law, it was hoped that greater success might be achieved in reducing traffic recidivism, accident involvement, and nontraffic recidivism than with traditional forms of intervention.

Goals

The goals of the project were:

1. To reduce recidivism and accident involvement among 16-18 year-old male habitual traffic offenders through a process of selective treatment of offenders with differing personality, social, and economic backgrounds to different treatment modalities optimal for the different types of offenders.

2. To evaluate the utility of demonstration-training environments for advanced students of the law or the behavioral sciences and police officers who are interested in social-action correctional work.

The earlier project in 1965-1966 contributed to the development of the goals for the present project. First, the idea advanced in the earlier program that probation and research complement one another in sentencing and treatment was preserved, but with the following significant innovation. It was directed at what has been noted as the most serious defect in sentencing and treatment—correlating the characteristics of offenders with optimal treatments to assure more accurate prediction (sentencing).

This innovative aspect of the major goal of the project involved two phases of treatment and inquiry. The first phase was purely descriptive, namely, describing the population under study, the treatment processes involved, and their success in relation to the recidivism and accident involvement of offenders sentenced sequentially into the program. The second phase utilized predictive sentencing models developed during the first phase of the project for sentencing offenders in the target population coming before the courts during this second phase. The validity of the predictive sentencing of offenders based upon their characteristics and the type of treatment they received was then measured with reference to the same criterion variables of recidivism and accident involvement.

Second, the tentative conclusion of the earlier program that 16-18 year-old persons having previously been convicted of four to five violations within the preceding year are most receptive to probationary techniques suggested the population for the present program with the further limitations that it should be confined to male persons in this age group and to persons having permanent residence in the Norman area. The restriction to males was made to avoid introducing into the treatment processes a variable that was thought might be significant and not readily subject to control and for the practical reason that the total docket of the court included very few females in the range of age and offenses under study. The restriction to permanent residents in the respective study areas was made both to confine the population under study to a common community background and to alleviate transient mobility problems.

Third, the internship feature of the earlier project was also generally successful. It was therefore continued in this project by using graduate students in law, psychology, and sociology and a police officer to administer the selected treatment processes of the program. Not only did this expanded approach continue to provide practical training in social-action correctional work for the persons involved, it also created an opportunity for evaluating the relative utility of the various disciplines in probation work.

Probation Strategy

The project involved only the sentencing of offenders following adjudication. It did not affect the determination of the innocence or guilt of the offenders. In the descriptive phase, 16-18 year-old Norman area male traffic offenders, upon conviction of three or more traffic violations within a period of one year were sequentially assigned to one of five different treatment modalities. These consisted of, first, the traditional sentence of the fine and, second, four experimentally innovative treatment modalities. The five treatment modalities were as follows:

Probation Group 1 Fine.
Probation Group 2 Individual counseling on deviant motivation to violate the traffic laws.
Probation Group 3 Group counseling on deviant motivation to violate the traffic laws.
Probation Group 4 Group counseling on driver's education.
Probation Group 5 Group counseling on consequences of illegal driving practices.

In the assignment of offenders to the treatment modalities, 16-18 year-old male traffic offenders convicted of three traffic offenses within a period of 12 months were sentenced sequentially in groups of six to one of the five different treatment modalities. The offenders were sentenced by a judge of the court and ordered to report to the chief probation officer of the court's Probation Division at a designated time for an intake session. The fined subjects attended the intake session, completed the forms, and took the tests to complete their obligation to the program. In all other cases, the fine was suspended by the court for a period of three months during the good behavior of the offender who, in addition to attending the intake session, was required to attend the sessions of the probation group to which he was assigned.

In the predictive phase (unlike the descriptive phase, and to enhance the validity of the data derived from the predictive phase), a "fine control group" was established through the generation of a table of random numbers by which the offender was sentenced in the first instance to either the fine control group or to predictive sentencing. In the case of the offender who was randomly fined, he was assessed a fine of $20, required to pay the fine, and released without testing, thus providing a pure control group against which to validate the predictive sentencing model. If the offender was randomly selected for predictive sentencing, he was tested on the critical variables employed in all five predictive sentencing equations. He was then fined or counseled depending upon the treatment that was determined to be optimal for him.

Research Strategy

Descriptive Phase

The study could have been approached from either a theoretical or empirical basis. The theoretical approach would have required the development of hypotheses of offender characteristics in relation to treatment effectiveness derived from generalized findings in criminology pertaining to the characteristics of offenders. Considering the particular class of offender involved in the present study and the relative paucity of knowledge concerning traffic offenders, their characteristics, and the deterrent process, the investigators leaned toward a more empirical approach. One such method would have been to assign offenders to different forms of treatment and simply observe the recidivism rates of the groups in each treatment modality. The treatment modality having the fewer recidivators would have then been selected as the optimal form of treatment. While this might have been a convenient approach, its simplistic nature would seem to obscure the complexity of the issues involved in the deterrent process. At the other extreme, data could have been gathered on the characteristics of the offenders in the target group before any attempt was made to describe the offenders, to develop treatment modalities, and to construct a differential treatment process. This approach had a significant time-consuming disadvantage.

Accordingly, the investigators took a middle-ground approach by combining a differential treatment process with the collection of data on the population under study. The research methodology had two phases: a descriptive phase and a predictive phase. The descriptive phase began December 15, 1968 and terminated May 31, 1972. It consisted of delineating the characteristics of the offenders studied, the treatment modalities, and the rate of traffic recidivism, nontraffic recidivism, and accident involvement among the groups. The five specific questions guiding this phase of the project were:

1. What are the characteristics of the offenders treated in the probation program?
2. How many offenders in the sample recidivate within one year after termination of treatment?
3. Are there significant differences in the rates of recidivism among the five treatment modalities?
4. Are there differences between offenders who recidivate and those who do not recidivate across all treatment modalities?
5. What differences are there between the offenders in each treatment modality who do recidivate and those who do not recidivate; that is, which of the variables discriminate between those who do and those who do not recidivate in each treatment modality?

Also, during the descriptive phase, hypotheses of optimal treatments among the five treatment modalities for different types of offenders were formulated and a predictive sentencing model was developed.

Predictive Phase

Utilizing the results of the descriptive phase and the personality-socioeconomic differences between recidivists and nonrecidivists within each group, prediction equations were developed for use in sentencing the offenders from the target group discriminately into that treatment group that would be optimal for them in reducing their recidivism. The predictive sentencing phase of the project was initiated in Norman, Oklahoma on June 1, 1972 to test the validity (cross-validation) of the predictive sentencing equations developed during the descriptive phase of the project. The same target population of 16-18 year-old male habitual traffic offenders was utilized. However, two innovations were introduced to enhance the validity and generalizability of the results. First, a randomly selected "fine control group" was established and, second, the predictive sentencing project was expanded to include four heterogeneous geographical areas of Oklahoma for a period of approximately one year. These areas were Tulsa, Lawton, Blackwell-Ponca City, and Ardmore-Madill-Durant. These areas provided maximum obtainable diversity among the geographical areas, provided a sufficient population base of 16-18 year-old offenders, and initially, at least, satisfied the requirement of a commitment of the appropriate public officials in the areas to fully cooperate in the implementation of the program in their areas.

Data Collection

In the descriptive phase, information was gathered either from the subject through testing or from other relevant sources in the following domains.

1. Family and social background
2. School
3. Personality
4. Court and police record of probationers
5. Court and police records of parents, siblings, and friends
6. Recidivism of the probationer

The data were reduced to identify a subset of all the variables that were minimally redundant and maximally efficient in conveying the information contained in the full set of variables. The following procedures were used:

1. Variables that showed negligible variance were eliminated.
2. Variables on which the great majority of probationers had no scores were eliminated.
3. The remaining variables were grouped into homogeneous sets and each set was subjected to principal components analysis, a technique that identifies independent sources of variation. The principal components factor matrix was then rotated to the varimax criterion to yield interpretable factors or dimensions of variation. Finally, variables that loaded high on a given factor (typically absolute values of 0.40 or more) and low on all other factors (typically absolute values of 0.25 or less) were retained for further considerations. Other variables were excluded.

As in the descriptive phase, in the predictive phase data was collected in the domains of family and social background, personality, school, court and police records, and recidivism. However, data collected during the predictive phase was greatly reduced over that of the descriptive phase. There were basically three reasons for the reduction: (1) data on variables showing minimal variance among subjects during the descriptive phase were not considered; (2) data on variables that could not be scored were eliminated; and (3) data was collected only on those variables that were determined in the descriptive phase to best measure the principal components.

Administrative Structure

The Legislative Fabric

The project was administered through both a Probation Division and a Research Division. The Probation Division administered the treatment processes and generated the data relevant to both the offender and the treatment process. The Research Division coded and analyzed the data relevant to research needs. During both the descriptive and predictive phases in the Norman area, the treatment processes were administered by the Probation Division of the Municipal Criminal Court of Norman, Oklahoma under the general supervision of the court's presiding judge. The judge was also the principal investigator of the research project and supervised the research organization responsible for the collection and analysis of the data. This dual role filled by the judge greatly facilitated the coordination of the vital and related work of both the probation and research divisions.

Article VII, Section 1 of the Oklahoma Constitution makes municipal courts in the state of Oklahoma a matter of general state concern by providing that municipal courts "shall continue in effect and shall be subject to creation, abolition or alteration by the Legislature by general laws."[1] Accordingly, state statutory law furnished, in the first instance, the legal authority for implementing the predictive sentencing program first in Norman and later in the four other regions of Oklahoma that were selected to test the sentencing scheme.

Fortunately, broad-based statutory authority existed from which to begin structuring the project in Norman, Oklahoma. Section 958.15 of Title 11 of the Oklahoma Statutes provides:

> Whenever any person shall be convicted in the Municipal Court of violating a municipal ordinance, the judge trying said cause, after sentence, may suspend said judgment or costs or both and allow said person so convicted to be released upon his own recognizance. Any person so released as provided herein shall be required to report at such times and to such person or officer as the judge shall

direct. Provided, if it shall be made to appear to the judge that such person so released has been guilty of the violation of any law after his said release, or is habitually associating with lewd or vicious persons, or is indulging in vicious habits, in that event said judge shall cause a warrant to be issued for said person and he shall be delivered forthwith to the place of confinement to which he was originally sentenced and shall serve out the full term for which he has been originally sentenced.[2]

This statutory authority, in turn, furnished the basis for the formalization of a Probation Division within the structure of the Municipal Criminal Court of Norman, Oklahoma. Sections 13-211(a) and (b) of the *Code of City of Norman* provide:

(a) The probation division of the Court shall assist that Court in the supervision of persons serving those suspended sentences and probation terms pronounced and adjudged by the Court.
(b) The Probation Division shall be staffed by probation officers appointed by the Presiding Judge, who shall also prescribe the duties of those officers.

In the other regions of Oklahoma, except Tulsa, Oklahoma, the same legislative authority furnished the legal basis for implementing the probation programs there. In Tulsa, though the statutory source of the authority was different, the substance was the same.[3]

The Research Division was organized independent of the court. This division functioned, first, under the auspices of the University of Oklahoma Research Institute and, more recently, under the University of Oklahoma Office of Research Administration.[a] This resulted largely from funding considerations and other practical considerations involved in the administration of the research grants that were made to support the project. For these reasons, legislative underpinning for the Research Division was unnecessary.

It should be noted that there was never any concern that a legislatively created Research Division within the Municipal Criminal Court would face any constitutional or other legal impediment. It was also conceivable that arrangements could have been made for either direct or indirect funding to the court for the creation and maintenance of a Research Division within the overall administrative structure of the court. However, given the anticipated limited duration of the project, establishment of the necessary administrative support within the court's structure was simply not feasible.

[a]The University of Oklahoma Research Institute was a nonprofit corporation organized under the laws of the State of Oklahoma to administer research grants for the University of Oklahoma and it managed the predictive sentencing program until 1974 when an enactment of the Oklahoma Legislature effectively required all research to be conducted within the structure of the University of Oklahoma. This led to the establishment of the Office of Research Administration within the University.

The Norman Organization

Separation of the Probation Division from the Research Division could have caused potentially serious problems in coordinating both the sentencing and research aspects of the project. In the first instance, it was absolutely essential that the sentencing judge adhere to the prescribed sentencing methodology adopted to implement the conceptual scheme. Likewise, at the probation stage, the testing and assignment of probationers to the proper treatment modality and adherence to the prescribed treatment format was also essential. If, for example, the sentencing judge were to depart from the sentencing scheme, or the probation counselor failed to follow the prescribed treatment format, there could be no assurance of the reliability of the data generated. Hence, effective *judicial supervision* of sentencing and probation was essential. At the same time, research control in the collection and analysis of data generated by the sentencing and probationary aspects of the project was essential. And in the end both these *judicial* and *research* functions had to be coordinated.

Moreover, separate staffing in the probation and research divisions was also essential to accommodate the varying expertise needed to achieve the objectives of the project. But the efforts of the personnel also had to be coordinated in an interdisciplinary setting if they were to function successfully in the combined effort.

The ultimate responsibility for coordinating both the judicial and research functions could, theoretically at least, be vested in the judge of the participating court and a separate director of research. Given the diversity of the two functions involved, perhaps even of intellectual orientation, the vesting of such responsibility in two different persons might have made the coordination between the judicial and research functions, at best, extremely difficult. Fortunately, this potential problem was resolved by one person assuming ultimate responsibility for the entire project in the dual role of both Presiding Judge of the court and Principal Investigator. Figure 2-1 diagrams the organization of the Norman project.

Probation Division. The Probation Division was supervised by a chief probation officer who was directly responsible to the Presiding Judge (Principal Investigator) of the court for the administration of the probation phase of the project. He was not charged, as such, with any responsibilities in the Research Division, except indirectly as they might arise in guarding the integrity of the research design. This included administering the probation program according to the research format specified in the Project Manual and the furnishing of insights to the investigators arising from his perspective of the program concerning the analysis of data.

More specifically, the chief probation officer's duties included, first, supervising the intake sessions to which the offender was sentenced for

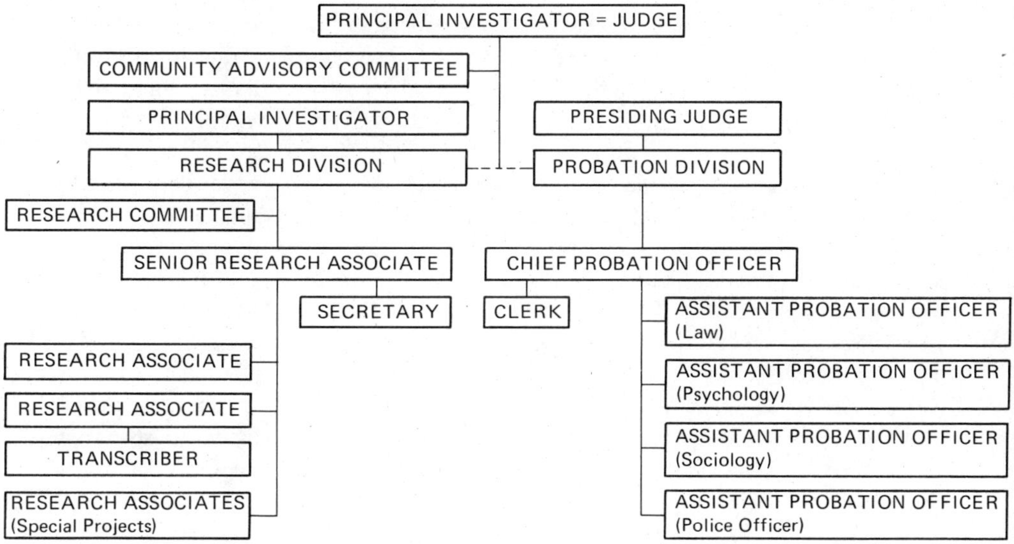

Figure 2-1. Norman Project Organization.

introduction into the project, scheduling treatment sessions, and supervising the assistant probation officers administering the treatment processes. Second, he scheduled orientation and training sessions for the assistant probation officers. Third, he supervised and assisted in the collection of data required by the research design and, in this connection, served as custodian of all records, tapes, correspondence, and other materials pertaining to the project. Further, his custodial responsibility included not releasing any data pertaining to the program to any person other than the personnel in the Probation or Research Divisions without the prior approval of the Presiding Judge. Fourth, he made monthly, semiannual, and annual reports to the Presiding Judge. These reports contained sections on general administration, personnel, administration of probation groups, data collection, statistical summaries of current intake, general summaries, conclusions, and recommendations.

The five assistant probation officers were representative of each of the four disciplines conceived as relevant to the project. These were law, psychology, sociology, and law enforcement. At the initiation of the project each assistant probation officer was assigned to one of the five treatment groups. The assistant probation officer assigned to Probation Group 1, the fine group, did not have any treatment responsibilities. Consequently, during the period he was assigned to this group he assisted the chief probation officer in the collection of data on all offenders, including data on the court and police records forms and school record forms. Each of the other assistant probation officers administered the treatment process of the particular group to which he had been assigned and according to the prescribed format. At the end of each three-month cycle, which concluded a treatment period, the assistant probation officers were rotated into the next succeeding probation group for a three-month period, and so on.

Finally, the administrative staff of the Probation Division was completed with a clerk, under the supervision of the chief probation officer. The clerk performed such secretarial and clerical duties for the chief probation officer and assistant probation officers as might be prescribed from time to time.

Research Division. The Research Division was supervised by the senior research associate who was directly responsible to the Principal Investigator (Presiding Judge). The responsibilities of this division extended into problem identification, conceptualization, adapting the research design, operationalization, interpreting the results, and writing interim and final reports. Research associates, working with the Senior Research Associate, assisted in these tasks. One research associate supervised data collection and coding and coordinated this responsibility with the chief probation officer and his assistants, who were given the responsibility of collecting the data. Other research associates were used from time to time during the project as the need arose, such as in assisting in the evaluation of data and the development of sentencing criteria at the end of the first stage of the project. The Principal Investigator took an active role in all of the Research Division's activities.

A Research Committee consisting of the project investigators and research associates made all major policy decisions concerning the research. This included decisions pertaining to the research design and its implementation, the collection and evaluation of the data, and the furnishing of varying guidance and support to the Research Division in accomplishing its tasks. Oftentimes the Research Committee served merely to ratify policies jointly derived by the Principal Investigator, the senior research associate, and the chief probation officer. On the other hand, Research Committee meetings sometimes served as the occasion for lively interdisciplinary debate that pitted the quantitatively oriented researcher against the qualitatively oriented researcher. The committee was thus often a valuable forum within which to deal with the interdisciplinary issues involved in the research design.

Selection of Personnel. All project personnel were selected by the Research Committee upon application and personal interview. This extended to both probationary and research personnel. In the case of probation officers' appointments, these were, of course, made by the Presiding Judge of the court by administrative order. However, given the significance of utilizing advanced students from different disciplines as assistant probation officers, the views of Research Committee personnel were relied upon heavily in making personnel decisions involving the Probation Division of the participating Norman court.

Regional Staff Responsibility and Authority

Probation and Research Structure. During the predictive phase from 1974-1975, in both the Norman area and the four heterogeneous areas (Tulsa, Lawton, Ponca City-Blackwell, Ardmore-Madill-Durant), a more elaborate administrative structure was employed. Separate probation divisions, as such, were not established in the participating municipal courts of the four heterogeneous areas. Each court, or area, had its own probation clerk to implement the probationary sentence, with the chief probation officer of the Norman court serving as the probation advisor. This had the dual advantage of centralizing and coordinating the probation work—essential to coordinating the research in the several diverse geographical areas. At the same time, this plan did not offend the integrity of, or interfere with, the organizational structure of the court involved where funding was not available or perhaps even necessary to establish a probation division.

As to research, independent research divisions were not conceived as either necessary or desirable. This was all coordinated within the Research Division in Norman to assure as much accuracy as possible in the collection, coding, and analysis of data. As in the case of Norman, the probation clerks in all areas administered the test instruments to obtain the raw data and score them for probationary purposes. The data was then transmitted to Norman for checking, coding, and analysis. Followup recidivism data was gathered by Norman research personnel. During the predictive phase of the project from 1973 to 1975, the administration of the project was carried out within the organizational structure diagrammed in Figure 2-2.

Selection of Personnel. Local residents, where available, were used to staff the probation clerk's office and the assistant probation officer (counselor) positions. For example, in Tulsa, students were selected from among students at the University of Tulsa's law, psychology, and sociology departments, while police officers serving as counselors were obtained from the local police departments in the communities involved. All research personnel utilized for the regional program were Norman-based personnel.

The same procedure utilized for selecting personnel for the Norman project was also utilized in the other areas with two modifications. Candidates were interviewed only by the Principal Investigator and the chief probation officer, and all appointments were made only with the concurrence of the judge of the participating court.

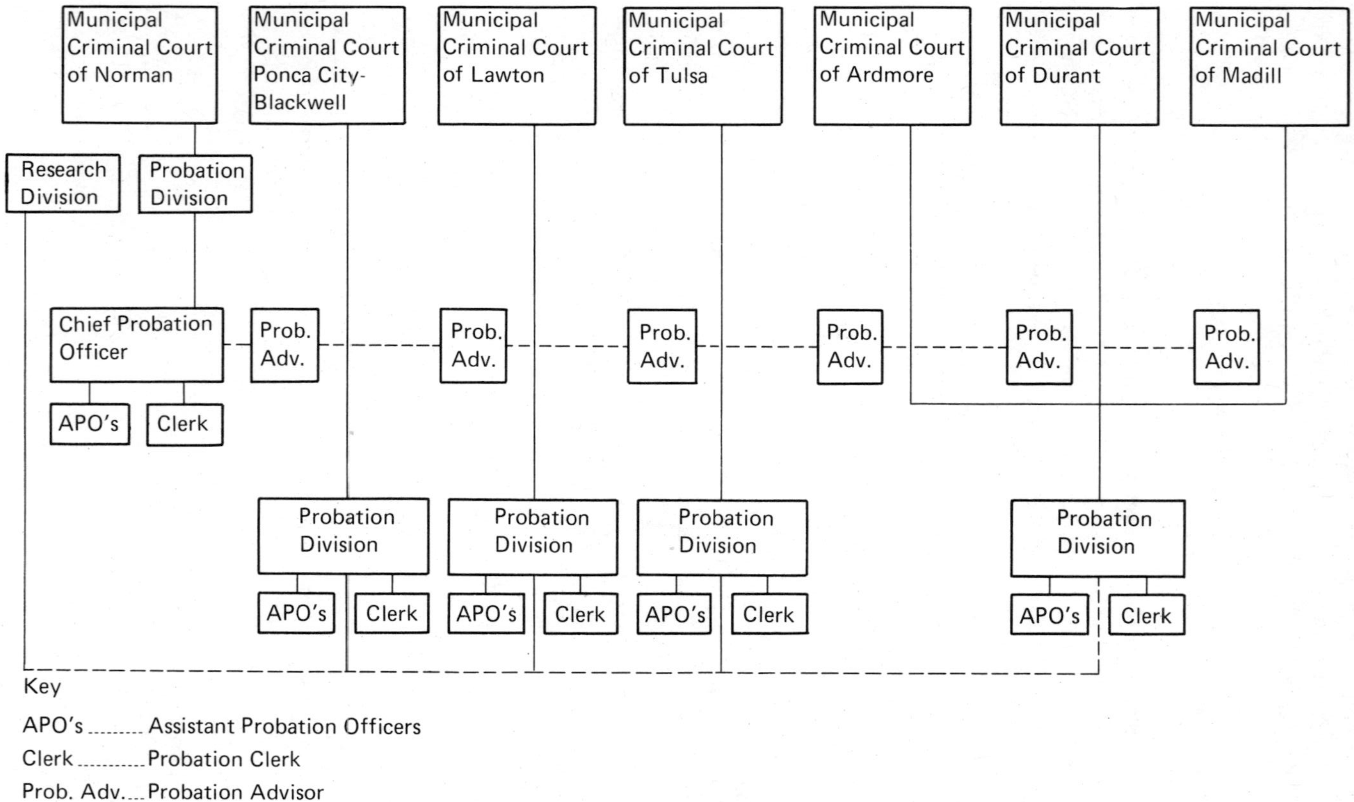

Figure 2-2. Organizational Chart for Predictive Sentencing Regional Project.

Community Advisory Committee

A Community Advisory Committee, consisting of representatives of various segments of the Norman community, was available as a link between the community and the project. It was intended as a means of securing the support of the community for the program, of providing a liaison between the program and the community, of helping to interpret the program to the community in any sensitive areas that might arise, and of having an additional source of combined expertise for critique of the project. In the end, the committee was only convened once at the inception of the project. Broad-based community support existed in Norman throughout the duration of the project and it was unnecessary to call on the committee for assistance.

Notes

1. *Okla. Const.*, Art. VII, Section 1. For a discussion of the organization of Oklahoma municipal courts under Article VII of the Oklahoma Constitution, see Whinery, "Organizing Municipal Courts in Oklahoma under the New Judicial Article," *O.B.A.J.* 39:2511, (1968). An earlier exhaustive analysis of the role and organization of municipal courts will be found in Whinery, "Policy, Legislation and Organization of Municipal Courts in Oklahoma," *Okl. L. Rev.* 18:1, (1965).
2. See also, *Code of City of Norman*, Oklahoma, Section 13-504.
3. See 11 Okl. St. §794.

3 Intervention

Sentencing and Intake

The intervention process began with a probationary sentence by the judge of the court after the offender had pled, or was found, guilty of the traffic violation. The project did not affect the determination of the innocence or guilt of the defendant. It involved sentencing only. It was imperative to the success of the program, both in its service to youthful offenders and in its research orientation, that no bias exist in the assignment of offenders to the treatment processes. At the same time, there had to be no element of injustice associated with the project. If the judge in a particular case had a strong tendency to treat the offender in a particular way, that offender was not assigned to the project. The project was not intended to experiment with youthful offenders simply for experimentation, nor was it operated in such a fashion. However, where sentencing into the program was indicated, upon a finding of guilty, the judge of the court imposed a probationary sentence and assigned the offender to the probation division of the court.

Once an offender had been assigned to the Probation Division, the probation clerk confirmed the eligibility of the offender by reviewing the probationer's driving record to ascertain that the probationer had committed three or more traffic offenses within a 12-month period. Further, the probation clerk made sure that the probationer was 16 to 18 years old and was a permanent resident of the local region. The probationer was then required to attend two intake sessions where the probation clerk administered the project's data gathering instruments. Following these intake sessions the probationer was assigned to one of the five treatment modalities. During the descriptive phase, a sequential assignment procedure was utilized; while during the predictive phase, probationers were assigned to that treatment group that was determined would be optimal for him in reducing his traffic recidivism.

If the probationer failed to comply with the requirements of the probationary sentence, the suspended fine was revoked and the probationer was taken out of the program. Failure to comply included either a refusal to attend the intake session or three absences without excuse from the probation sessions. In either event, the chief probation officer notified the Presiding Judge of the court who then initiated procedures to return the probationer to the court for revocation of the suspended sentence and payment of the suspended fine. The offender was then removed from the project, though his file was retained during the duration of the project for comparative data purposes.

Treatment Modalities

Following the intake process the probationer was scheduled for his probation sessions in accordance with the sentence imposed, either sequentially or predictively, depending upon the phase of the project. Except for those who were fined at the time of sentencing and released following intake, the subjects were counseled for 12 hours at the rate of one hour per week. A format for each treatment group provided the specific kind of intervention stratagem designed to implement the conceptual scheme and for subsequent evaluation of the effect of the program to provide some assurance that the offenders assigned to a particular treatment modality would all be exposed to the same process.

Description of Treatment

The outlines for the probation groups were as follows.

Probation Group 1: Fine and/or testing group. This group was used as a form of control in both the descriptive and predictive phase in an attempt to measure the effectiveness of the fine in comparison to the more innovative treatments devised for the project.

Probation Groups 2 and 3: Counseling format.

Session 1	Getting acquainted
Session 2	Law and society
Session 3	Law and punishment
Session 4	Teenagers and driving
Session 5	Peer group relationships
Session 6	Family
Session 7	Family relationships
Session 8	Self: present offense
Session 9	Self: driving and other behavior
Session 10	Self: school
Session 11	Self-acceptance and goals
Session 12	Value of sessions

The only difference between groups 2 and 3 was the difference between individual counseling used in Group 2 and group counseling used in Group 3. The two approaches were utilized in an attempt to determine if the interaction of a group setting would produce different results than those obtained through individual counseling.

These treatment modalities were approached from the theoretical position of Glasser's *Reality Therapy*, since it was deemed most appropriate to short-term counseling.[1] *Reality Therapy* essentially emphasizes the fulfillment of one's needs to be loved and feel worthwhile toward oneself and others within the reality of the world in which one lives and without depriving another of the ability to fulfill similarly his needs. This approach had been found to be very successful with delinquent girls as well as with other types of populations.[2] Perhaps more importantly, it has been found to constitute an approach that can be successfully used by the nonprofessional counselor.[3]

In these treatment modalities, Session 1, Getting Acquainted, the probationer was asked why he believed he was sentenced to probation. He was also given an opportunity to express his feelings concerning the offense, what he believed the purpose of the sessions were, and what, if anything, would be accomplished by them.

During Session 2 the probationer was encouraged to express his views concerning the general purpose of law. Why do we have laws? What does the probationer think of the laws? Does he think they work? Which ones does he believe should be changed? What would the probationer's law be for (whatever area is mentioned, such as drinking beer)? What is the policeman's relationship to law? What characteristics does the probationer attribute to a good policeman? To whom does the probationer think the laws apply? Does the probationer believe that teenagers are being "picked on"? Does the law apply to the group of fellows the probationer hangs around with? If a fellow driving a new Cadillac went 10 miles over the speed limit and behind him was a fellow doing the same thing in an old Chevrolet, which fellow would the policeman stop? Does the probationer believe everybody breaks the law? Who gets caught? Who gets away with breaking the law?

Session 3 focused on the prevention of law violations. Why do people keep getting caught for violating the same laws over and over again? What can we do to keep people from continually violating the law? What will work? Is punishment a good method? Will it work for people generally? When did the probationer first start violating the traffic laws? How long has he been committing traffic offenses? Why is he stopped for traffic violations and others are not? How does he feel toward the police officer and the judge? The offense on which the probationer was placed in the program was discussed. Does the probationer feel responsible? Does he believe the sentence he received is fair?

Session 4 dealt with teenagers and their driving habits. Does the probationer like to drive a car or motorcycle? Why? The probationer was asked to describe his feelings when operating a car, or motorcycle. Does the probationer feel it is necessary to own a car? Does he own a car? What kinds of things are as important, or more important, to the probationer than owning a car? Does the probationer believe the rules governing the operation of a motor vehicle are different for teenagers than for adults? Are the rules enforced differently for teenagers than for adults?

In Session 5 peer group relationships were discussed with the probationers. Are adults unable to understand teenagers? In what ways? Why? Are the same things as true in other places as they are in Norman? What does the adult community in Norman expect of teenagers as a group? What are the probationer's feelings about what adults think of teenagers? Is it important to the probationer what adults think, or is he more concerned with what teenagers think? Who are your friends? How different is what the probationer's friends think and what adults think? Is it more important what adults think or what the probationer's friends think?

Session 6 focused on the probationer's parents and their attitudes toward law and discipline. Does the probationer believe his parents are good or poor examples of complying with the law? What are the attitudes of the parents toward traffic laws? Do they regard these laws as important? Is it important for adults to obey them? For teenagers to obey them? How do the parents react toward the probationer's present and past offenses? Do they approve, disapprove, or are they indifferent? Do they react to different offenses differently? If so, which ones? Does the probationer know why? Is the probationer disciplined at home? What types of conduct cause the parents to discipline the probationer? What type of discipline is imposed by the parents? How does the probationer feel about this discipline?

Session 7 again focused on the family but dealt more specifically with family life and relationships among siblings. What is the character of the home life of the probationer? Does the probationer and his family eat together and engage in social and recreational activity together? What are the smoking, drinking, social, and religious habits of the home? How many brothers and sisters does the probationer have? (Here the same topics were developed with the probationer concerning siblings as in Session 6.) Is the attitude of probationer's parents toward the siblings respecting their offenses and behavior the same as in the case of the probationer? Are all teenagers disciplined similarly in the home, or are they treated differently? Does the probationer talk to his parents? Can he talk to them? Does he have any desire to talk to them? What subjects do they discuss? Does he talk to brothers and sisters? Can he talk to them? Does he have any desire to talk to them? What subjects do they discuss? Does he have a preference for talking to either parents or brothers and sisters? What are the parents aspirations and expectations for the probationer? For the siblings? Do they differ?

Session 8 shifted the focus to the probationer and asked why the probationer committed the offense for which he was placed in the program. Why did he commit the other offenses?

Session 9 again focused on the probationer and dealt with the relationship between his driving behavior and other types of behavior. Why do these similarities or differences exist? What are the probationer's feelings, and behavior, toward his parents, in general and specifically? What are the probationer's feelings, and behavior, with respect to school, in general and specifically?

Sessions 10 and 11 turned to the probationer's self-conception, self-acceptance, and goals. Does the probationer feel that he is misunderstood? Who misunderstands him? Why is he misunderstood? Does the probationer have anyone with whom to share his thoughts? What is the probationer's degree of self-acceptance? How does he feel he is accepted by others, both boys and girls? What are the probationer's goals in life? What is the probationer working forward to? Is it important to have purposeful goal-seeking? What are the dangers of aimlessness? Do self-acceptance and purposeful goal-seeking have any relationship, or lack of relationship, to the commission of the offenses that brought him into contact with law enforcement officials?

Finally, Session 12 was a wrap-up session. What has the probationer learned in the sessions? Of what value have the sessions been to him? What are his feelings concerning the sessions? Have they served a useful purpose?

Probation Group 4 Counseling Format.

Session 1	Pretreatment drivers examination
Session 2	Types of vehicles and their characteristics
Session 3	Driving compartment
Session 4	The driver, his qualifications, and responsibilities
Session 5	Session 4 continued
Session 6	Traffic laws–rules of the road
Session 7	Rules of the road, signs, signals, and markings
Session 8	Science of motion
Session 9	Other users of the road
Session 10	Road and intersection variables
Session 11	Defensive driving
Session 12	Posttreatment testing

Group 4 was essentially an informational group aimed at dealing with the probationer's knowledge of automobiles, their use on the roads and highways, and the rules and regulations governing their use. Actual use of and instruction in the automobile was not involved. Considerable time was employed in the use of the lecture technique, though questions and group discussion were encouraged where relevant and appropriate to the particular subject matter being considered at the time.

Probation Group 5 Counseling Format.

Session 1	The nature of the traffic problem
Session 2	Damage to persons (emphasis on offender)

Session 3	Extent of the traffic problem
Session 4	The traffic control effort
Session 5	Damage to persons (emphasis on offender)
Session 6	Damage to persons (emphasis on persons other than offender)
Session 7	Damage to persons (emphasis on victim's family)
Session 8	Damage to persons (emphasis on the innocent victim)
Session 9	Damage to persons (emphasis on offender)
Session 10	Damage to property (emphasis on the vehicle involved)
Session 11	Evaluation
Session 12	Summary and conclusions

This treatment group was designed to change the youthful traffic offender's values (what they consider right and wrong in connection with driving) by placing heavy emphasis on those consequences of illegal driving practices that most people consider bad. The strategy involved a certain kind of logic; for example, pain is undesirable; illegal driving is more likely to produce pain than legal driving; therefore, illegal driving is undesirable. Another example: the loss of a loved one is undesirable; illegal driving is more likely to produce such a loss than legal driving; therefore, illegal driving is undesirable. Examples with the premise "death is undesirable" or "destruction of property is undesirable" were used in the same way.

This treatment group was not concerned with the consequences of being caught and punished but rather with the consequences of engaging in those acts defined by the law as wrong. Dissuasion by threatening punishment was thus avoided. One reason for this was the hope of developing effective interaction leading to change of values. Threats of punishment may have changed behavior but not values. The concern of treatment Group 5 was not simply with change of behavior but also with change of values or motivation. The logic here was that knowledge of consequences of getting caught might lead simply to "defensive illegal driving" in order to avoid getting caught. A person whose deviant motivation was being suppressed by the threat of being caught may have sought another way of expressing this motivation that could be equally problematic to society although not related to illegal driving. Thus the concern was not simply with deterring an inclination to engage in acts that were defined as wrong, but with changing the offender's orientation toward such acts so that he would be less inclined to engage in them.

Session 1 (The nature of the traffic problem). The specific goal here was to give the probationers a knowledge of and an appreciation for the problem (of moving motor vehicles safely) that has led to the traffic laws now on the books. It was assumed that such knowledge (in combination with other knowledge) would force the conclusion that illegal driving practices are undesirable.

Session 2 (Damage to persons: emphasis on the offender). Presentation of Film: "Signal 30" (33 minutes). The specific goal in this session was to give the offender knowledge of possible consequences of illegal driving practices that are generally considered undesirable with emphasis on injury to the offender. The means used was an impact-type film that should shake them up quite a bit. It was assumed that the film would illustrate in a very dramatic way that illegal driving practices are genuinely undesirable.

Session 3 (Extent of the problem). The specific goal here was to give them knowledge of damage to persons and property in the United States each year as a result of accidents. The assumption was that most, if not all, accidents are the result of illegal driving practices.

It was assumed, of course, that knowledge of damage to persons and property as a result of accidents would force the conclusion that illegal driving practices are undesirable (certainly for the victims if not for the country as a whole).

Session 4 (The traffic control effort). The specific goal here was to give the probationers knowledge of the *total effort* to control traffic, presenting them with the big picture and indicating that the law or law enforcement is only one part of the total traffic control effort. There are at least two other components to this effort: education and engineering. The engineering effort includes not only traffic engineering but also engineering in vehicle production itself.

Hopefully, this information gave them a perspective on the control effort that would influence their behavior. It was assumed that this knowledge would suggest the conclusion that a great many people are concerned about them and their safety; that as a nation we are engaged in a total-push program to "solve" the problem, that law enforcement is only one part of this effort, and one that we invoke only when all else fails.

Emphasis was placed on the fact that the police are the absolute last resort when the education and engineering efforts have failed. A point to get across was that if the day should ever come when compliance with the law is voluntary, then the police will be unnecessary.

Session 5 (Damage to persons: emphasis on the offender). Presentation of a case history: "The Case of R.D." (30-minute taped interview). This session consisted of a taped interview with a former delinquent and victim of a serious traffic accident. R.D. was born and reared in Norman and was a member of one of the more notorious gangs in this area in the 1950s. He tells of repeated violations of traffic laws and the accident that led to his present crippled condition. He states in detail some of the consequences of being paralyzed and some of the changes in his philosophy of life that have taken place as a result of the accident. Note was taken of the tendency for R.D. to make himself and the driver appear less culpable than they probably were. This is to be expected, of course, as the consequences of their driving practices were obviously quite serious.

Session 6 (Damage to persons: emphasis on persons other than the offender). Presentation of a case history: "More on R.D." (30-minute taped interview). This session was a continuation of Session 5, but with a slight change in emphasis. In this session there was more emphasis on the adverse consequences of illegal driving practices for persons other than the offender. Use is made of additional portions of the interview of R.D. and covers the reaction of his first wife, his mother and father, and others with whom he was associated.

During this session as well as in Session 5, a discussion of disfigurement in relation to both the offender and others around him was an effective way of pointing up adverse consequences. Death seems to be an abstract concept to offenders in this age group, but disfigurement is not.

Session 7 (Damage to persons: emphasis on the victim's family). Presentation of a film: "Anatomy of an Accident" (30 minutes). This probation session was built around the film, "Anatomy of an Accident." The film shows the effects of an accident on the victim's family.

Session 8 (Damage to persons: emphasis on the innocent victim). Presentation of a case history: "The Case of Linda" (30-minute taped interview). This session was based on a taped interview with Linda. Linda describes the situation of her accident, the short- and long-term consequences of her injuries, her feelings toward future use of an automobile, the money losses as a result of the accident, and the effects of the accident on her family.

Session 9 (Damage to persons: emphasis on the offender). Presentation of a film: "The Unteachables" (26 minutes). The film, "The Unteachables," was employed to emphasize problems relating to injuries received by the offender.

Session 10 (Damage to property: emphasis on the vehicles involved). Presentation of a film: "Broken Glass." The film, "Broken Glass," provided a focal point for this session. Damage to the automobile touches home, money-wise, with the probationers. In discussions, the probationers might recall similar accidents in which they were involved and the amount of money they spent repairing their cars.

Session 11 (Evaluation). Session 11 was basically an evaluation of changes in the probationer's orientation during the course. A typical evaluation of this type involved a measurement of orientation at the beginning of the course and again at the end.

One of the main goals of this session was to obtain some notion of the effectiveness of the program in conveying certain ideas. Evaluative responses to the following statements and questions were elicited from the probationers at this particular session.

1. One of the more obvious consequences of illegal driving practices is getting caught by the police and in some sense punished. But there are other consequences one might list. These were explored.

2. The probationer was then asked to state as accurately as he could the likelihood that these consequences would occur to persons who continually engaged in such illegal driving practices.

3. Finally, the probationer was asked to consider what the "good" and "bad" implications for him might be of these consequences of illegal driving behavior.

Session 12 (Summary and conclusions). This session was a kind of "cooling out" session in which the probationers could vent their hostility and leave the program with the feeling that they had had the opportunity to express themselves.

Recording Counseling Sessions

Recordings were made of the counseling sessions for three reasons. First, it permitted the monitoring of the sessions for content as a kind of quality control to determine that all probationers were exposed to approximately the same treatment format within each type of treatment modality. Second, the recordings were used as training aids for replacements in counselor positions and provided continuity throughout the project. Third, they served as a means for self-evaluation by probation counselors. While the use of the tape recorder may have cut down on the spontaneity and freedom of expression in the critical early phase of the treatment process, both counselor and counselee appeared accustomed to it in later treatment sessions.

Moreover, the recordings were made with the full knowledge of the probationer and an assurance of anonymity. The probationers were told the following with respect to the taping of the sessions.

The purpose of the tape recorder is to obtain accurate records. Anytime you want to say something "off the record," we will turn off the machine.

Treatment Monitoring

The development of a predictive sentencing model, and its subsequent use for predictive sentencing, dealt solely with the relation between offender characteristics and treatment outcome. That is, given a particular offender, which treatment should he be sentenced into so that the probability of nonrecidivism is highest? This process of predictive sentencing assumed, however, that the specific contents of a treatment for a particular offender would be the same for any other offender sentenced into that treatment. At the inception of the project a firm policy decision was made that the chief probation officer monitor the recordings of the treatment sessions to evaluate the assistant probation officer in his delivery of the treatment. This policy provided the investigators with data for eventually evaluating whether the counseling processes were equivalent for all probationers.

Descriptive Phase

During the descriptive phase, offenders were sequentially assigned to treatment groups in groups of six. The first six offenders sentenced were assigned to Group 1, the second six to Group 2, and so on. After six offenders had been assigned to Group 5, the process was repeated. This scheme was adopted in lieu of a pure random assignment, although random assignment would have been preferable. However, random assignment was finally determined to be impractical for several reasons. First, given the size of the sample, it would have taken an indefinite period of from one to four months to fill any one of the five treatment groups. This would have resulted in substantial disparity in the time commitments of the probationers. Second, even in the interests of research, to unduly delay treatment for formation of a treatment group by random sampling might introduce confounding variables into the research design that random sampling is ordinarily expected to overcome. Third, a random sampling technique would have posed significant problems in administration, such as scheduling intake sessions, scheduling treatment group sessions, and distributing the time commitment and work load evenly among all personnel connected with the project.

Predictive Phase

Norman

During the predictive phase, the wide range of anticipated rates of intake afforded the opportunity of: (1) cross-validating the predictive sentencing model in Norman; (2) simultaneously replicating both the sequential sentencing phase and the predictive sentencing phase (cross-validation of the project in Tulsa); (3) fully replicating the predictive sentencing phase in Lawton; and (4) assessing the utility of operating the single best innovative treatment in the small towns of Ardmore-Madill-Durant and Ponca City-Blackwell.

In Norman, unlike the descriptive phase and to enhance the validity of the data derived from the predictive phase, a "fine control group" was established through the generation of a table of random numbers by which the offender was sentenced in the first instance to either the fine control group or to predictive sentencing. In the case of the offender who was randomly fined, he was assessed the fine of $20, required to pay the fine, and released without testing, thus providing a pure control group against which to validate the predictive sentencing model. If the offender was randomly selected for predictive sentencing, he was tested on the critical variables employed in all five predictive sentencing equations. He was then fined or counseled depending upon the treatment that was determined to be optimal for him after computing his predicted number of traffic recidivisms (PNTR) for each of the five treatment modalities.

Tulsa

The offenders were randomly divided into two groups: one for sequential sentencing and the other for predictive sentencing. The sequentially assigned offenders represented replication of the descriptive phase of the Norman project, with the modification of overassigning offenders to Group 2 (individual psychological counseling), which showed the lowest rate of traffic recidivism in Norman. The predictively sentenced offenders were further randomly divided into a pure control group (fine control group) and a group predictively sentenced in accordance with the Norman procedure.

Lawton

The offenders sentenced in Lawton were randomly divided into two groups: one group represented a pure control group (fine control group), and the other group was predictively sentenced in accordance with the Norman procedure.

Little Cities

In the Ponca City-Blackwell and Ardmore-Madill-Durant areas the offenders were again randomly divided into two groups: one group represented a pure control group (fine control group), and the other group was sentenced into Group 2 (individual psychological counseling).

Criterion Variables

Recidivism

A common assumption within the criminal justice system has been that *recidivism,* the commission of offenses after adjudication, is one of the most significant indicators of the success or failure of sentencing programs. Accepting this assumption, the investigators initially adopted recidivism as the criterion variable with which to measure the success or failure of the treatment, with a period of one year following treatment constituting the time component of the recidivism criterion variable. Later, in the case of some probationers, it also included recidivism in the three years following the first year.

The actual number of offenses in the recidivism year were utilized to determine the rate of recidivism. However, police and court data were available only for probationers remaining in the Norman area and generally not accessible in other jurisdictions where the probationer might have committed offenses following treatment. The recidivism data was thus susceptible to bias arising from differences in the amount of time that the probationers might have spent in the Norman area. For example, in an extreme case, a probationer who had spent no time in the Norman area after treatment would have been considered a nonrecidivator simply because the available police and court data were incomplete.

Weighted Recidivism

To minimize the limitations of this approach, a weighting scheme was devised whereby the number of posttreatment convictions could be calculated proportionate to the actual amount of time spent in the Norman area during the recidivism year. Ideally, one would want to know, on a daily basis, the actual time each probationer spent within the Norman area during the recidivism year. The constant monitoring required to obtain such data was simply not feasible. The other extreme is no knowledge of the extent of the presence of the probationer in the Norman area during the recidivism year, which is the result of simply examining the number of posttreatment year convictions. The compromise solution selected was determining the number of half-months spent by each probationer in the Norman area during the recidivism year. There were two advantages to dividing the recidivism year into 24 half-month periods. First, the actual time spent by the probationer in the Norman area could be relied upon with more assurance. Second, it provided a basis for extrapolating the number of recidivisms that might be attributable to an offender spending less than 24 half-months in the Norman area.

The actual time spent, in half-months, in the Norman area by the 213 probationers sentenced during the descriptive phase of the project is summarized in Table 3-1. The distribution by treatment group of half-months spent in the Norman area by the probationers is set forth in Table 3-2.

This data was collected at the end of the recidivism year by contacting each probationer or some person acquainted with the probationer (hopefully, a reliable source of information) to determine the number of half-months the probationer spent in the Norman area. Table 3-3 summarizes the distribution of the sources of information.

Table 3-1
Half-Month Distribution of Probationers during Descriptive Phase

	Half-Months	*Number*	*Percent*
	0	4	1.9
	1	1	0.5
	2	1	0.5
	3	0	0.0
	4	2	0.9
	5	0	0.0
	6	2	0.9
	7	2	0.9
	8	4	1.9
	9	1	0.5
	10	3	1.4
	11	1	0.5
	12	6	2.8
	13	1	0.5
	14	7	3.3
	15	2	0.9
	16	1	0.5
	17	0	0.0
	18	4	0.9
	19	1	0.5
	20	5	2.3
	21	4	1.0
	22	8	3.8
	23	9	4.2
	24	131	62.0
Subtotal		200	94.5
No contacts		13	6.1
Total		213	100.6[a]

[a]Total does not equal 100 percent due to rounding error.

Table 3-2
Distribution of Probationers in Norman Area by Half-Months and Treatment Group During Descriptive Phase

Half-months	*Group 1*	*Group 2*	*Group 3*	*Group 4*	*Group 5*
0	1			2	1
1					1
2		1			
3					
4		1			1
5					
6	1		1		
7		1	1		
8	2	2			
9					
10	1	1			1
11	1				
12	2	3			1
13		1			
14	3		1	1	2
15	2			1	
16		1			
17					
18	1			1	2
19		1			
20	2		1	1	1
21	1	1	1		1
22	1	2	1		2
23		5	2	2	
24	29	17	27	33	25
Unable to Contact	2	3	2	2	4

Table 3-3
Distribution in Sources of Information about Probationers in Norman Area during Recidivism Year

	Number	*Percent*
Subject	47	23.5
Mother	84	42.0
Father	31	15.5
All other relatives	19	9.5
Other	19	9.5
Total	200	100.0

As mentioned, in addition to gathering data on actual time spent in the Norman area, the half-month approach also enabled the investigators to adjust the actual frequency of offenses and calculate weighted recidivism thereby extrapolating for one year the recidivism rate for each probationer.

The weighted recidivism score was calculated as follows: Weighted recidivism (WR) = Actual recidivism X Weight, where:

$$\text{Weight} = \frac{\text{24 half-months}}{\text{Number of half-months of recidivism year spent in Norman area}}$$

It follows from the foregoing formula that a probationer who spent 18 half-months (that is, 3/4 of a recidivism year) in the Norman area had his actual recidivism multiplied by 1.33 to produce his weighted recidivism score. This weighting scheme consisted of a simple extrapolation and was based on the assumption that each person had a constant recidivism rate. Obviously, this assumption was not tenable for every case; however, the use of the weighting scheme was justified by the expectation that weighted recidivism data lead to more valid conclusions than actual recidivism data. To further enhance the validity of weighted recidivism data, no probationer was included in the analysis unless he had spent at least six half-months in the Norman area. Also, because of the simplifying assumption that the recidivism rate was constant, the recidivism scores were not stratified beyond trichotomization: zero, one, or more than one traffic offense.

Traffic Recidivism. Not only did the investigators assume from the beginning that recidivism generally was a reliable measure of antisocial behavior, it was also assumed that traffic recidivism was reflective of actual driving behavior, and hence both recidivism generally and traffic recidivism specifically were criteria of the success or failure of a particular sentencing strategy or treatment modality.

It was nevertheless recognized that traffic recidivism might be only partially dependent on the frequency of traffic violations and partially dependent on other variables, such as the amount of driving done during periods of intensive traffic law enforcement. However, an independent study in 1972 of 16-17 year-old male Norman High School students who had not been sentenced in the project disclosed, first, a very low level of association between the number of traffic citations the students reported and the amount of time they reported driving during intervals in which a high number of traffic citations were issued. This strongly suggested that the number of traffic citiations received did not depend upon the amount of driving done or the time of day in which the driving was done. Second, the study disclosed an association between the number of traffic citations the students reported and the frequency with which they reported having violated traffic laws. In conclusion, there appeared to be a direct relationship between citations and violations: nonprobationers reporting frequent violations reported receiving many traffic citations.[4]

Moreover, in a second independent study it was found that there was no significant relationship between car characteristics, car stickers, reported number of traffic violations, and number of traffic citations. This result lent further credence to the notion that entry into the probation program depended on actual driving behavior.[5] And both studies tended to support the notion that traffic recidivism was a valid criterion for determining the success or failure of the project goals.

Accident Involvement. Even given the general validity of traffic recidivism as a measure of the success or failure of the project goals, the question arose whether traffic recidivism was the most relevant measure of treatment success given the argument that the enforcement of traffic laws is to protect society from personal injury and property damage. Since there is a significant social cost in the apprehension, prosecution, and sentencing of traffic law violators independent of property damage and personal injury caused by illegal driving behavior, reduction in traffic recidivism is a desirable goal in any sentencing scheme. But this objective does not necessarily address itself to the issue of reducing property damage and personal injury, which is also a desirable (and perhaps more important) goal in any sentencing scheme.

The criterion variable, "accident involvement," was therefore added for the precise purpose of focusing attention on the importance of measuring the success of the treatment modalities independent of the reduction in traffic recidivism. Specifically, would the different treatment interventions successfully reduce property damage and personal injury resulting from a reduction in dangerous driving behavior? Further, the selection of accident involvement as a criterion variable enabled the investigators to examine empirically the relationship between traffic recidivism, i.e., illegal driving behavior, and accident involvement, i.e., dangerous driving behavior.

Nontraffic Recidivism. An underlying concern throughout the duration of the study was the association between the danger posed to society by the habitual traffic offender and the danger posed to society by him in the commission of nontraffic offenses. If there was a significant relationship between the commission of traffic offenses and nontraffic offenses by the habitual traffic offender, early differential treatment could lead to decriminalization generally. To measure this relationship it was necessary to employ nontraffic recidivism as a criterion of the success or failure of the treatment strategies.

Typically too much emphasis has been placed on only one aspect of behavior in judging the success or failure of sentencing schemes. And, more often than not, not enough emphasis has been placed by sentencing judges on the objectives they are trying to achieve in the sentencing process. The three-fold criteria of traffic recidivism, accident involvement, and nontraffic recidivism permitted a more realistic assessment of the effectiveness of the treatment modalities as correctional devices in achieving the intent of the law to protect society. Moreover, they also provided a realistic basis for the empirical comparison of the relationship between illegal driving behavior, dangerous driving behavior, and other antisocial conduct.

Notes

1. Glasser, William, *Reality Therapy* (New York: Harper and Row, 1965).

2. Rachin, Richard L., "Reality Therapy: Helping People Help Themselves," *Crime and Delinquency* 20:1974, p. 45.

3. Ibid.

4. See *Final Report, Predictive Sentencing of 16-18 Year-Old Male Habitual Traffic Offenders*, University of Oklahoma Office of Research Administration (1976), Appendix IV-3, p. IV-3-1.

6. Ibid., Appendix IV-4, p. IV-4-1.

4 Outcomes

Descriptive Phase

Sample Size

The total number of probationers sequentially sentenced into the project during the descriptive phase was 257, with a minimum of 40 and a maximum of 45 probationers being assigned to each of the five treatment modalities. Of the total intake of 257, 214 completed treatment, 40 dropped out of the program prior to completion of treatment, and 3 were not included in the analyses because they left the jurisdiction after treatment.

It should be pointed out that the 214 probationers who completed treatment also remained in the Norman area the minimum of three months during their recidivism year deemed essential for validly extrapolating recidivism rates for the duration of the 12-month recidivism year. Seventy-five percent of the drop-outs left the program for reasons beyond their control rather than an unwillingness to comply with the terms of the probationary sentence. An analysis of probationers refusing to comply would have been of considerable interest and significant to the overall goals of the study during the descriptive phase, but due to the small number of such persons, no meaningful inferences could be drawn.

The methodology of sequential assignment was discussed at length by the investigators at the inception of the project and all were aware that random assignment would have been preferable. However, random assignment was finally determined to be impractical for several reasons. First, given the size of the sample, it would have taken an indefinite period from one to four months to fill any one of the five treatment groups and a minimum of five months to fill all five different groups. This would have resulted in substantial disparity in the time commitments of the probationers. Second, even in the interests of research, to delay treatment unduly for formation of a treatment group by random sampling might introduce confounding variation into the research design. Third, a random sampling technique would have posed significant problems in administration, such as scheduling intake sessions, scheduling treatment group sessions, and distributing the time commitment and work load evenly among all personnel connected with the project. Accordingly, the decision was made to assign sequentially, but with the qualification that the sample be analyzed to determine that the groups were evenly matched in relation to the descriptive variables.

Two studies were conducted to ascertain whether any systematic bias was introduced into the sample, either by sequential assignment or by abnormal fluctuation in the court's docket or sentencing procedures. Using program ANOVAR,[1] a separate one-way analysis of variance was conducted using all 223 sequentially assigned probationers, except drop-outs, together with the 321 project variables associated with these probationers. Of the grand total of 321 independent variables, 78 were categorical (arbitrarily scaled) and nonsuitable for analysis of variance, while 243 were at least quasiordinal (scaled in ascending or descending order), thereby being at least marginally appropriate for analysis of variance. Of the 243 variables that were at least quasiordinal, 12, or 5.3 percent, of 243 were significantly different at the 0.05 level among treatment groups. The conclusion reached by these analyses confirmed the fact that the distribution of characteristics of offenders among treatment groups approximated that to be expected under random assignment of offenders to treatment groups. As to abnormalities in docketing or sentencing, a comparison of the total traffic docket of the Municipal Criminal Court of Norman with project intake by quarter-year periods during the descriptive phase disclosed an asynchronous relationship. It was found that entry into the program was significantly correlated ($r = 0.50$, $p = 0.01$) with the total traffic docket when entry into the project was lagged by six months. This result has considerable face validity in view of the fact that three traffic convictions were requisite for entry into the project, thus providing some assurance that intake was not being systematically biased due to either abnormal fluctuations in the court docket, docketing procedures, or erratic sentencing.

Further study was undertaken to determine whether the project was reaching its intended target group of habitual traffic violators. It appeared plausible that those offenders entering into the program were doing so because of other factors besides their actual driving behavior. They could have been "singled out" because they drove during peak enforcement hours, they exhibited controversial or offensive bumper stickers,[2] or for other less obvious reasons.[3] Comparison of 16-17 year-old probationers with a randomly selected group of 16-17 year-old nonprobationers from Norman High School revealed that probationers were significantly different from nonprobationers on several background variables. Nonprobationers were more education oriented, held higher status occupations, had fathers with more formal schooling, and were less car oriented than probationers. Also, there were no significant differences in the self-reported number or kinds of bumper stickers and the time and amount of driving between probationers and nonprobationers. Further, and most important, probationers reported more frequent traffic law violations; thus, the project appeared to be reaching its targeted population, and entry into probation depended on actual driving behavior.

Treatment Effectiveness

A comparison of the relative effectiveness of the five different treatment modalities in relation to the three criteria of traffic recidivism, accident involvement, and nontraffic recidivism revealed that generally the Group 2 individual counseling treatment was most successful.

In addition, the five project treatment modalities are compared to a sixth modality (quasi-control fine group 6). Group 1 of the project (fine) partially filled the need for a control group but suffered from the possibility of contamination due to the extensive testing involved. At the same time, it was not practical to develop a testing-free control group from the population under study due to its limited size. Group 6, consisting of 140 offenders, represented a partial solution to this problem in that it was composed of members of the same population selected by the same criterion as with Groups 1 through 5 of the project but free from testing and coming from the earlier time period of January 1, 1964 through December 15, 1968.[4]

Tables 4-1 and 4-2 report dichotomized traffic recidivism and trichotomized weighted traffic recidivism respectively.

An examination of Table 4-1 discloses that with dichotomized traffic recidivism during the descriptive phase treatment Groups 2 and 5 were not only superior to treatment Group 1, but additionally, Groups 2 and 5 were the most effective of all treatment modalities in reducing traffic recidivism.

In Table 4-2 traffic recidivism is trichotomized into zero, one, or more than one recidivisms. Inspection of Table 4-2 demonstrates the superiority of individual psychological counseling over the fine treatment with respect to the commission of multiple traffic recidivisms. This superiority is also manifested in the other innovative treatment modalities, although not as strongly as in the case of individual psychological counseling.

Chi-square statistics were also computed between Group 1 (fine group) and each of the four innovative treatments. In the case of dichotomized traffic recidivism, none of the probabilities of chi-square statistics attained the traditional 0.01 or 0.05 level of significance. That is, while Group 2 appeared to be a superior form of treatment, the difference, while unlikely, may have been attributable to chance. However, with regard to trichotomized traffic recidivism, the probability of the Group 2 versus Group 1 chi-square statistic reveals a significant difference below the traditional 0.05 level ($p = 0.0445$).

Chi-square statistics were also computed between Group 6 (the quasicontrol group) and each of the five different treatment modalities. While Group 6 is not significantly different from Groups 1, 3, 4, or 5, the difference between Group 6 and Group 2 is significant at the 0.0069 level. The facile interpretation that Group 2 probationers recidivated significantly less than Group 6 (the quasicon-

Table 4-1[a]
Number and Percentage of Probationers in Groups 1 through 6 with Either Zero, or One or More Traffic Recidivisms

Traffic Recidivisms	*Group 1 (Fine)*	*Group 2 (Individual Psychological Counseling)*	*Group 3 (Group Psychological Counseling)*	*Group 4 (Drivers Education)*	*Group 5 (Counseling on Consequences)*	*Group 6 (Quasi-control Fine)*[b]
Zero	13 (32%)	23 (52%)	16 (37%)	14 (33%)	17 (39%)	40 (29%)
One or More	28 (68%)	21 (48%)	27 (63%)	28 (67%)	27 (61%)	100 (71%)
Total	41 (100%)	44 (100%)	43 (100%)	42 (100%)	44 (100%)	140 (100%)

[a]It should be pointed out that traffic recidivism in this case was not weighted by the amount of time a subject remained in the Norman area, although all subjects in Groups 1 through 5 were in the area at least three months.

[b]No allowance was made for the possibility that Group 6 subjects did not remain in Norman during the entire recidivism year, hence their traffic recidivisms were not weighted and are therefore probably understated.

Table 4-2
Number and Percentage of Probationers in Groups 1 through 5 with either Zero, One, or More than One Traffic Recidivism

Weighted Traffic Recidivisms	*Group 1*	*Group 2*	*Group 3*	*Group 4*	*Group 5*
Zero	13 (32%)	23 (52%)	16 (37%)	14 (33%)	17 (39%)
One	7 (17%)	11 (25%)	12 (28%)	12 (29%)	10 (23%)
More than one	21 (51%)	10 (23%)	15 (35%)	16 (38%)	17 (39%)
Total	41 (100%)	44 (100%)	43 (100%)	42 (100%)	44 (100%)

trol group) must be viewed with caution in light of two rival hypotheses. The first is that the difference might be attributed to preexisting differences in age and amount of highest fine. The second is that Group 6 is not a contemporaneous control group. Additionally, Group 6 consisted of 96 more subjects than Group 2. With an analysis based on 188 subjects, even relatively small differences could have yielded statistically significant results.

The effectiveness of the treatments and the predictive sentencing scheme was initially intended to be evaluated on the basis of a one-year follow-up. To this point all evaluations have indeed been based on the one-year follow-up. However, in order to accumulate enough probationers to permit sample sizes large enough to furnish reliable information, the project extended over a period of some seven years. Seven years is an extremely long duration for a social action research project. This very fact made possible a four-year follow-up of the recidivism and accident involvement of the earlier probationers, which is unfortunately all too rare. Table 4-3 reports the mean differences in traffic recidivism between the two groups for this four-year follow-up recidivism period.

It should be observed that over the four-year period Group 2 individual counseling exhibited a lower recidivism rate than the Group 1 fine group. The pattern and magnitude of these differences are viewed as strong evidence that the superiority of individual counseling over the fine control during the descriptive phase cannot be reasonably attributable to random fluctuations in the data. Even disregarding the extent of the differences, note that the probability that a given group would be better than another group four times in a row would happen by chance one out of 16 times. (This is computed simply by the formula P = Particular event/All possible events = $(1/2)^4 = 1/16 = 0.06$.) A detailed account of the implications of this striking outcome will be discussed in Chapter 5. Comparable data for the other three treatment modalities is not reported, since they exhibited relatively weak effectiveness in relation to Group 2 individual counseling. With this in mind, a follow-up across all groups was not warranted in relation to the comparative cost of such a follow-up.

Table 4-3
Mean Values for Traffic Recidivism between Groups 1 and 2 for the Four-Year Post-treatment Recidivism Period

Groups	*Number of Subjects*	*Year One*	*Year Two*	*Year Three*	*Year Four*
1	34	0.65	0.47	0.47	0.29
2	32	0.44	0.31	0.34	0.19

Accident Involvement. Table 4-4 reports the posttreatment dichotomized rate of accident involvement among the five different treatment modalities.

Again, Groups 2 and 5 were not only better than Group 1 but additionally, Groups 2 and 5 disclosed the best results of all groups on the criterion of accident involvement. While the absolute magnitude of the differences between the two best treatments and the fine treatment are close, namely 6 percent, the pattern of superiority of these two innovative treatments is consistent. Moreover, it is also interesting to observe that the percentage of people in the fine group subsequently involved in accidents is one and one-half times as high as in these other two innovative treatments.

In the four-year follow-up, a pattern consistent with that of traffic recidivism emerged. Table 4-5 reports the comparative rates of accident involvement between Groups 1 and 2. It is to be observed that again Group 2, the individual counseling modality, disclosed a lower accident rate than Group 1 which, as mentioned, is consistent with the observed results with respect to traffic recidivism in the four-year follow-up period.

Nontraffic Recidivism. Table 4-6 reports dichotomized nontraffic recidivism across all five treatment modalities. Again a pattern emerged that was consistent with those found for traffic recidivism and accident involvement; namely, all four treatments showed better results than the fine group, albeit by a small margin.

Table 4-4
Number and Percentage of Probationers in Groups 1 through 5 Involved in Zero, or One or More Accidents in the Recidivism Year

Accident Involvement	*Group 1*	*Group 2*	*Group 3*	*Group 4*	*Group 5*
Zero	34 (83%)	39 (89%)	30 (70%)	33 (79%)	39 (89%)
One or more	7 (17%)	5 (11%)	13 (30%)	9 (21%)	5 (11%)
Total	41 (100%)	44 (100%)	43 (100%)	42 (100%)	44 (100%)

Table 4-5
Mean Values for Accident Involvement between Groups 1 and 2 for the Four-Year Posttreatment Recidivism Period

Groups	*Number of Subjects*	*Year One*	*Year Two*	*Year Three*	*Year Four*
1	34	0.12	0.15	0.12	0.06
2	32	0.03	0.16	0.06	0.00

Table 4-6
Number and Percentage of Probationers in Groups 1 through 5 with either Zero, or One or More Nontraffic Recidivisms

Nontraffic Recidivisms	*Group 1*	*Group 2*	*Group 3*	*Group 4*	*Group 5*
Zero	30 (73%)	38 (86%)	37 (86%)	37 (88%)	42 (95%)
One or More	11 (27%)	6 (14%)	6 (14%)	5 (12%)	2 (5%)
Total	41 (100%)	44 (100%)	43 (100%)	42 (100%)	44 (100%)

Again a similar pattern emerged when examining nontraffic recidivism between Groups 1 and 2 over the four-year period following treatment. Table 4-7 reports these findings. It should be noted when examining Table 4-7 that the definition of a juvenile under Oklahoma law was changed to include 17 and 18 year-old males effective April 4, 1972, thus seriously diminishing the reported number of nontraffic offenses.[5] Nevertheless, the greater effectiveness of Group 2 was still evident. Table 4-8 summarizes the results by reporting the means of each treatment group on all criterion variables discussed in the preceding sections.

Model Building

Probationer Characteristics

The question of the characteristics of the probationers was of central importance throughout the duration of the project. Was there sufficient but not excessive homogeneity in the characteristics of the probationers to make differential prediction feasible? Two independent analyses were conducted to isolate the characteristics of the probationers sentenced during the descriptive phase of the project. The first was performed as a pilot study early in the project when the data on only 144 probationers were available and the second when the data on

Table 4-7
Mean Values for Nontraffic Recidivism between Groups 1 and 2 for the Four-Year Posttreatment Recidivism Period

Groups	*Number of Subjects*	*Year One*	*Year Two*	*Year Three*	*Year Four*
1	32	.26	.12	.12	.03
2	32	.12	.06	.09	.03

Table 4-8
Mean Values on Criterion Variables

Outcome Variables	*Group 1*	*Group 2*	*Group 3*	*Group 4*	*Group 5*
Dichotomized traffic recidivisms	0.68	0.48	0.63	0.67	0.61
Trichotomized traffic recidivisms	1.15	0.70	0.98	1.05	1.00
Dichotomized nontraffic recidivisms	0.27	0.19	0.19	0.12	0.04
Dichotomized accident involvement	0.17	0.11	0.30	0.21	0.11

all 219 descriptive phase probationers were available. This final analysis utilized the 33 variables reported in Table 4-9.

As in the pilot study, four highly dissimilar types emerged from hierarchical grouping analysis.[6] The discriminant function computed upon these probationer types yielded a probability that the types were samples from the same population of less than 1 in 10,000. Further, these groups differed markedly along at least three dimensions or roots. The variables that best described the dimensions were:

Dimension 1: MMPI 14
Dimension 2: Age at intake into the probation program
Dimension 3: Number of male friends

MMPI 14, the F scale, is composed of items rarely endorsed by "normals," where extremely high F scores are associated with either carelessness, confusion, illiteracy, or with emotional distress. Age at intake is the age in years of the probationer at the time of his intake into the probation program. Number of male friends is based upon the probationer's answer to the question: "Would you list your close friends and his or her sex?"

Table 4-9
Thirty-Three Variables Used in Discriminant Function Analysis of the Four Types Emerging from Hierarchical Grouping

Variable Number	*Items*
1	Length of residence
2	Father's schooling
3	Family support
4	Other source of income
5	Number of jobs in past year
6	Number of siblings
7	Male friends
8	Female friends
9	Friends drag
10	Club memberships
11	Own car
12	Dream car
13	Work on family car or cycle
14	Summer work
15	Drink-self
16	Weekday TV-viewing
17	Number of school transfers
18	Average study time
19	Quit and enlist
20	Mom's expectations
21	Self-expectations
22	College essential
23	School offices
24	Age at intake
25	MMPI 6
26	MMPI 9
27	MMPI 10
28	MMPI 11
29	MMPI 14
30	Greatest traffic fine
31	Age at first traffic charge
32	Nature of present offense
33	Mother's contact

Inspection of the results reveals that probationers of Type 1 were *lowest* on MMPI 14, were *oldest* at age of intake, and had a *moderate* number of male friends. Type 2 probationers were characterized by *low* scores on MMPI 14, *moderate* on age of intake, and were *highest* on number of male friends. Type 3 subjects scored *high* on MMPI 14, were *youngest* at age of intake, and had *few* male friends. Type 4 subjects scored *highest* on MMPI 14, were rather *old* at intake, and had *few* male friends.

Second, could these typologies be utilized as predictors of optimal treatment? While four discreet probationer types emerged in these analyses, which made prediction feasible, these offender types could not be used as predictors for a predictive sentencing program because of insufficient sample size. Rather, it was found necessary to use multiple regression techniques to build a predictive sentencing model.

As a final assessment of the feasibility of predictive sentencing, an analysis was performed to determine if systematic differences existed between those probationers who recidivated and those probationers who did not recidivate after treatment. Discriminant function analysis with 83 probationers having zero traffic recidivisms and 131 probationers with one or more traffic recidivisms yielded a probability of less than 0.0001 that the two groups were samples from the same population. Table 4-10 lists the variables used in this analysis.

The variables that maximally differentiated recidivators from nonrecidivators were club membership and school office. More than twice as many nonrecidivators belonged to clubs or held school offices as compared to recidivators. Additionally, nonrecidivators scored lower on MMPI 14 (the validity scale), and only 34 percent of the nonrecidivators as opposed to 47 percent of the recidivators had been convicted of reckless or careless driving before entering the program. These findings must be viewed with circumspection since probationers receiving different treatments were combined for purposes of this analysis. In all events, the feasibility of predictive sentencing was indicated in that recidivators were clearly different from nonrecidivators.

Predictive Sentencing Equations

The development of a predictive sentencing model and the resultant optimal sentencing of offenders in the target group based on the differences in the characteristics between recidivators and nonrecidivators within each treatment modality began in January 1972 when 115 sequentially assigned probationers from the descriptive phase had completed their recidivism year. A predictive sentencing model, designated "A," was constructed at the first stage of model building on 14 MMPI variables using multiple discriminant function analyses. While the discriminant functions of Model "A" showed significant discrimination between recidivators and nonrecidivators within each treatment group, and hence permitted accurate prediction of recidivism, the complexities involved in routinely using these functions for predictive sentencing argued against their use.

A new approach was then employed for constructing a test Model "B" and the "Final Model" with these refinements: (1) in addition to the 14 MMPI variables, 32 more variables were employed, some of which were the best

Table 4-10
Variables Used for Discriminating Probationers Who Recidivated from Probationers Who Did Not

1. Length of residence	24. Self-expectations
2. Father's schooling	25. College essential
3. Family support	26. School offices
4. Other source of income	27. Age at intake
5. Number of jobs in past year	28. MMPI 1 (Hypochondriasis)
6. Number of siblings	29. MMPI 2 (Depression)
7. Friends	30. MMPI 3 (Hysteria)
8. Male friends	31. MMPI 4 (Psychopathic deviate)
9. Female friends	32. MMPI 5 (Masculinity-femininity)
10. Significant others	33. MMPI 6 (Paranoia)
11. Friends drag race	34. MMPI 7 (Psychothenia)
12. Club memberships	35. MMPI 8 (Schizophrenia)
13. Own car	36. MMPI 9 (Hypomania)
14. Dream car	37. MMPI 10 (Social introversion)
15. Work on family car or cycle	38. MMPI 11 (Anxiety)
16. Summer work	39. MMPI 12 (Repression)
17. Drink-self	40. MMPI 13 (Ego strength)
18. Weekday TV-viewing	41. MMPI 14 (Validity, F scale)
19. Number of school transfers	42. Most serious traffic offense
20. Average study time	43. Greatest traffic fine
21. Quit and enlist	44. Age at first traffic charge
22. Mom's expectations	45. Nature of present offense
23. Father's expectations	46. Mother's police contact

measures of the principal components of the full set of available variables, and the remainder were variables chosen on a priori grounds by the investigators; (2) the medians of all these 46 variables were calculated separately for recidivists and nonrecidivists within each of the five groups to supply values for missing data in place of the less desirable, though simpler, method of substituting means for missing data; and (3) linear regression was substituted for the multiple discriminant function because, in this instance, the former yielded equivalent results but had the added advantage of ease in explanation to lay persons using them, such as the mathematically unsophisticated probation clerks.

Finally, after many UNICON[a] analyses were performed separately for each

[a]Program UNICON is similar to stepwise linear regression, because it computes the amount of criterion-related variance explained by each predictor variable and the "unique" contribution to criterion-related variance of each predictor variable, also referred to as the *squared semipartial correlation*. That is, in terms of linear regression, UNICON calculates the

of the five treatment groups, the variables that accounted for the maximum amount of "unique" criterion-related variance in each treatment group were selected for use as predictors for the particular group.

Multiple linear regression analyses were then employed to produce the "Final Model" for the predictive phase of the project.

Group 1: Predicted number of traffic recidivisms (PNTR) = (–0.2754) (Other source of income) – (0.3027) (Club membership) + (0.0091)(MMPI 9) + 0.2977

Group 2: PNTR = (–0.0310)(MMPI 6) + (0.0341)(MMPI 9) + (0.0217)(MMPI 10) – 1.2005

Group 3: PNTR = (–0.3128)(School offices) + (0.0135)(MMPI 14) – 0.1464

Group 4: PNTR = (0.0788)(College essential) – (0.4541)(School offices) + 0.6531

Group 5: PNTR = (–0.4545)(Friends drag race) – (0.0172)(MMPI 11) + 2.0142

The equations differ from those of Model "B" in two respects. In Group 4 the least-squares regression weights are different due to the addition of three probationers who had completed their recidivism year from the descriptive phase. In Group 5 the variable "Friends drag race" was substituted for "Father's schooling" because this resulted in more subjects being assigned to Group 5 without any appreciable loss in overall accuracy of classification. Also, data from five additional probationers were available for analysis.

The variables employed in this model are explained in Table 4-11.

The classification of a probationer using the predictive sentencing model could be accomplished by:

1. Multiplying his score on each variable used in the sentencing equation by the raw regression weight associated with that variable.
2. Summing the products formed in step 1 to derive his predicted number of traffic recidivisms (PNTR).
3. The probationer would then be assigned to that treatment in which his (PNTR) was lowest. He would be classified a recidivator if his PNTR was greater than 0.5 and a non-recidivator if his PNTR is equal to or lower than 0.5.

---

difference between R^2 of the full model, consisting of all predictors, and R^2 of the restricted model, consisting of the full model without the single predictor in question. Each predictor is dropped in turn from the full model thereby enabling the analyst to gauge quickly the "unique" criterion-related variance of each of several predictors. In summary, identical results could have been achieved using stepwise linear regression, but by first employing UNICON, variables having little "unique" criterion-related variance were more quickly eliminated.

Table 4-11
Final Model Predictor Variables and Their Relation to Success within Treatment Groups

Group 1 (Fine)

1. *Club membership:* If the probationer belongs to a club, he is *less* likely to recidivate.
2. *MMPI 9, Hypomania:* The lower the probationer's score on hypomania, the *less* likely he will recidivate.
3. *Other sources of income:* If the probationer's family has no source of income in addition to parent's wages or business income, he is *less* likely to recidivate.

Group 2 (Individual psychological counseling)

1. *MMPI 6 Paranoia:* The higher the probationer's score on paranoia, the *less* likely he is to recidivate.
2. *MMPI 9, Hypomania:* The lower the probationer's score on hypomania, the *less* likely he is to recidivate.
3. *MMPI 10, Social introversion:* The lower the probationer's score on social introversion, the *less* likely he is to recidivate.

Group 3 (Group psychological counseling)

1. *School office:* Probationers who have held one or more school office are *less* likely to recidivate.
2. *MMPI 14, Validity (F):* The lower the probationer's score on the validity scale, the *less* likely he is to recidivate.

Group 4 (Driver's education)

1. *College essential:* Probationers whose parents feel college is essential are *less* likely to recidivate.
2. *School office:* Probationers who have held one or more school office are *less* likely to recidivate.

Group 5 (Consequences)

1. *Friends drag race:* Probationers whose friends do not drag race are *less* likely to recidivate.
2. *MMPI 11, Anxiety:* The higher the probationer scores on anxiety, the *less* likely he is to recidivate.

As an example, suppose a probationer scored as in Table 4-12 on the predictor variables employed in the final model:

With these scores, a probationer's PNTR for Group 1 would be computed as follows:

1. $\text{PNTR} = 0 \times (-.2754) - 1 \times (0.3027) + 60 \times (0.0091) + 0.2977$
2. $\text{PNTR} = 0 - 0.3027 + 0.5460 + 0.2977$
3. $\text{PNTR} = 0.5410$ for Group 1

Similarly, his PNTR for each of the other four treatment groups would be:

Table 4-12
Scores on the Predictor Variables of the Final Predictive Sentencing Model for a Hypothetical Probationer

Variable	*Score*
Other source of income	0
Club membership	1
Number of school offices	1
College essential	1
Friends' drag race	1
MMPI 6	62
MMPI 9	60
MMPI 10	43
MMPI 11	38
MMPI 14	46

Group 2	–0.5526
Group 3	0.1618
Group 4	0.2778
Group 5	0.9061

Thus this probationer would be predicted a recidivator in Groups 1 and 5 and a nonrecidivator in Groups 2 through 4. However, he would be assigned to Group 2, since his PNTR for this group was lowest.

To explicate the use of the model and to assure the correct assignment of predictively sentenced probationers, matrices were tabulated in such a manner as to enumerate all possible regression scores. Use of these matrices allowed the probation clerks to figure a PNTR by simply referring to the probationer's scores and reading the PNTR from the appropriate entry in the matrix. This freed the probation clerks from having to do any arithmetic computations.

Assessment of the Model before Cross Validation

The limited duration of the project necessitated the initiation of predictive sentencing before all 214 probationers of the descriptive phase had completed their posttreatment recidivism year. In consequence, the "Final Model" was developed when only 159 probationers had completed their posttreatment recidivism year. The basic technique for assessing the accuracy of the "Final Model" was the accuracy with which the model classified recidivators and nonrecidivators. The accuracy of classification of the 159 probationers using the "Final Model" sentencing equations is reported in Table 4-13.

Table 4-13
Accuracy of Classification within Groups (Final Model)

Actual Status	Classification				
	Group 1				
	Recidivist		*Nonrecidivist*		*Total*
Recidivist	23	76.7%	3	37.5%	26
Nonrecidivist	7	23.3%	5	62.5%	12
Total	30	100%	8	100%	38
	Group 2				
	Recidivist		*Nonrecidivist*		*Total*
Recidivist	12	80%	2	14.3%	14
Nonrecidivist	3	20%	12	85.7%	15
Total	15	100%	14	100%	29
	Group 3				
	Recidivist		*Nonrecidivist*		*Total*
Recidivist	19	76%	1	14.3%	20
Nonrecidivist	6	24%	6	85.7%	12
Total	25	100%	7	100%	32
	Group 4				
	Recidivist		*Nonrecidivist*		*Total*
Recidivist	20	83.3%	1	14.3%	21
Nonrecidivist	4	16.7%	6	85.7%	10
Total	24	100%	7	100%	31
	Group 5				
	Recidivist		*Nonrecidivist*		*Total*
Recidivist	12	80%	5	35.7%	17
Nonrecidivist	3	20%	9	64.3%	12
Total	15	100%	14	100%	29

It must be clearly borne in mind that the figures cited for accuracy of optimal assignment represent upper boundaries that may have been approximated but not reached, because linear regression capitalizes on systematic trends in the data and errors unique to the particular sample upon which it was based. However, when applied to a new set of probationers, it was still reasonable to expect a considerable improvement over the policy of simply fining offenders or sentencing them to the treatment group in which the recidivism rate was lowest.

Additional analyses to test the efficacy of the equations were performed. First, the question was raised whether the same regression equation might not work equally well for all groups. To test this notion as rigorously as possible, but without cross-validation, the variables of each prediction equation were applied separately to each of the five groups of probationers. In doing so, rather than using the regression weights from the prediction equation, the regression weights were permitted to take on those values that maximized R^2 in each instance and thereby minimize the differences in R^2 between the predictive sentencing equation and the second best equation for each group. Figure 4-1 shows that the differences in R^2 for Groups 1, 3, and 4 were quite low. In contrast, the differences in R^2 for Groups 2 and 5 were substantial. Therefore the variables of the predictive sentencing equations did not work equally well for all groups, especially for Groups 2 and 5, which have proven to be the best groups across all

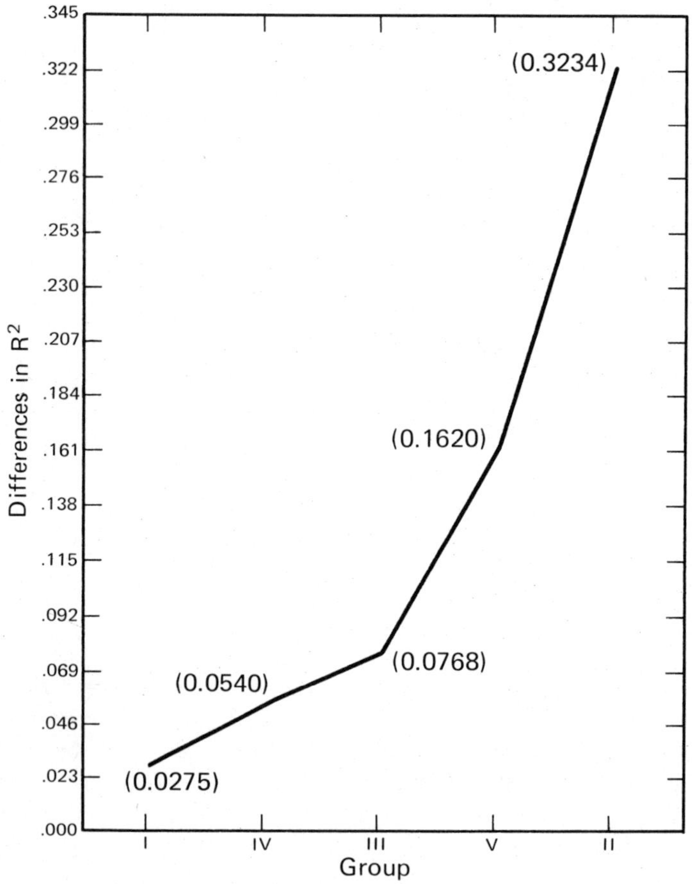

Figure 4-1. Differences in R^2 between the Predictive Sentencing Equation and the Second-Best Equation for Each Group.

outcome variables. Second, the variables in each of the predictive sentencing equations were applied separately to all 159 probationers. The R^2 in each case was essentially zero, indicating differential treatment effects.

The possibility was also considered that substantial numbers of probationers would be predicted to recidivate in each group thus seriously limiting the utility of this particular predictive sentencing scheme. The results, however, indicated the opposite. Figure 4-2 shows that 85.5 percent of the 159 probationers were predicted not to recidivate in at least one of the groups.

When all 214 descriptive phase subjects had completed their recidivism year, a further assessment of the "Final Model" was undertaken. Table 4-14 shows the distribution of probationers across treatment groups and the differences in the number of probationers by treatment group based on 159 and 214 probationers, respectively. First, R^2's were recomputed across 214 probationers using the predictive sentencing equations. The resulting shrinkage of the R^2's was appreciable but, in each case, at least 12 percent of the criterion variance

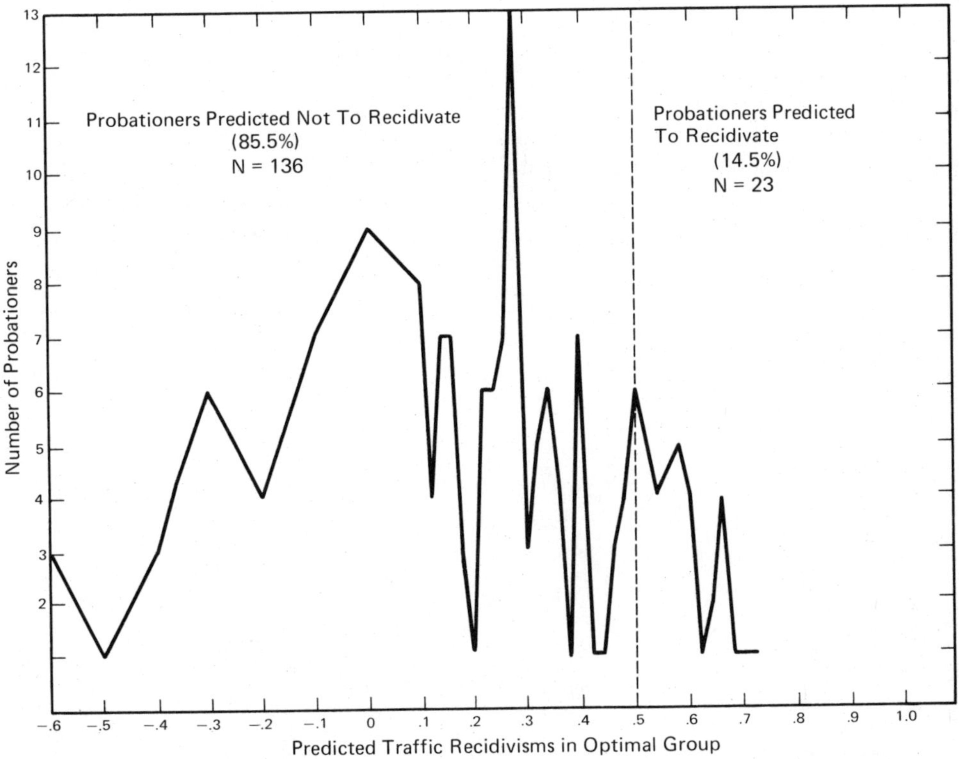

Figure 4-2. Frequency Polygon of Minimum Predicted Traffic Recidivisms for All 159 Probationers.

Table 4-14
Distribution of Sequentially Assigned Probationers Completing Recidivism Year

Group	*159 Probationers*	*214 Probationers*	*Difference*
1	39	41	3
2	29	44	15
3	32	43	11
4	31	42	11
5	29	44	15

(recidivism) was still explained by each predictive sentencing equation (see Table 4-15). Second, of utmost practical significance was the fact that the accuracy of classification remained stable despite the shrinkage in the R^2's caused by the addition of the 55 new probationers. Table 4-16 compares the accuracy of classification of the predictive sentencing equations using both 159 probationers and 214 probationers.

Ideally, it would have been most desirable to delay predictive sentencing until a model could have been constructed on all 214 sequentially assigned probationers. However, empirical research must frequently be conducted within personnel, budgetary, and time constraints that are inconsistent with ideal research conditions. Nevertheless, the generally promising results derived from the assessment of the predictive sentencing model based on the recidivism data obtained from only 159 probationers justified the initiation of predictive sentencing.

Predictive Phase

Sample Size

The total number of probationers sentenced into the program is set forth in Table 4-17 by region and by treatment group.

Table 4-15
R^2 Results

Group	*R^2 (159 Probationers)*	*R^2 (Applied to 214 Probationers)*
1	0.29	0.28
2	0.46	0.12
3	0.23	0.16
4	0.32	0.17
5	0.24	0.12

Table 4-16
Comparison of Accuracy of Classification of the Final Model Based on 159 and 214 Probationers (The figures for the 159 subjects are in parentheses)

Actual Status	Classification: Recidivist			Nonrecidivist			Total
Group 1							
Recidivist	25	76%	(77%)	3	38%	(38%)	28
Nonrecidivist	8	24%	(23%)	5	68%	(62%)	13
Total	33	100%		8	100%		41
Group 2							
Recidivist	15	71%	(80%)	6	26%	(14%)	21
Nonrecidivist	6	29%	(20%)	17	74%	(86%)	23
Total	21	100%		23	100%		44
Group 3							
Recidivist	26	76%	(76%)	1	11%	(14%)	27
Nonrecidivist	8	24%	(24%)	8	89%	(86%)	16
Total	34	100%		9	100%		43
Group 4							
Recidivist	25	76%	(83%)	3	33%	(14%)	28
Nonrecidivist	8	24%	(17%)	6	67%	(86%)	14
Total	33	100%		9	100%		42
Group 5							
Recidivist	19	76%	(80%)	8	42%	(36%)	27
Nonrecidivist	6	24%	(20%)	11	58%	(64%)	17
Total	25	100%		19	100%		44

Table 4-18 compares the actual with the projected intake based on the extrapolation from the population described in Table 4-17. Again, in all expansion areas, as in the case of the descriptive phase, there was not a sufficient number of drop-outs to warrant independent analysis of this subset of the target population.

In all areas except Lawton, the differences between the projected and actual intake were neither surprising nor did they jeopardize the research strategy. The projections were, after all, based on the Norman experience but were applied to areas intentionally selected for their differences from Norman. Second, procedures in traffic enforcement and traffic court administration differed in the

Table 4-17
Distribution on Intake in the Different Regions

	Region					
Group	*Norman*	*Tulsa Sequential*	*Tulsa Predictive*	*Lawton*	*Blackwell-Ponca City*	*Ardmore-Durant-Madill*
Fine control	32	97		5	11	17
1	10	12	5	0	–	–
2	36	16	83	9	11	17
3	0	18	12	0	–	–
4	0	15	6	0	–	–
5	7	11	18	0	–	–
Dropout	28	26		4	3	2
Total	113	72 (319)	221	18	25	36

Table 4-18
Actual Intake Compared with Projected Intake

City	*Actual*	*Projected*
Norman	113	84
Tulsa	319	492
Lawton	18	108
Ponca City-Blackwell	25	48
Ardmore-Madill-Durant	36	48
Total	476	780

regions, which may have accounted for some of the discrepancy between projected and actual intake. In Norman, more offenders than anticipated were sentenced into the program, a fact that might have been attributable to an increase in the Norman police force during the predictive phase.

With respect to intake in Lawton, it is very strange that a town of approximately 74,000 persons yielded fewer offenders in the target group than in regions having less than half of Lawton's population. Further, in all other regions, actual intake approached 50 percent or better of the projected intake, while in Lawton only 13 percent of the projected intake was attained. Leaving aside all other possible explanations, however likely, for this low intake rate, the most reasonable conclusion to be derived from this data is that a significantly lower number of citations were issued to the target population in Lawton.

Temporal and Regional Stability of Probationer Characteristics

Studies of probationer characteristics from both the descriptive and predictive phases were completed for purposes of determining the temporal and regional stability of the population under study. This was of both practical and theoretical interest. It seemed reasonable that the more nearly constant the characteristics of habitual traffic offenders from different periods of time and from different regions, the greater the generalizability and consequent utility of any predictive sentencing scheme. The best possible overall estimate in the temporal and regional stability among probationers across time and regions was based, first, on the 29 variables listed in Table 4-19 that were available from 358 probationers. These probationers consisted of 221 from the Norman descriptive phase, 53 from the Norman predictive phase, 61 from Tulsa, and 23 from the little cities. The 29 variables available for all probationers used in these analyses were derived from 39 best measures of the principal components of the 321 variables describing the probationer characteristics of 221 descriptive phase probationers. These 39 measures were then modified as follows to produce the 29 variables used:

1. Selection of only those variables that were available for probationers from both the descriptive and predictive phases and from all regions
2. Use of the five MMPI variables that were used in the predictive sentencing model.

These variables are listed in Table 4-19.

Second, using these variables and the available probationers, discriminant analyses were run to assess the degree of similarity between the probationers from the various regions and time periods. The overall discrimination among the foregoing regional and time groups was significant ($F = 2.19$, $p < 0.00$), disclosing that on some of the 29 variables the probationers from different regions and time periods are dissimilar. Given these differences, it was then of particular interest to determine whether they arose from variables employed in the predictive sentencing equations or from variables apparently unrelated to success or failure of the treatment modalities.

To test this hypothesis, the above analyses were again performed using the 10 variables employed in the predictive sentencing equations. See Table 4-11. In this second analysis, the overall discrimination among the temporal and regional groups was not significant ($F = 1.14$, $p > 0.05$). These results were encouraging because the characteristics identified by the variables used in the predictive sentencing model did not vary among the different temporal and regional groups.

Table 4-19
Variables Used for Study of Probationers' Characteristics

Variable Number	*Item*
1	Length of residence
2	Father's schooling
3	Family support
4	Other source of income
5	Number of jobs in past year
6	Number of siblings
7	Male friends
8	Female friends
9	Friends drag
10	Club membership
11	Own car
12	Dream car
13	Work on family car or cycle
14	Summer work
15	Drink-self
16	Weekday TV viewing
17	Number of school transfers
18	Average study time
19	Quit and enlist
20	Mom's expectations
21	Self-expectations
22	College essential
23	School offices
24	Age at intake
25	MMPI 6
26	MMPI 9
27	MMPI 10
28	MMPI 11
29	MMPI 14

Treatment Effectiveness

Traffic Recidivism. As in the descriptive phase, the criteria variables traffic recidivism, accident involvement, and nontraffic recidivism were utilized in all geographical locations to determine the relative effectiveness of the treatment modalities. Tables 4-20 and 4-21 report Norman probationers dichotomized traffic recidivism and trichotomized weighted traffic recidivism, respectively.

An examination of Table 4-20 discloses that with dichotomized traffic

Table 4-20

Number and Percentage of Norman Probationers in Fine Control and Groups 1, 2, and 5 with either Zero, or One or More than One Traffic Recidivism

Traffic Recidivisms	*Fine Control*	*Group 1*	*Group 2*	*Group 3*[a]	*Group 4*[a]	*Group 5*
Zero	8 (31%)	1 (11%)	4 (19%)			2 (22%)
One or more	18 (69%)	8 (89%)	17 (81%)			7 (78%)
Total	26 (100%)	9 (100%)	21 (100%)			9 (100%)

[a]No probationers were treated in these groups during the predictive phase.

Table 4-21

Number and Percentage of Norman Probationers in Fine Control and Groups 1, 2, and 5 with either Zero, One, or More than One Traffic Recidivism

Weighted Traffic Recidivism	*Fine Control*	*Group 1*	*Group 2*	*Group 3*[a]	*Group 4*[a]	*Group 5*
Zero	8 (31%)	1 (11%)	4 (19%)			2 (22%)
One	8 (31%)	1 (11%)	6 (29%)			0 (0%)
More than one	10 (38%)	7 (78%)	11 (52%)			7 (78%)
Total	26 (100%)	9 (100%)	21 (100%)			9 (100%)

[a]No probationers were treated in these groups during the predictive phase.

recidivism during the predictive phase, unlike the descriptive phase, neither treatment Group 2 nor 5 was significantly more effective than Group 1 or the fine control in reducing traffic recidivism. In Table 4-21, weighted traffic recidivism is trichotomized into zero, one, or more than one recidivisms, where recidivism was weighted by the number of half-months the subject spent in the Norman area. The results were not appreciably different from those based on dichotomized traffic recidivism.

Tables 4-22 and 4-23 report similar traffic recidivism data for Tulsa, including both the sequentially and predictively sentenced probationers. Again, as in the case of Norman, there is neither statistical nor practical differences among the groups using traffic recidivism as the criterion.

Table 4-24 reports the traffic recidivism and treatment groups of the 10 Lawton probationers. No statistical analyses were undertaken on these probationers because of the extremely small sample size.

Tables 4-25 and 4-26 report similar traffic recidivism for the Little Cities. Again there is no appreciable difference between the fine control and the Group 2 counseling group.

In Norman there was again an opportunity to follow-up predictively sentenced probationers from fine control and Groups 1 and 2, though in this instance it was limited to two years. Table 4-27 reports the mean differences in traffic recidivism between these groups.

Accident Involvement. Table 4-28 reports the relative effectiveness of the treatment modalities in Norman using accident involvement as the criterion variable. Interestingly, Group 2 appears to be the most effective treatment modality, but this might be viewed with caution since there were only eight accidents.

Table 4-29 reports the accident involvement data for Tulsa for both the sequentially and predictively sentenced probationers. Again, as in the case of traffic recidivism for Tulsa, there does not appear to be any appreciable difference in treatment modality effectiveness.

In the little cities, as in Norman, the Group 2 treatment modality appears to be more effective in reducing accident involvement than the fine control group. Table 4-30 reports these results for the little cities.

As in the case of traffic recidivism, Norman probationers' rate of accident involvement was determined for a two-year follow-up period. Table 4-31 reports these mean differences in accident involvement for the two-year follow-up period.

Nontraffic Recidivism. Tables 4-32 through 4-34 report nontraffic recidivism for Norman, Tulsa, and the little cities. None of the treatment modalities appear to be more effective than any other treatment modality in reducing nontraffic recidivism.

Table 4-22

Number and Percentage of Tulsa Probationers in Fine Control and Groups 1 through 5 with either Zero, or One or More than One Traffic Recidivism

Traffic Recidivism	*Fine Control*	*Group 1*	*Group 2*	*Group 3*	*Group 4*	*Group 5*
			Sequentially Sentenced			
Zero		1 (14%)	1 (9%)	4 (27%)	0 (0%)	2 (33%)
One or more		6 (85%)	10 (91%)	11 (73%)	12 (100%)	4 (67%)
Total		7 (100%)	11 (100%)	15 (100%)	12 (100%)	6 (100%)
			Predictively Sentenced			
Zero	14 (22%)	1 (25%)	8 (14%)	0 (0%)	0 (0%)	6 (75%)
One or more	51 (78%)	3 (75%)	50 (86%)	9 (100%)	3 (100%)	2 (25%)
Total	65 (100%)	4 (100%)	58 (100%)	9 (100%)	3 (100%)	8 (100%)

Table 4-23
Number and Percentage of Tulsa Probationers in Fine Control and Groups 1 through 5 with either Zero, One, or More than one Traffic Recidivism

Weighted Traffic Recidivism	*Fine Control*	*Group 1*	*Group 2*	*Group 3*	*Group 4*	*Group 5*
			Sequentially Sentenced			
Zero		1 (14%)	1 (9%)	5 (33%)	0 (0%)	2 (33%)
One		0 (0%)	2 (18%)	1 (7%)	1 (8%)	1 (17%)
More than one		6 (86%)	8 (73%)	9 (60%)	11 (92%)	3 (50%)
Total		7 (100%)	11 (100%)	15 (100%)	12 (100%)	6 (100%)
			Predictively Sentenced			
Zero	14 (22%)	1 (25%)	8 (14%)	0 (0%)	0 (0%)	6 (75%)
One	12 (18%)	0 (0%)	11 (19%)	1 (11%)	0 (0%)	0 (0%)
More than one	39 (60%)	3 (75%)	39 (67%)	8 (89%)	3 (100%)	2 (25%)
Total	65 (100%)	4 (100%)	58 (100%)	9 (100%)	3 (100%)	8 (100%)

Table 4-24
Number of Traffic Recidivisms of Lawton Probationers

Probationer	*Treatment Group*	*Number of Recidivisms*
1	2	1
2	1	0
3	2	1
4	Fine control	0
5	Fine control	2
6	2	3
7	Fine control	0
8	2	2
9	Fine control	0
10	Fine control	0

Table 4-25
Number and Percentage of Little Cities' Probationers in Fine Control and Group 2 with either Zero, One or More than One Traffic Recidivism

Traffic Recidivism	*Fine Control*	*Group 2*
Zero	8 (31%)	8 (35%)
One or more	18 (69%)	15 (65%)
Total	26 (100%)	23 (100%)

Two-Year Follow-Up. Again, two-year follow-up nontraffic recidivism data was available in Norman. Table 4-35 reports the mean differences.

Summary. During the descriptive phase, across all three criteria, individual counseling proved superior not only to the fine control but also to the other three innovative treatments. Not surprisingly, during the predictive phase the model assigned the preponderance of available probationers in all regions to Group 2, individual counseling. Given this preponderance of probationers assigned to individual counseling, little can be said about the differential predictive effects of the other innovative treatments. This reflects the failure of these innovations in the descriptive phase for the Norman area and, perhaps more important, is indicative of the impracticablity of these treatment modalities for the target population in question. An inspection of the recidivism and accident involvement criteria, in contrast to the descriptive phase, discloses that the powerful treatment effects of individual counseling vanished during the predictive phase. In the case of traffic recidivism, none of the innovative treatment modalities employed in any region were significantly better than the

Table 4-26
Number and Percentage of Little Cities' Probationers in Fine Control and Group 2 with either Zero, One, or More than One Traffic Recidivism

Weighted Traffic Recidivism	*Fine Control*	*Group 2*
Zero	8 (31%)	8 (35%)
One	4 (15%)	3 (12%)
More than one	14 (54%)	12 (52%)
Total	26 (100%)	23 (100%)

Table 4-27
Mean Values for Traffic Recidivism in Norman between Fine Control, Group 1, and Group 2 for the Two-Year Posttreatment Recidivism Period

Groups	*Number of Subjects*	*Year One*	*Year Two*
Fine control	16	0.69	0.62
Group 1	8	0.88	0.88
Group 2	13	0.92	0.54

fine control groups. Moreover, in Tulsa, where the Norman sequential sentencing was replicated simultaneously, the results of predictive sentencing disclosed no greater utility than sequential sentencing or fine control. In Lawton the failure of the experiment to generate any more than 10 probationers renders interpretation impossible. In the little cities, where probationers were randomly assigned only to fine control and Group 2, traffic recidivism results favored the Group 2 treatment modality over the fine control, but this could be attributable to random fluctuation.

In Norman as to accident involvement, the treatment effect of Group 2 over the fine control is appreciable, but attribution of the difference to sampling error cannot be ruled out. In the other regions, innovative treatment was not clearly demonstrated to reduce accident involvement in comparison with fine control.

In the case of nontraffic offenses, some superiority of the innovative treatments over fine control group is indicated, but interpretation is again difficult because of a low base rate that may be associated with the 1972 statutory change in the Oklahoma law making records of persons in the target population confidential.

Adherence to Treatment

As noted earlier, at the inception of the project a firm policy decision was made that the chief probation officer monitor the recordings of the treatment sessions

Table 4-28
Number and Percentage of Norman Probationers in Fine Control and Groups 1, 2, and 5 Involved in Zero, One or More than One Accidents in the Recidivism Year

Accident Involvement	*Fine Control*	*Group 1*	*Group 2*	*Group 3*[a]	*Group 4*[a]	*Group 5*
Zero	20 (80%)	7 (78%)	19 (95%)			9 (100%)
One or more	5 (20%)	2 (22%)	1 (5%)			0 (0%)
Total	25 (100%)	9 (100%)	20 (100%)			9 (100%)

[a]No probationers were treated in these groups during the predictive phase.

Table 4-29
Number and Percentage of Tulsa Probationers in Fine Control and Groups 1 through 5 Involved in Zero, or One or More than One Accidents in the Recidivism Year

Accident Involvement	*Fine Control*	*Group 1*	*Group 2*	*Group 3*	*Group 4*	*Group 5*
Sequentially Sentenced						
Zero		7 (100%)	9 (82%)	12 (80%)	8 (67%)	4 (67%)
One or more		0 (0%)	2 (18%)	3 (20%)	4 (33%)	2 (33%)
Total		7 (100%)	11 (100%)	15 (100%)	12 (100%)	6 (100%)
Predictively Sentenced						
Zero	49 (75%)	4 (100%)	43 (74%)	8 (89%)	3 (100%)	6 (75%)
One or more	16 (25%)	0 (0%)	15 (26%)	1 (11%)	0 (0%)	2 (25%)
Total	65 (100%)	4 (100%)	58 (100%)	9 (100%)	3 (100%)	8 (100%)

Table 4-30
Number and Percentage of Little Cities' Probationers in Fine Control and Group 2 Involved in Zero, or One or More than One Accidents in the Recidivism Year

Accident Involvement	*Fine Control*	*Group 2*
Zero	4 (50%)	12 (75%)
One or more	4 (50%)	4 (25%)
Total	8 (100%)	16 (100%)

Table 4-31
Mean Values for Accident Involvement Among Fine Control, Group 1, and Group 2 for the Two-Year Posttreatment Recidivism Year

Groups	*Number of Probationers*	*Year One*	*Year Two*
Fine control	16	0.13	0.38
Group 1	8	0.25	0.12
Group 2	13	0.08	0.00

to evaluate the assistant probation officer in his delivery of the specified treatment. This policy provided the investigators with some assurance that the counseling process was roughly equivalent for all probationers, and as a result of this policy, it is believed that, generally, the prescribed treatment was the delivered treatment. However, the nature of any counseling process, be it reality therapy, gestalt therapy, or drivers education, is an aggregate of many separate processes. For this reason, more precise measurement was attempted to analyze the treatments themselves so that those processes within the treatments that were associated with successful outcomes, that is, no recidivism, might be isolated with greater particularity.

This analysis of the treatments was guided by four questions. First, to what extent were the treatment contents in adherence to the prescribed curricula? Second, in the case of Groups 2 and 3, to what extent were the treatments in adherence to Reality Therapy? Third, to what extent was the degree of adherence to the prescribed curricula and/or Reality Therapy positively related to nonrecidivism? Fourth, was there some other process not included in the prescribed curricula or in Reality Therapy that was more strongly related to nonrecidivism?

The answer to these questions necessitated a reliable and valid measurement of the content of the treatment sessions. Ultimately, this measurement was attempted using the *Harvard Fourth Psychosociological Dictionary* with the *General Inquirer* system for content analysis.[7] Analyses of these measures

Table 4-32

Number and Percentage of Norman Probationers in Fine Control and Groups 1, 2, and 5 with either Zero, or One or More than One Nontraffic Recidivisms

Nontraffic Recidivism	*Fine Control*	*Group 1*	*Group 2*	*Group 3*[a]	*Group 4*[a]	*Group 5*
Zero	24 (92%)	9 (100%)	21 (100%)			8 (89%)
One or more	2 (8%)	0 (0%)	0 (0%)			1 (11%)
Total	26 (100%)	9 (100%)	21 (100%)			9 (100%)

[a]No probationers were treated in these groups during the predictive phase.

Table 4-33

Number and Percentage of Tulsa Probationers in Fine Control and Groups 1 through 5 with either Zero, or One or More than One Nontraffic Recidivisms

Nontraffic Recidivisms	*Fine Control*	*Group 1*	*Group 2*	*Group 3*	*Group 4*	*Group 5*
			Sequentially Sentenced			
Zero		6 (86%)	10 (91%)	15 (100%)	12 (100%)	6 (100%)
One or more		1 (14%)	1 (9%)	0 (0%)	0 (0%)	0 (0%)
Total		7 (100%)	11 (100%)	15 (100%)	12 (100%)	6 (100%)
			Predictively Sentenced			
Zero	61 (94%)	3 (75%)	55 (95%)	8 (89%)	3 (100%)	7 (88%)
One or more	4 (6%)	1 (25%)	3 (5%)	1 (11%)	0 (0%)	1 (12%)
Total	65 (100%)	4 (100%)	58 (100%)	9 (100%)	3 (100%)	8 (100%)

Table 4-34
Number and Percentage of Little Cities' Probationers in Fine Control and Group 2 with either Zero, or One or More than One Nontraffic Recidivisms

Nontraffic Recidivism	*Fine Control*	*Group 2*
Zero	20 (77%)	22 (96%)
One or more	6 (23%)	1 (4%)
Total	26 (100%)	23 (100%)

Table 4-35
Mean Values for Nontraffic Recidivism between Fine Control, Group 1, and Group 2 for the Two-Year Posttreatment Recidivism Period

Groups	*Number of Subjects*	*Year One*	*Year Two*
Fine control	16	0.12	0.06
Group 1	8	0.00	0.12
Group 2	13	0.00	0.08

suggested that the dictionary categories or tags were of rather low reliability. Nevertheless, an attempt was made to determine the degree of relationship between recidivism and those categories with less questionable reliabilities.

The results of a pilot study utilizing the *General Inquirer* system did disclose a significant relationship between the expected and observed rank orderings for treatment Groups 2, 3, 4, and 5, though Groups 4 and 5 were best on the special purpose categories, as was expected. However, when treatment modality assessment on Groups 2 and 3 was submitted to comprehensive human validation, there was little indication that computer-assisted monitoring measured the degree of adherence to the curriculum or to Reality Therapy in Groups 2 and 3.

This failure, while partly attributable to *General Inquirer*, is in a large measure due to the inadequacy of the *Harvard Fourth Psychosociological Dictionary* in describing real, ongoing, counseling processes. This inadequacy is reflective of two primary defects. First, from a theoretical viewpoint, very little is known about what takes place within a one-to-one counseling situation. (If it works, why? What should distinguish a successful counseling encounter from an unsuccessful encounter?) This lack of a theoretical framework accounts for the lack of a systematic classification of the *Harvard IV* categories as they were applied to a counseling process.

Second, from a more practical viewpoint, there appears to be little rhyme or reason behind the design of the categories in the *Harvard IV* dictionary. The categories were found to be redundant and overlapping, so that when it was used to tap some rather abstract themes, multiinterpretations resulted.

These results in the evaluation of the Group 2 (3) treatment certainly suggest that whenever one attempts to examine the communication between a counselor and counselee, much attention must be given to the dictionary to confine it to those realms where knowledge is highest. This is not to say that computer-assigned monitoring is not to be attempted; rather, it needs to be done within a well-defined framework and on a scale less grandiose than *Harvard IV*. Also, it appears that at the present state of the art, no computer-assisted monitoring should be undertaken without a comprehensive human validation. Certainly, the cost of such an undertaking is great. But given the possible policy implications for future counseling processes, the benefits of a well-conceived and well-executed computer-assisted monitoring scheme far outweigh the costs. Certainly, a major disappointment of the treatment modality assessment was its failure to shed any light on the surprising and strange results of the predictive phase Group 2 treatment. In the end, it can only be surmised that the counseling process for Group 2 treatment was roughly equivalent for all probationers based on the systematic monitoring of the sessions by the chief probation officer.

Notes

1. Veldman, D.J., *Fortran Programming for the Behavioral Sciences* (New York: Holt, Rinehart and Winston, 1967).

2. Heussenstamm, F.K., "Bumper Stickers and the Cops," *Trans-Action* (February 1971), pp. 32-35.

3. Pepinsky, Harold E., "Police Decision-Making," in Don M. Gottfredson, (ed.), *Decision-Making in the Criminal Justice System: Reviews and Essays* (Rockville, Md.: National Institute of Mental Health, Center for Studies of Crime and Delinquency, 1975), pp. 40-43.

4. See Volume II, *Final Report, 16-18 Year-Old Male Habitual Traffic Offenders*, University of Oklahoma Office of Research Administration, 1976, Appendix IV-6, p. IV-6-1.

5. See 10 *Okla. Stat.* §1101(a) and 1111.

6. Veldman, *Fortran Programming*; Tarver, Don, *Personal Communication*, 1972.

7. Stone, Philip J., Dunphy, Dexter C., Smith, Marshall S., and Ogilvie, Daniel M., *The General Inquirer: A Computer Approach to Content Analysis* (Cambridge, Mass.: The M.I.T. Press, 1966).

5 Conclusions

Sentencing Model Reevaluated

Summary of Treatment Effectiveness

Figures 5-1, 5-2, and 5-3 summarize the traffic recidivism, accident involvement, and nontraffic recidivism results reported in detail in Chapter 4 for all three phases of the project, namely, the preprobation, descriptive, and predictive phases. In the case of the predictive phase only the fine control and Group 2 treatment modality findings are disclosed for each region. This is done to permit evaluation only on groups with a minimum of 20 probationers, to enhance the reliability of interpretations, and to promote clarity in summarizing the findings. The results from the Lawton region are not reported for the reasons already explained in Chapter 4.

In the case of traffic recidivism, notice that while the fine control remained stable throughout the three phases of the project, the effectiveness of Group 2 individual counseling declined sharply from the Norman descriptive phase to the Norman, Tulsa, and Little Cities predictive phase. Group 2, except in Tulsa, continued to show relatively greater effectiveness in reducing accident involvement throughout the project than the fine control groups. The same results occurred in the case of nontraffic recidivism. It is true, as reported earlier, that a legislative change in the keeping of court records, could have conceivably affected these results, but, in any case, they should have been affected equally across all groups within random fluctuation.

The Practical Efficiency of the Model

The evaluation of the sentencing model is confined to the Group 2 equation within the model. Too few probationers were sentenced into the other modalities to permit evaluation of the relative effectiveness of the other sentencing equations of the model. Inspection of Figure 5-1 discloses that persons predictively sentenced into group individual counseling in both Norman and Tulsa had higher traffic recidivism rates than the fine control group. Clearly, the overall practical efficiency of the model (reliable reduction in traffic recidivism) was null, at least, during the years of the predictive phase. On the other hand, in the case of Norman and the Little Cities, an inspection of Figures

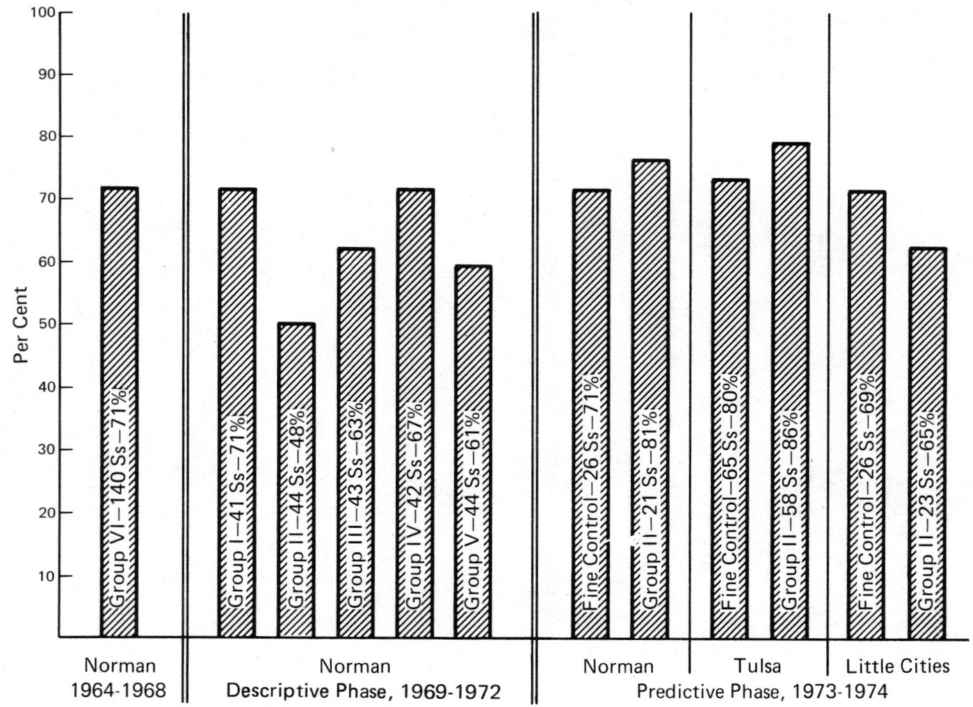

Figure 5-1. Traffic Recidivism across the Three Phases of the Project for Groups Having a Minimum of Twenty Probationers.

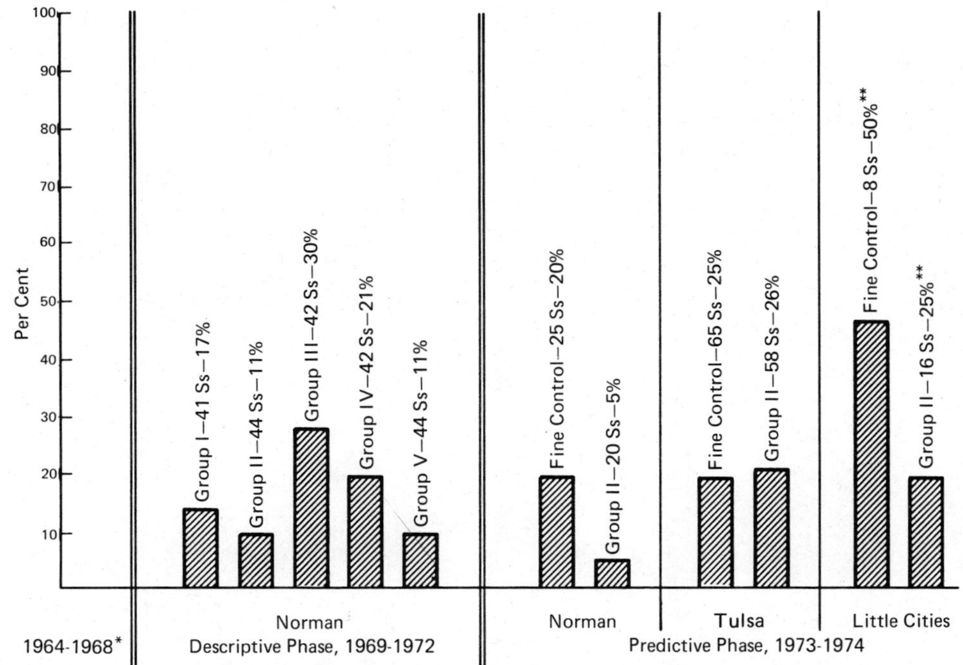

* No comparable data to Group VI. Only traffic recidivism data available for this period.

** The same 23 probationers were used in compiling this data, but some were not counted because records of accident involvement were questionable.

Figure 5-2. Accident Involvement across the Descriptive and Predictive Phases of the Project for Groups Having a Minimum of Twenty Probationers.

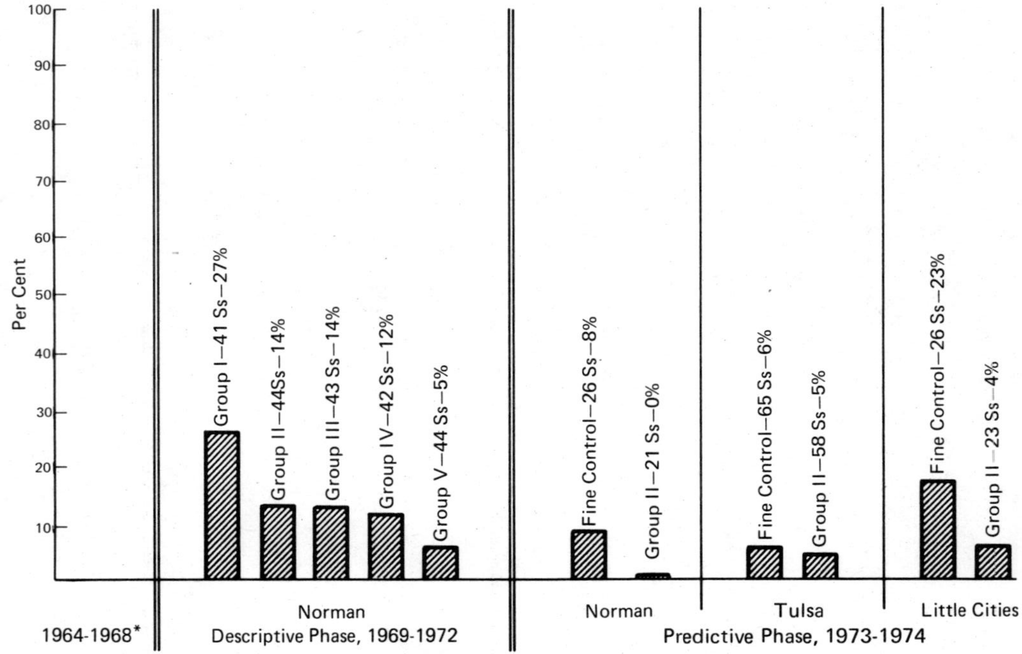

* No comparable data to Group VI. Only traffic recidivism data available for this period.

Figure 5-3. Nontraffic Recidivism across the Descriptive and Predictive Phases of the Project for Groups Having a Minimum of Twenty Probationers.

5-2 and 5-3 discloses that Group 2 individual counseling showed lower accident involvement and nontraffic recidivism than the fine control group. In consequence, there exists the perplexing picture of the sentencing equation failing on the one criterion variable and succeeding on the other two in Norman and the Little Cities, assuming that the low base rate for accident involvement and nontraffic recidivism does not affect the interpretation. The assessment of the practical efficiency of the sentencing equation is then further confounded by its failure in Tulsa on accident involvement and nontraffic recidivism.

The Theoretical Efficiency of the Model

Another dimension on which to judge the efficacy of the sentencing equation is its theoretical efficiency, namely, the predictive power of the equation independent of its practicality. Two measures were employed. The first and the more common measure was to calculate the cross-validated R^2. In Norman, this R^2 between predicted traffic recidivism and observed traffic recidivism was 0.06. The correlation between the predicted and the observed traffic recidivism when both were dichotomized at their respective medians (0.23 for predicted traffic recidivism and 1.5 for observed traffic recidivism) was 0.23. In the little cities the R^2 between predicted traffic recidivism and observed traffic recidivism was 0.46.

In Tulsa the results were equivocal. For probationers who completed treatment before October 1, 1973, the correlation between the predicted traffic recidivism and the observed traffic recidivism was 0.23. On the other hand, for probationers completing treatment after October 1, 1973, the correlation between the predicted traffic recidivism and the observed traffic recidivism was zero.

There were too few subjects in Norman and the little cities to permit calculation of cross-validated R^2 by time of treatment. By conventional standards the preponderance of the results of Norman, little cities, and early Tulsa probationers indicate strong theoretical validation of the sentencing equation. This fact must be weighed against the equation failure with respect to late probationers in Tulsa, which is suggestive of a significant time factor in cross-validating the predictability of any sentencing equation.

A second approach in evaluating the theoretical efficiency of a model is to examine the accuracy of classification by employing the sentencing equation. Recall in Chapter 4 this approach was used for a post hoc assessment of the predictive sentencing model utilizing the 214 sequentially sentenced probationers. Further, determining the accuracy of classification consisted of counting the number of recidivators who were predicted to recidivate plus the number of nonrecidivators who were predicted not to recidivate. A probationer was predicted to recidivate if his predicted recidivism score (PNTR) was greater than the cut-point of 0.50; he was predicted not to recidivate if his score was less than or equal to 0.50. Table 5-1 sets forth the accuracy of classification for those probationers sentenced into Group 2 across each region.

Examination of this table reveals that a substantial number of probationers were inaccurately classified as nonrecidivators. This result is not, however, inconsistent with the findings that treatment effectiveness was null; yet, at the same time, the cross-validated R^2's were substantial. That is, the average rate of recidivism has increased, so that the median at which to divide the recidivism scale falls at 1.5. Table 5-2 again presents the accuracy of classification of the Group 2 sentencing equation across each region. In Table 5-2, however, probationers are classified as recidivators only if they committed two or more traffic offenses in their posttreatment recidivism year.

While the accuracy was still not perfect, there was, nevertheless a marked improvement indicating that the model has some theoretical efficiency, although at a higher average rate of recidivism.

An evaluation of the sentencing equation for Group 2 thus discloses that while it looks very good theoretically, its practical utility is null. One possibility for increasing the practical utility of the sentencing equation would be to change the decision-rule made during the descriptive phase in the direction of being more selective in assigning probationers to Group 2. This increased selectivity would be achieved by lowering the cut-point dividing predicted recidivators from

Table 5-1
Accuracy of Classification of the Group 2 Sentencing Equation across Each Region

Actual Status	Classification		
Norman			
	Recidivist	*Nonrecidivist*	*Total*
Recidivist	4 (100%)	13 (76.5%)	17
Nonrecidivist	0 (0%)	4 (23.5%)	4
Total	4 (100%)	17 (100%)	21
Tulsa Predictive			
	Recidivist	*Nonrecidivist*	*Total*
Recidivist	3 (100%)	47 (85.5%)	50
Nonrecidivist	0 (0%)	8 (14.5%)	8
Total	3 (100%)	55 (100%)	58
Little Cities			
	Recidivist	*Nonrecidivist*	*Total*
Recidivist	8 (88.9%)	7 (50.0%)	15
Nonrecidivist	1 (11.1%)	7 (50.0%)	8
Total	9 (100%)	14 (100%)	23

Table 5-2
Accuracy of Classification of the Group 2 Sentencing Equation across Each Region Where Recidivism is Dichotomized

Actual Status	Classification		
Norman			
	Recidivist	*Nonrecidivist*	*Total*
Recidivist	3 (75.0%)	8 47.1%)	11
Nonrecidivist	1 (25.0%)	9 (52.9%)	10
Total	4 (100%)	17 (100%)	21
Tulsa Predictive			
	Recidivist	*Nonrecidivist*	*Total*
Recidivist	2 (66.7%)	37 (67.3%)	39
Nonrecidivist	1 (33.3%)	18 (32.7%)	19
Total	3 (100%)	55 (100%)	58
Little Cities			
	Recidivist	*Nonrecidivist*	*Total*
Recidivist	7 (77.8%)	5 (35.7%)	12
Nonrecidivist	2 (22.2%)	9 (64.3%)	11
Total	9 (100%)	14 (100%)	23

predicted nonrecidivators. This greater selectivity could be expected to reduce the recidivism rate, but at the expense of confining treatment to relatively few probationers. If, for example, in Norman, only probationers with predicted traffic recidivisms of less than 0.23 (cut-point) were assigned to individual counseling, then only 36 percent of the probationers eligible for the program could be treated. This is in contrast to the descriptive phase where an *anticipated* 85 percent of the eligible probationers could have been successfully treated if all those with predicted traffic recidivisms of less than 0.50 (cut-point) would have been assigned to their optimal treatment.[1]

The Anomalous Results

Prior to the initiation of the predictive phase, the adequacy of the model was evaluated in a variety of ways, as reported in Chapter 4. The results of each assessment favored the testing of the model in the cross-validation experiment. The subsequent assessment of the theoretical efficiency of the model supported these earlier confirmatory analyses. Yet the outcomes were clearly inconsistent with these expectations. Moreover, the outcomes were internally contradictory. First and foremost, why was Group 2 individual counseling less effective in reducing traffic recidivism in the predictive phase than in the descriptive phase?

This contradiction is heightened by the persistence of the treatment effectiveness of Group 2 over a four-year follow-up period for those probationers who were counseled during the descriptive phase. Moreover, why should Group 2 be less effective in reducing traffic recidivism but remain relatively effective in reducing accident involvement and nontraffic recidivism. Figure 5-4 provides a graphic depiction of these anomalies for the Norman area. The other areas are not shown due to the short time span during which the project was operated in these areas.

Finally, returning to theoretical efficiency, why was the cross-validated R so high, but the practical efficiency of the Group 2 sentencing equation so low? In short, the equation predicts with considerable fidelity in Norman, but even those probationers sentenced in accordance with the model fared no better with respect to traffic recidivism than those probationers assigned to fine control. Why?

There are numerous conventional explanations that could possibly account for the contradictory conclusions. The first of these is that there was no treatment effect operating. Rather, a Hawthorne effect was mistaken for a treatment effect. That is, the observed differences in the mean levels of traffic recidivism should be attributed to novelty and expectancy on the part of probationers and probation officers rather than the administration of the treatment itself. In short, Group 2's effectiveness was merely a placebo diminishing with the passage of time. Another explanation would be that apparent differences between groups and across time were merely artifacts of changes in enforcement practices, court procedures, probationary practices, and administrative control over the project. Still another plausible explanation for the varying shifts in effectiveness is a marked change in the characteristics of the target population. A final explanation is that the results are nothing more than the product of research error, including the acquisition, coding, and processing of data.

The difficulty with attributing the results to Hawthorne effects are at least twofold. First, with reference to the probationers, most of the treatment groups never looked reliably better than the fine control group. If Hawthorne were operating, one would suppose the expectancy would be the same for all treatment groups. However, is there any apparent Hawthorne evident only in Group 2? Recall that Group 2, the treatment group that maximized individual attention and interpersonal relation between probationer and probation officer, was also the treatment group that looked best in relation to fine control. Assuming that this caused a Hawthorne effect, one would expect a decline in the effectiveness of Group 2 treatment over time. The strongest contrary evidence is based on the fact that fewer probationers who were individually counseled in the second year of the project recidivated than probationers counseled in the first year of the project, and fewer probationers counseled in the third year recidivated than those counseled in the second year. This pattern is just the opposite of what is expected from a Hawthorne effect.

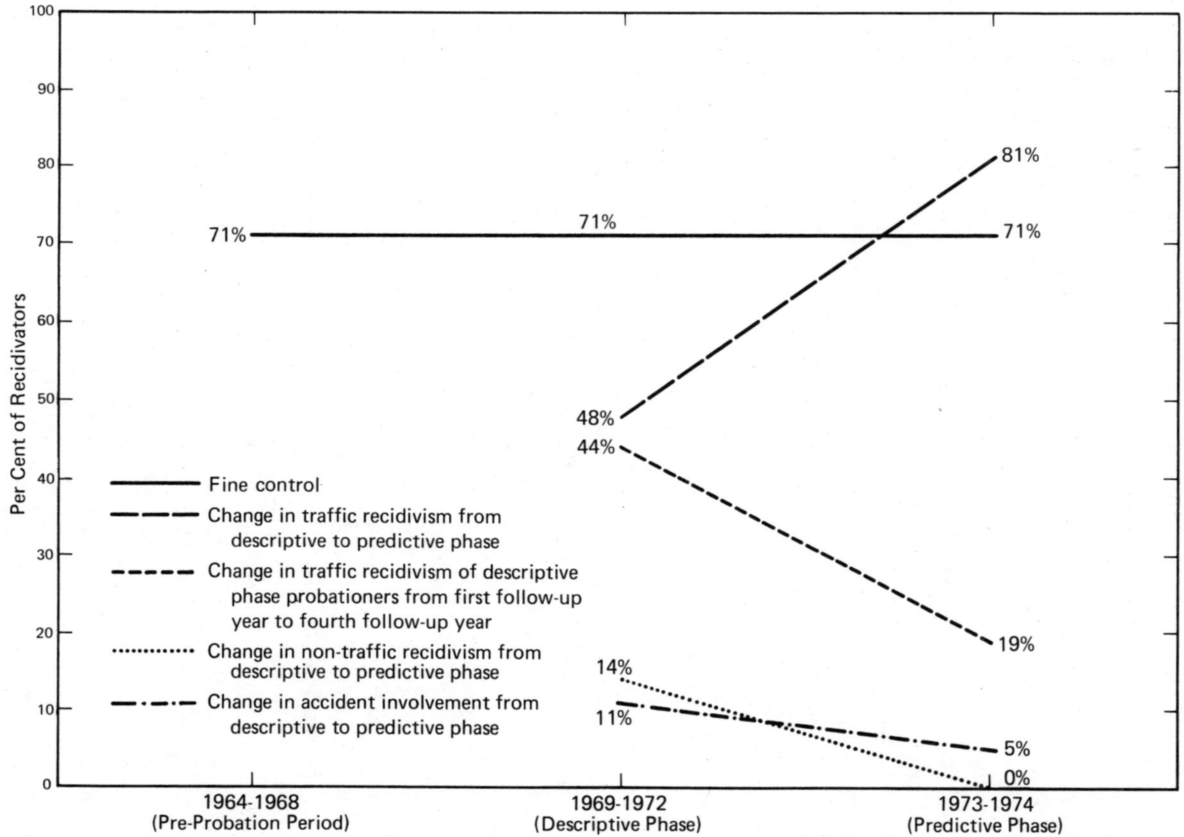

Figure 5-4. Anomalous Group 2 Traffic Recidivism Results Compared with the Fine Control Group for the Norman Area for Three Project Periods.

To test the Hawthorne hypothesis further, the same group of fine control and Group 2 probationers were followed up not just one year, but into their second, third, and fourth years. There were 34 probationers in Group 1 and 32 probationers in Group 2 who were followed up. A pattern of outcome supporting the Hawthorne interpretation would be an initial difference between the means of the two groups, followed by a rapid convergence of the means. Also, if the initial difference were based on random fluctuation only, then one would expect that no consistent pattern favoring Group 2 over fine control would be found. Even if Group 2 had exerted some true effect, one would still expect marked dissipation in its effectiveness with the passage of time.

Quite to the contrary, as Figure 5-5 clearly indicates, not only were the Group 2 people superior during the entire year by year four-year follow-up period, but also the slopes of the trend lines for the two groups were parallel throughout the period. Further, the differences between the two groups over the four-year period are statistically reliable. ($F = 4.887$, $p = 0.028$, $df = (1,64)$). Not only does this vitiate the Hawthorne hypothesis, further, it undermines the rival hypothesis of negligible treatment effect against the background of random fluctuation.

Second, a Hawthorne effect could have operated through the assistant probation officer (counselor) rather than the probationer. If this were the case, one would expect the assistant probation officer's expectancies to be highest, and most likely to be fulfilled, in the earlier stages of the project. This would be reflected in an immediate short-term effectiveness. However, the persistence of Group 2 treatment effectiveness during the descriptive phase would again seem to refute this argument.

On the other hand, the predictive phase of the project did not operate for sufficient duration to generate either the number of probationers or the time span required for an assessment of possible Hawthorne effects in this phase. It is interesting to note that in Tulsa the individual counseled probationers who terminated treatment early in the predictive phase fared somewhat better on traffic recidivism than did their later counterparts, which raises a suspicion of a Hawthorne effect there. (These differences were not, however, significant. Yet, it is also true that the predictive model cross-validated strongly on early probationers and not at all on later probationers.) Further, the effects of Hawthorne phenomena could not be distinguished from any other confounding factor that may have affected treatment. Moreover, even if there was a Hawthorne effect operating during the predictive phase, it could hardly serve to explain the inconsistent results of the project.

One might also surmise that unplanned changes in practices unrelated to treatment, such as law enforcement practices, court procedures, probation practices, and control over the administration of the project, might account for the differences in the outcome between the descriptive and predictive phases.

As to enforcement practices, in Norman there was a substantial increase in

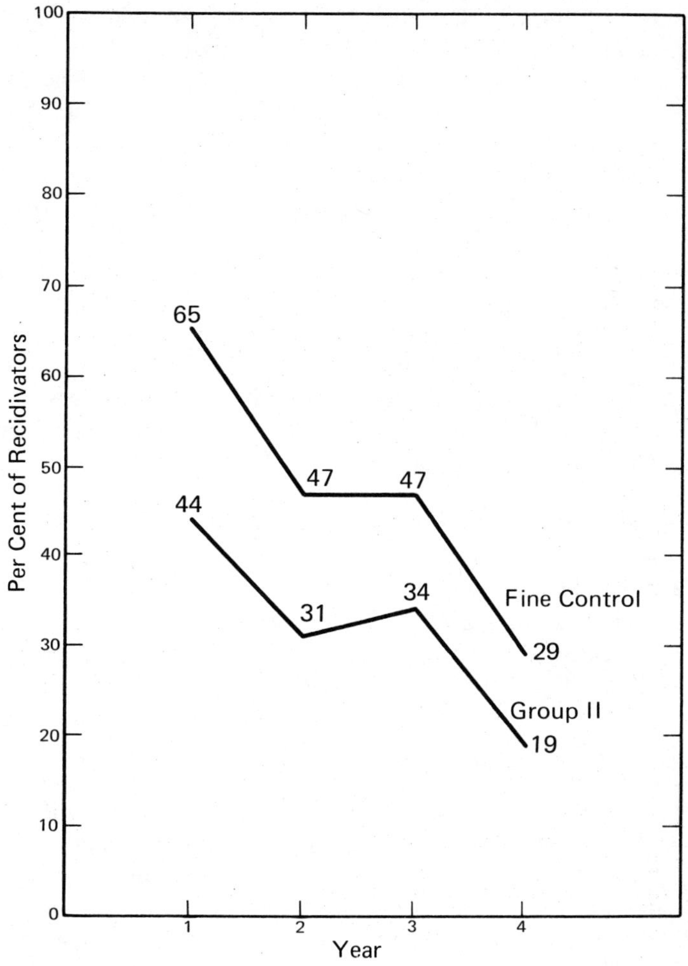

Figure 5-5. Effectiveness of Group 2 over Fine Control by Years in Reducing Traffic Recidivism among Probationers Fined or Counseled during Descriptive Phase.

police personnel during the duration of the project with accompanying changes in enforcement equipment, such as the number of police and radar units. One may also surmise that there was change in the covert enforcement policy of the police agency from time to time during the project. For example, an increase in the number of traffic citations written would be expected to increase the mean traffic recidivism rate for all groups equally. But how could this act to alter selectively the differences in mean levels between groups? This would be true only if the police could discern individually counseled probationers from fine controls and systematically base the issuance of citations on this knowledge. This is clearly implausible. It is even less plausible that the police could penetrate the social milieu of the counseled probationers and alter their attitudes and behaviors in the driving situation. Their capacity to directly affect the counseling session was null.

In court procedures, it is believed that there was minimal change in the Norman area that might have affected the number of probationers refusing treatment or the attitude of court personnel toward probationers entering the program. In other project areas, such as Tulsa, where control over the judicial administration of the project was indirect at best, there is more reason to believe that there might have been periodic changes in court procedures that might have influenced outcome.

In probationary practices, there was a substantial reduction in testing time in the Norman area from 4 to 6 hours during the descriptive phase to 1 to 1½ hours during the predictive phase. There were changes in the probationary counseling personnel throughout the duration of the project.

General administrative control, or the lack of it, could be a substantial factor in influencing the extent of fidelity to the research design. There is, indeed, some evidence that administrative control was lacking in some regions. Among participating judges this was manifested by behavior ranging from adequate judicial supervision, to lack of direct ongoing involvement, to supreme indifference. Also, in Tulsa there is evidence that intake into the program fluctuated with the recency and duration of visits by Norman project personnel to assist in the operation of the program there. Another source of variation associated with administrative control could be in the availability and accuracy of records and the mode of record keeping, both statewide and locally.

However pernicious these factors and the variations in them might have been, by the logic of the Fisherian randomized design, both fine control and individually counseled groups should have been equally affected within random fluctuation by these factors. For example, effective April 4, 1972 in Oklahoma, male persons 18 years of age or younger were redefined as juveniles thus making their records confidential and correspondingly less accessible for data collection. At the same time, it will be noted from Figure 5-4 that there was a significant decline in nontraffic recidivism in the Norman area that could be explained by this fact alone. However, while mean levels in nontraffic recidivism would be affected, differences in mean levels would not be. Inspection of Figure 5-3 discloses just this state of affairs.

With respect to marked change in the population of interest, the argument might be made that the project simply "skimmed the cream," the probationers changed, there was a maturation of the probationers, or there was a change in expectancies. However, first, the multiple discriminant function based on the 10 variables in the sentencing model (thought to be most related to traffic recidivism) indicated no difference over time. Second, again by the logic of randomized assignment, differences in the target population could affect mean levels but not differences in mean levels.

Finally, as to research error, it might be divided into either random or systematic error. The random component might understate or attenuate existing relationships in the data, but it is unlikely that random error would actually introduce such spurious relationships as disclosed. Systematic error can only be evaluated by the reader in light of the data disclosed.

Treatment Effectiveness Deterioration

In conclusion, none of the conventional explanations seem adequate to explain the four anomalous results of the project. In point of fact, what happened to cause the deterioration in treatment between the descriptive and predictive phases? It was hoped that the analyses described earlier to explain the treatment failure would at least partially solve the riddle. However, these analyses served only to increase the dilemma and produce additional anomalies. Moreover, the conventional explanations, such as Hawthorne effects, changes in enforcement policy, probation practices, or administrative control, are all useful for explaining changes in mean levels of groups, but they seem hardly adequate to explain the anomalous pattern of differences in mean levels among groups on the three different project criterion measures.

The single most important result triggering a less orthodox evaluation of project results was the dramatic decline in Group 2 treatment effectiveness between the descriptive and predictive phases of the project. A simple and direct test of the relationship between the change in the rate of traffic recidivism and the change from the descriptive to the predicted phase is shown in the chi-square analysis reported in Figure 5-6.

Certainly these results underscore the dramatic decline in Group 2 treatment effectiveness between the descriptive and predictive phases of the project. Also, during the descriptive phase, Group 2 was appreciably better than all other treatment modalities, at least, in reducing traffic recidivism. Hence, with the formulation of the Group 2 predictive sentencing equation and the exhaustive supportive statistical analyses, the question became not whether Group 2 would be an improvement over the fine control, but what the magnitude of the improvement associated with the degree of cross-validation of the model would be. The later demonstrated theoretical efficiency of the model during cross-validation was supportive of these earlier expectancies of the overall efficiency of the Group 2 treatment. But even given these earlier expectancies, it did not occur to the investigators at the beginning of the predictive phase that the treatment effect would be so susceptible to deterioration over time.

Traffic Recidivism

Phase		0	One, or More	
	Descriptive Phase	23	21	44
	Predictive Phase	9	25	34
		32	46	78

Chi Square = 4.26
p = .03
df = 1

Figure 5-6. Chi-Square between Descriptive and Predictive Phases and Traffic Recidivism.

The decline in Group 2 treatment effectiveness, the failure of the conventional approaches to explain the anomalies, and the differential loss in treatment effectiveness between individually counseled probationers and the fine controls, despite the randomized experimental design, all pointed to some external event undermining the treatment process itself.

If, indeed, some yet unaccounted for external event was operating to affect the treatment, this event was not detected until all of the outcome data had been analyzed. Why? Research rarely examines the treatment itself for changes in quality over time or the independent factors that might influence the quality of the treatment. A substantial reason for this is that the research technology for measuring the quality of the treatment is still in its infancy. As reflected in Chapter 4, a substantial effort within the context of this project was mounted to directly evaluate the quality of the treatment. This enterprise failed and, more important, failed to suggest possible independent variables that caused the quality of the treatment to decline over time. Further, research in the behavioral sciences is usually of such short duration that an assessment of treatment effect over a sufficient period of time in relation to fluctuations in other independent variables is impossible. Precisely for these reasons, namely, the extreme difficulty of measuring the quality of treatment over time, the short duration of most research projects, and the consequent prevention of detection of these problems, the literature has little, if anything, to say about strategies for dealing with this gap.

Exogenous Variables and Project Outcomes

What changes in the social climate coinciding with the change from the descriptive to the predictive phases of the project could have undermined treatment effectiveness? The two most evident changes occurring around the time of the transition from the descriptive to the predictive phases of the project were the loss in faith of government associated with the Watergate scandal and the onset of the peculiar recession characterized by simultaneously increasing inflation and unemployment. As to the former, there are studies that disclose that there was a significant decline in the public's trust in the presidency during the period 1972-1974, which in turn might have impacted on the attitudes of probationers and counselors toward government generally.[2] Relative to the influence of economic conditions on behavior, M. Harvey Brenner put the question and its associated answer in his 1973 work *Mental Illness and the Economy* as follows:

> Under what historical conditions does society become "unglued," and what society-wide factors (if any) are responsible for basic instabilities in social relations? . . .
>
> There is reason to believe that changes in the economy have the most pervasive impact on the life of a society and its individual members.[3]

Empirical assessment of the effect on the project of the loss of faith in government was not undertaken because, first, the necessary data was not available on a yearly/regional basis and, second, there was no theoretical linkage reported in the literature between this type of variable and crime or emotional stress. On the other hand, both yearly/regional data on the economy and theoretical linkages of the state of economy to crime[4] and to mental health[5] have been explicated. With this as a starting point, other exogenous data were also examined that, first, related to the economic conditions, second, to those conditions that might be viewed as stress indicators, third, related to traffic law enforcement, and fourth, related to crime.

The exogenous data that was analyzed is set forth by year in Appendix 5A. As indicated, the variables selected were unemployment, consumer price index, automobile registration, Norman policemen assigned to field activity, gasoline consumption, Norman municipal court traffic docket, and crime rate. In each instance the unit of measurement and the source of the information are specified.

The selection of the exogenous variables that conceivably could have affected traffic recidivism was guided, first, by the more recent econometric literature suggesting a strong relationship between crime rate and unemployment and other economic indices,[6] second, by literature relating traffic citations to transportation and law enforcement variables and, third, by the observed dramatic increase in the nationwide crime rate during a period beginning in 1972, which paralleled the crime statistics for the Norman region.[7]

The chi-square analysis previously reported in Figure 5-6 provided an indirect measure of a possible relationship between unemployment and traffic recidivism, since unemployment also showed a dramatic increase in 1971, prior to the initiation of predictive sentencing in 1972. This comparison lagged unemployment one year behind the variable it sought to explain in accordance with the literature that suggests that the effect of unemployment on stress and crime is felt approximately one year after the occurrence of unemployment.[8] For example, in correlating unemployment with traffic recidivism, the unemployment rate for 1971 would be matched with the traffic recidivism rate of 1972, 1972 unemployment with 1973 traffic recidivism, and so forth. Since the results of this chi-square analysis, together with the rise in unemployment, suggested an association between unemployment and traffic recidivism consistent with the literature, further analyses seemed warranted.

Description and Interrelationships of Exogenous Variables

Table 5-3 gives the means and standard deviations for each of the exogenous variables for 1968 through 1973, and Table 5-4 is the correlation matrix for the same variables across the same period.

Notice that the variables police in field, gasoline consumption, and the Municipal Criminal Court traffic docket were also reported in Table 5-4 as additional variables by dividing each by total automobile registrations to obtain an approximation in the rate adjusted for increases in the number of cars being operated for the years in question. This was the best approximation possible given the data available. Note the high degree of correlation among the exogenous variables, reflecting the fact that most increased over time. The most pronounced exceptions to the monotonic, though not necessarily linear, in-

Table 5-3
Means and Standard Deviations for the Exogenous Variables

Variable	*Mean*	*Standard Deviation*
Unemployment rate	4.0	0.7
Consumer price index	127.3	12.4
Automobile registrations	42026.1	5587.2
Police in field	62.3	15.5
Gasoline consumption	17046.1	1274.0
Court traffic docket	9056.9	1950.6
High school drop-out rate	5.5	0.5
Crime rate	3525.8	1249.8
Police in field/automobile registrations	0.0	0.0
Gasoline consumption/automobile registrations	0.4	0.0
Court traffic docket/automobile registrations	.21	0.0

Table 5-4
Correlation Matrix of Exogenous Variables

	Dichotomized traffic recidivism	*Unemployment rate*	*Consumer price index*	*Auto registration*	*Police in field*	*Gas Consumption*	*Court traffic docket*	*High school drop-out rate*	*Crime rate*	*Dichotomized unemployment rate*
Dichotomized Traffic Recidivism	1.00									
Unemployment Rate	0.19	1.00								
Consumer Price Index	0.13	0.80	1.00							
Auto Registration	0.19	0.93	0.94	1.00						
Police in Field	0.16	0.90	0.96	0.97	1.00					
Gas Consumption	0.22	0.84	0.82	0.93	0.93	1.00				
Court Traffic Docket	0.15	0.88	0.93	0.96	0.99	0.94	1.00			
High School Drop-out Rate	0.23	0.58	0.28	0.43	0.29	0.28	0.07	1.00		
Crime Rate	0.22	0.89	0.92	0.98	0.96	0.96	0.91	0.42	1.00	
Dichotomized Unemployment Rate	0.24	0.92	0.80	0.90	0.83	0.77	0.69	0.77	0.88	1.00

creases are unemployment, high school dropout rate, and traffic court docket. A reliable association between unemployment and project outcome variables was found. The chi-square analysis of the relationship between unemployment and dichotomized traffic recidivism resulted in a chi-square of 3.46 ($p = 0.06$, $df = 1$). With trichotomized recidivism the chi-square was 5.23 ($p = 0.07$, $df = 2$).

Table 5-5 reports the results of the comparison of traffic recidivism between low and high unemployment using analysis of variance.

In performing these analyses, unemployment was lagged a year behind traffic recidivism for Norman individually counseled probationers. Further, unemployment was dichotomized into high unemployment (greater than 4 percent) and low unemployment (less than 4 percent). Notice that the strength of the association between unemployment and traffic recidivism varied between 0.022 and 0.073 as a function of the scaling of traffic recidivism and the hypothesis testing technique used. Hence, there does appear to be a reliable relationship between unemployment and traffic recidivism.

If school dropout rate, like unemployment, is dichotomized into low and high dropout rate at 5.5 percent, there is a reliable association, though less significant than in the case of unemployment, between the dropout rate and traffic recidivism. For dichotomized traffic recidivism the chi-square was 2.71 ($p = 0.10$, $df = 1$) while for trichotomized traffic recidivism the chi-square was 3.69 ($p = 0.16$, $df = 2$).

Table 5-6 reports the results of the comparison of traffic recidivism using the low and high dropout rate with analysis of variance.

Earlier it was mentioned that the "traffic law enforcement" variables were adjusted to obtain an approximation in the rate adjusted for the number of cars being operated for the years in question. The correlation of these variables with traffic recidivism is reported in Table 5-7.

Table 5-5
Summary Table on Analysis of Variance on Traffic Recidivism between Dichotomized Low and High Unemployment

	Source	*D.F.*	*Sum of Squares*	*Mean Squares*	*F Ratio*	*F Prob.*
Dichotomized traffic recidivism	Between groups	1	1.05	1.05	4.53	0.037
	Within groups	76	17.63	0.23		
	Total	77	18.68			
Trichotomized traffic recidivism	Between groups	1	3.94	3.94	5.45	0.022
	Within groups	76	54.94	0.72		
	Total	77	58.88			

Table 5-6
Summary Table on Analysis of Variance on Traffic Recidivism between Low and High Drop-out Rate for Norman High School

	Source	*D.F.*	*Sum of Squares*	*Mean Squares*	*F Ratio*	*F Prob.*
Dichotomized traffic recidivism	Between groups	1	.87	0.87	3.71	0.058
	Within groups	76	17.81	0.23		
	Total	77	18.68			
Trichotomized traffic recidivism	Between groups	1	2.50	2.50	3.37	0.070
	Within groups	76	56.39	0.74		
	Total	77	58.89			

Table 5-7
Correlation Matrix for Traffic Law Enforcement Variables, Unemployment, and Traffic Recidivism

	Unemployment	*Police/Auto*	*Gas/Auto*	*Court/Auto*	*Traf. Recid.*
Unemployment	1.00				
Police/auto	0.85	1.00			
Gasoline/auto	−0.78	−0.78	1.00		
Court/auto	0.09	0.37	−0.53	1.00	
Traffic recid.	0.29	0.22	−0.26	0.22	1.00

Crime

Chi-square statistics were also computed between dichotomized and trichotomized traffic recidivism and low and high crime rates, where the crime rate was dichotomized at 3000 property crimes per hundred thousand population during the period 1968 to 1973. The chi-square for dichotomized traffic recidivism was 2.72 ($p = 0.10$, $df = 1$) and for trichotomized traffic recidivism it was 4.24 ($p = 0.12$, $df = 2$).

Table 5-8 reports a summary of analysis of variance on traffic recidivism and low and high crime rates.

Summary of Exogenous Data Analysis

Figure 5-7 (a and b) gives a graphical representation of the relationships between traffic recidivism, the high school dropout rate, unemployment, and the crime

Table 5-8
Summary Table on Analysis of Variance on Traffic Recidivism between Low and High Property Crime Rates

	Source	*D.F.*	*Sum of Squares*	*Mean Squares*	*F Ratio*	*F Prob.*
Dichotomized traffic recidivism	Between groups	1	0.86	0.86	3.61	0.058
	Within groups	76	18.02	0.24		
	Total	77	18.88			
Trichotomized traffic recidivism	Between groups	1	3.19	3.19	4.37	0.038
	Within groups	76	55.49	0.73		
	Total	77	58.68			

against property rate. Notice the association between the increase in unemployment and the corresponding increases in high school dropouts and the increase in crimes against property during the period 1968 to 1974. The addition of Figure 5-7c shows a similar association, at least in the acceleration for the period 1971-1974, between unemployment rate, high school dropout rate, crimes against property rate, and court traffic caseload rate. Interestingly, this longitudinal data for unemployment, high school dropout rate, and crimes against property are consistent with a cross-sectional study by Fleischer in 1963.[9] If these exogenous data are then again graphically compared to Group 2 individual counseling recidivism rates, a similar association appears. See Figure 5-8.

Note from Figure 5-7 and 5-8 that it is precisely at the point where Group 2 treatment effectiveness fails that a marked increase in unemployment, high school dropouts, and, correspondingly, crime against property increases markedly. This general association between unemployment and Group 2 traffic recidivism, as indicated by the chi-square statistics, is suggested by the probability of the chi-squares (p = 0.062 and 0.073). Accordingly, there is reason to believe that the economy, as measured by the variable unemployment, somehow had an adverse effect on the Group 2 treatment effectiveness insofar as traffic recidivism is concerned beginning in 1972. This is particularly striking when one observes in Figure 5-8 the relatively high consistency in the effectiveness of the fine in reducing recidivism throughout the period 1965 through 1974.

These findings are also consistent with recent findings on the importance of economic factors in explaining social ills, particularly crime rate. The analyses of this study extend this work to traffic recidivism in a controlled experimental setting, whereas previous work has been confined to retrospective, aggregated, ecological studies. Ideally, the explanatory variable would not be an aggregated yearly/regional unemployment figure but rather the actual economic status of the probationer and his family. Contrary to the entire paradigm of social intervention to reduce delinquency based on psychological, sociological, and criminological factors,[10] it appears that the prevailing economic climate cannot be ignored in judging the efficacy of social intervention. It is of even more than slight interest that economic factors conceivably even permeate efforts in the psychosocial remediation of poor driving behavior.

An Explication of Project Anomalies

The question still remains whether the exogenous factors explain the four anomalies described earlier that defied conventional explanations. To recapitulate, the anomalies are: first, why was Group 2 individual counseling less effective in reducing traffic recidivism in the predictive phase than in the descriptive phase, second, why did the sentencing equation demonstrate considerable theoretical efficiency and yet, at the same time, so little practical utility; third, why did Group 2 in the descriptive phase remain persistently effective over a four-year follow-up period extending into the predictive phase; and, fourth, why should Group 2 remain relatively effective in reducing accident involvement and nontraffic recidivism during the predictive phase while having no effect on traffic recidivism during the same period?

Admittedly, these anomalous results may be the product of chance occurrence. Certainly, it is true that the significance of the relationship between the exogenous factors and traffic recidivism did not all attain the traditional 0.05 level of significance. Rather, they ranged from the 0.02 to the 0.16 level of significance and, in the case of unemployment, from 0.02 to 0.07. The preponderance of the data, together with the results disclosed in other studies, suggests that there was a relationship between the exogenous factors of unemployment and crime generally and traffic recidivism of individually counseled probationers specifically. The single factor most suggestive of a genuine rather than a spurious nature of the unemployment situation is the very fact that the unemployment explanation seemingly handles all four anomalies. In contrast, in the case of ad hoc explanations there tend to be about as many as there are anomalies to be explained. Indeed, in accounting for the dramatic decrease in Group 2 treatment effectiveness in the predictive phase, it would appear that unemployment may be that variable that can differentially affect control groups and treated groups despite the protection of randomization.

One can thus theorize that a mechanism by which the state of the economy could attenuate treatment is through an interrelationship in the loss of credibility of reality therapy's insistence upon individual responsibility with no allowance for mitigating circumstances, together with the preoccupations over one's own precarious economic circumstances on the part of both counselor and counselee.

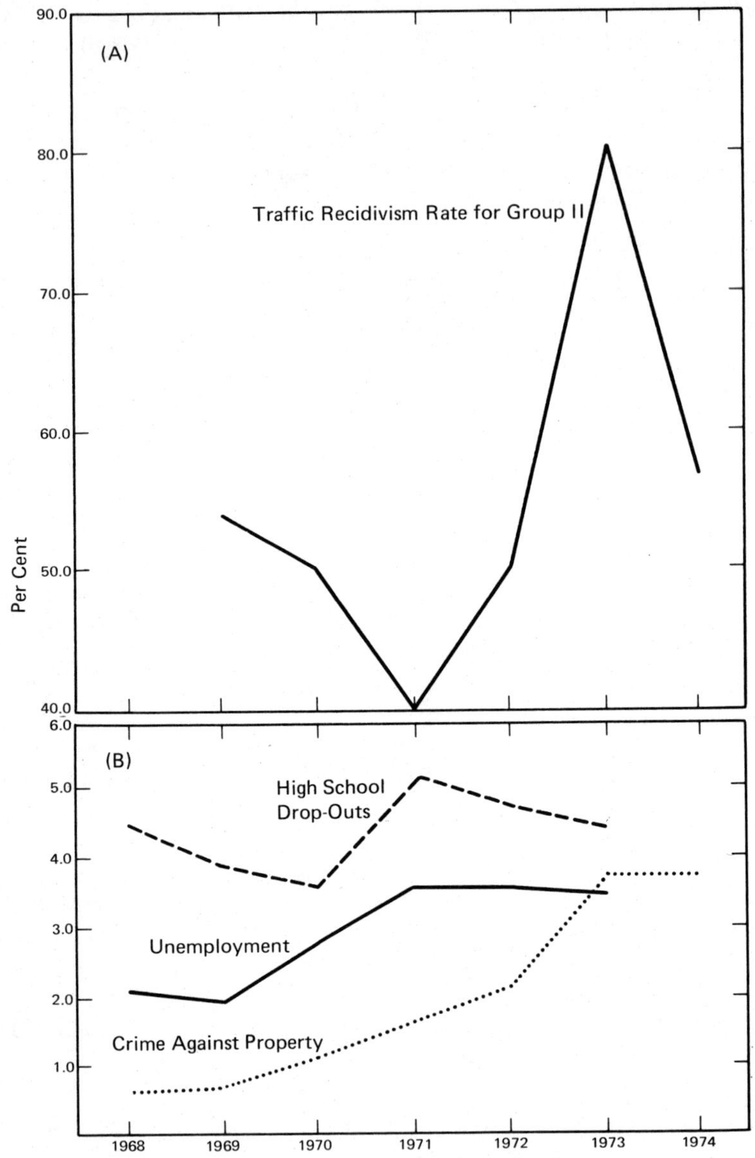

Figure 5-7. a. and b. Comparison of Increase in Group 2 Traffic Recidivism with the Increase in High School Drop-Out Rate, Unemployment, and Crime against Property. c. Norman Municipal Court Traffic Caseload Divided by the Number of Automobile Registrations for Cleveland County, 1968 through 1974.

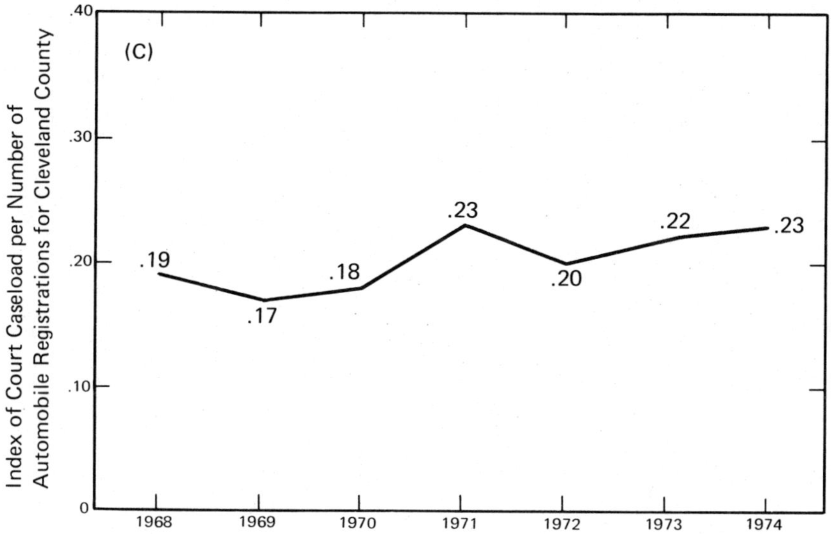

Second, if economic conditions are associated with treatment effectiveness, would this not also account for the continuing theoretical efficiency of the sentencing equation (predictability) and at the same time the loss in its practical utility. This is illustrated by Figure 5-9, where the observed points of recidivism continue to lie close to the regression line, but the regression line itself intercepts the *y* axis at a higher point than before. This indicates the loss of treatment effectiveness but the continuation of predictability. Thus people who were predicted to do well in predictive sentencing fared better than those predicted to do poorly, but on the average, as stated earlier, "probationers sentenced in accordance with the model fared no better than those probationers assigned to random controls."

With reference to the third anomaly, Figure 5-10 depicts the persistence of Group 2 treatment effectiveness in the descriptive phase in comparison with the effectiveness of the fine control and Group 2 treatment in the predictive phase. To the degree that the state of the economy affects the treatment process, one may then argue that a counseling process undertaken during reasonably good (economic) times and unattenuated by external factors will produce different immediate effects from attenuated counseling. And, further, one would expect that the results of such unattenuated treatment would persist over time. Indeed, it is precisely this pattern that is observed from the four-year follow-up of the descriptive phase Group 2 treatment.

An overall conceptualization of the suggested interrelationships between

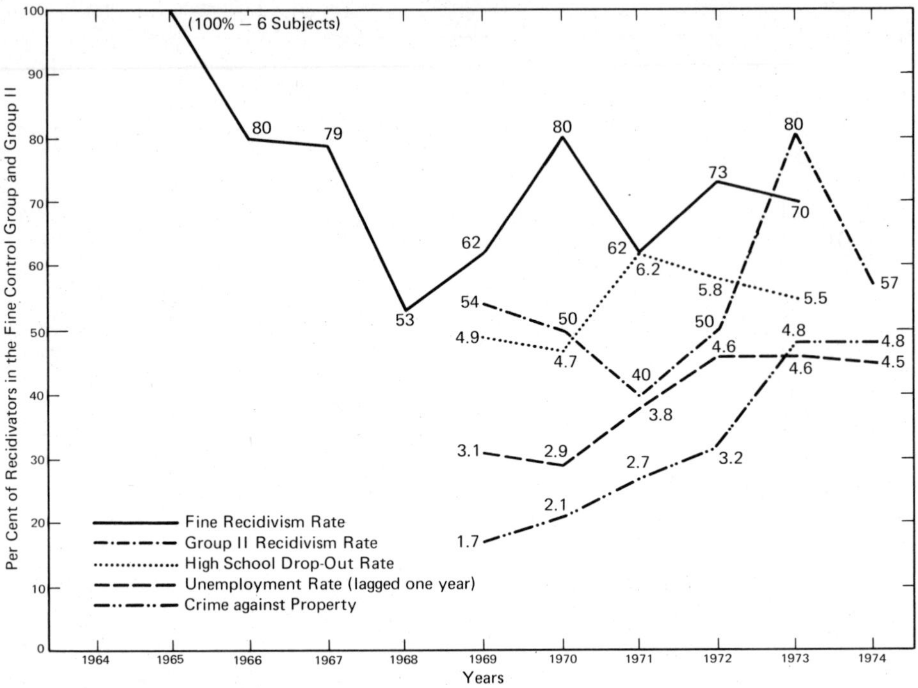

Figure 5-8. Comparison of Increase in Group 2 Traffic Recidivism with Fine Control Group and the Increase in High School Drop-out Rate, Unemployment, and Crime Against Property.

treatment, the treatment process, treatment outcome, and economic conditions is diagrammed in Figure 5-11. Again, notice that in this conceptualization, the randomized control design does not protect the integrity of the design from this sort of external contaminate, since the contaminate acts exclusively on the treatment processes whether it is the relationship of counselor and counselee, the rationale of the counseling technique, or the sensitivity produced within the treatment process.

Finally, in an effort to explain the fourth anomaly, does this conceptualization explain the difference in outcome between traffic recidivism, accident involvement, and nontraffic recidivism. Recall that for the predictive phase, the mean level for Norman Group 2 traffic recidivism was 0.81, while accident involvement and nontraffic recidivism was 0.05 and 0.0 respectively. While these differences may not be reliable because of the low base rate, to the extent that they are reliable, the results again appear consistent with the foregoing conceptualization of the treatment process. The influence of economic condi-

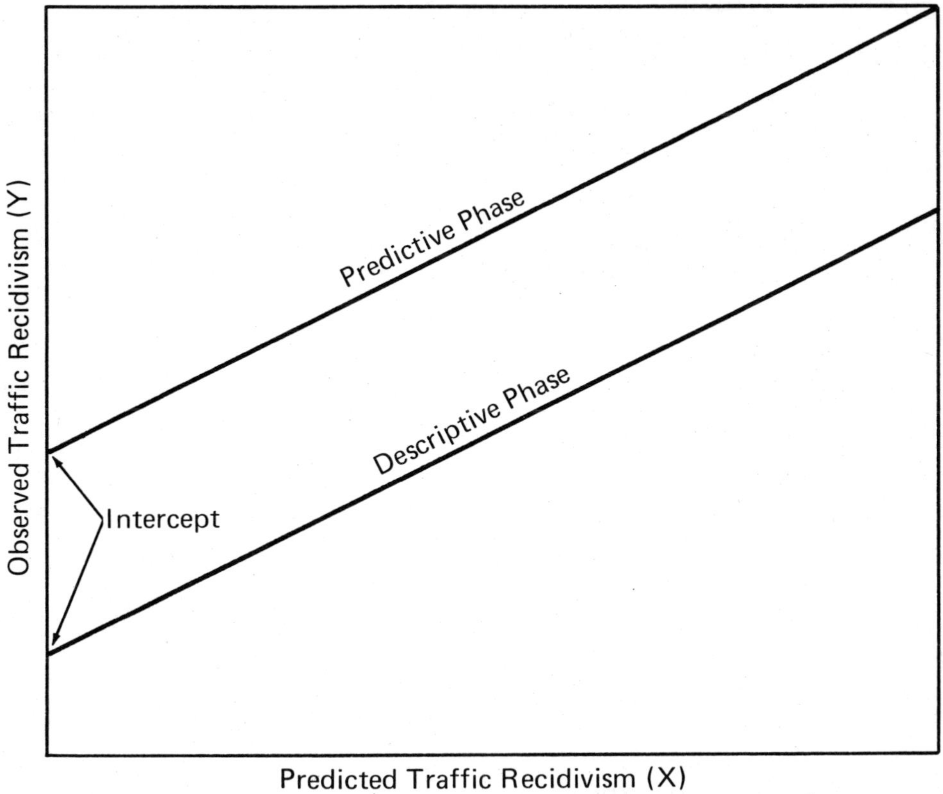

Figure 5-9. Changes in Treatment Outcome with Continuing Predictability.

tions (or other external stress factors) may be such that a probationer's sensitivity to violating a traffic law is diminished. It is reasonable to hypothesize that there are degrees in dangerousness in driving and the propensity to indulge in more dangerous behavior is proportionate to the emotional state of the person, which in turn may be affected proportionately by the influence of the state of the economy on a person in the driving situation. These degrees of dangerousness may be measurable by a dimension bounded at the lower end by no traffic violations and no accident involvement, traffic violations at the midpoint, and by both traffic violations and accident involvement at the other extreme. A person treated in good times may be sensitized to not violating the traffic laws as well as avoiding accidents, but a person treated in less favorable times may not develop a sensitivity to avoiding traffic tickets but rather will develop a sensitivity to not becoming involved in accidents.

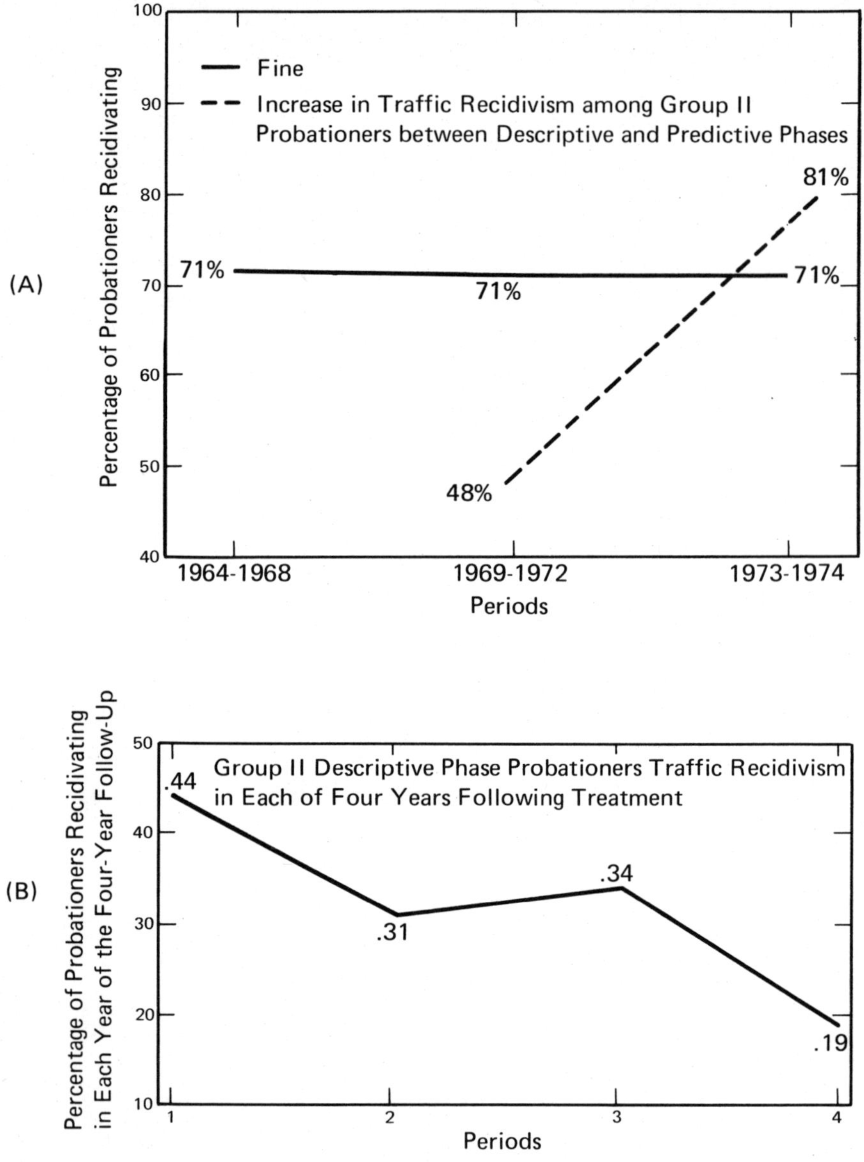

Figure 5-10. Comparison of Fine Control, Group 2 Treatment Effectiveness in Predictive Phase and Persistence of Group 2 Treatment Effectiveness for Persons Counseled during Descriptive Phase.

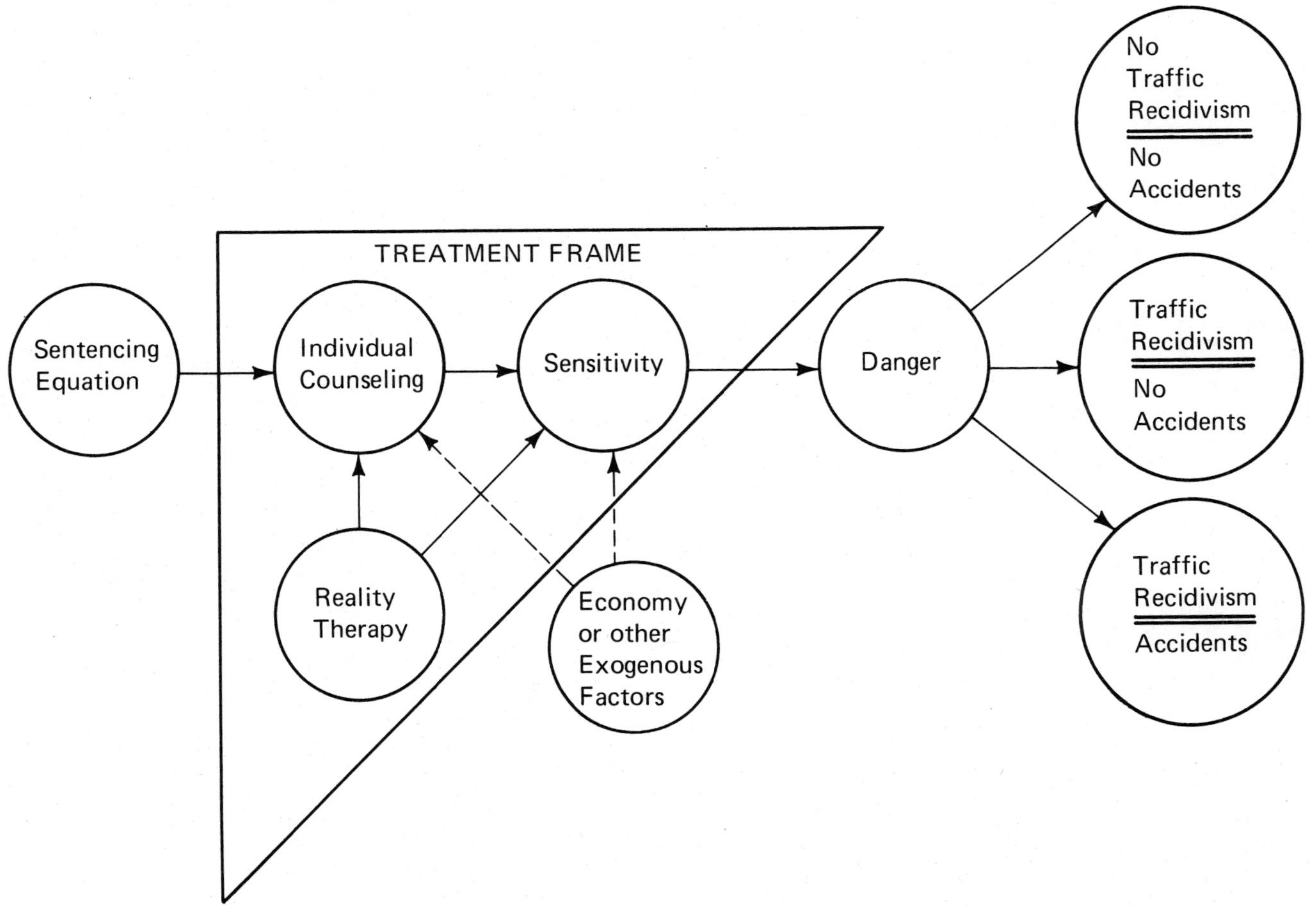

Figure 5-11. Conceptualization of Relationship between Sentence, Treatment, Danger, and Exogenous Factors.

In summary, the expectations of the investigators were certainly not met by the results or conclusions derived from this study of the predictive sentencing of habitual teenage traffic offenders. This is attributable, in part, to the investigators' confidence in the research design and their control over the experimental conditions, at least insofar as the Norman predictive phase was concerned. Beyond this, however, there was also strong statistical support at the end of the descriptive phase to bolster this confidence and warrant the initiation of the predictive phase of the project for the purpose of cross-validating the sentencing model. The investigators were aware of the fact that cross-validation is a hazardous undertaking but were insensitive to the possibility that a strong external factor might affect the treatment process in spite of the protection afforded by randomized control groups.

Ironically, the unexpected results led to conclusions that raise additional questions concerning the sentencing process not contemplated at the inception of the project. If, as suggested, there is a significant interaction between treatment effect and conditions external to the treatment, then the sentence involves an understanding of more than simply the psychosociological characteristics of the offender in relation to a particular treatment. It must allow for and deal with any such external condition, or exogenous factor, whether it is the state of the economy, as manifested by unemployment, or some other external environmental factor influencing either the probationer, the probation officer, or a combination of both in the treatment process. Moreover, if the interaction between the treatment process and conditions external to treatment may differentially affect success of treatment depending upon the time the treatment is administered and the measurement of success that is used (traffic recidivism, or accident involvement, or nontraffic recidivism), then should not greater attention be paid by the sentencing judge to the particular outcome that he hopes to derive from imposition of his sentence (treatment), the type of treatment imposed, and the time when it is imposed. Yet to ask this question may also suggest that the sentencing judge will have neither the resources, the time, nor the expertise to manipulate such attenuating subtleties in sentencing as to justify the use of judicial intervention in *sentencing* habitual traffic offenders.

Finally, though the conclusions were unexpected, they certainly afforded the investigators some basis for evaluating the utility of the particular sentencing model employed in the project for sentencing 16-18 year-old male habitual traffic offenders. Moreover, the results and accompanying conclusions permit some empirical evaluation of predictive sentencing and its practical utility in the sentencing process.

Notes

1. See Chapter 4, Figure 4-2, p. 63.

2. *IRS Newsletter*, Institute for Social Research, The University of Michigan, Summer 1975.

3. Brenner, M. Harvey, *Mental Illness and the Economy* (Cambridge, Mass.: Harvard University Press, 1973).

4. Fleisher, Belton M., "The Effect of Unemployment on Juvenile Delinquency," *Journal of Political Economy* 71:6 (December 1963).

5. Brenner, *Mental Illness.*

6. Brenner, ibid.; Fleisher, "The Effect of Unemployment on Juvenile Delinquency."

7. *Chicago Tribune*, November 18, 1975.

8. Brenner, *Mental Illness*; Fleisher, Belton M., *The Economics of Delinquency* (Chicago: Quadrangel Books, 1966).

9. Fleisher, "The Effect of Unemployment on Juvenile Delinquency."

10. Galliher, John F., and McCartney, James L., "The Influence of Funding Agencies on Juvenile Delinquency Research," *Social Problems* 21:1 (Summer 1973).

Appendix 5A

Table 5A-1.

	1963	*1964*	*1965*	*1966*
Economic				
Unemployment rate, OKC metro. area, Oklahoma Security Commission	3.7	3.8	3.6	3.2
Consumer Price Index, National, U.S. Dept. of Commerce, 1967 = 100	91.7	92.9	94.5	97.2
Stress Variables				
Admissions to the Cleveland[a] County Mental Health Center				
Traffic Law Enforcement				
Automobile Registration, Oklahoma Tax Commission, no. of automobiles registered in Cleveland County	22,242	24,158	26,522	22,517
Police in Field, Norman Police Department, no. of officers assigned to field		31	31	36
Gasoline consumption, Oklahoma Retail Trade & Tax Commission, sales in 1000 gal. for City of Norman		11,361	11,875	11,856
Municipal Criminal Court Traffic Docket, Municipal Criminal Court of Norman, no. of adjudications per year			2,605	4,940
High School Drop-outs				
Norman High School Drop-outs for grades 10-12				
Crime Generally				
Rate of FBI Part I crimes against property known to police per 100,000 population FBI *Uniform Crime Reports.* Number of robberies, burglaries, larcenies, and motor vehicle thefts.		1611.5	1407.7	1651.2

[a]This data was not analyzed. Further, the number of State Mental Hospital admissions was going to be employed. However, this data was not available in time for inclusion in the report.

1967	*1968*	*1969*	*1970*	*1971*	*1972*	*1973*	*1974*
3.2	3.1	2.9	3.8	4.6	4.6	4.5	4.5
100.0	104.2	109.8	116.3	121.3	125.3	133.1	147.7
362.0	462.0	596.0	603.0	726.0	656.0	574.0	563.0
29,023	31,162	33,074	36,018	39,245	42,927	46,952	48,213
41	40	36	46	59	62	74	81
13,525	14,120	15,059	15,858	16,723	16,472	18,632	17,891
5,136	5,906	5,687	6,685	9,067	8,697	10,559	11,260
4.4	6.6	5.5	4.9	4.7	6.2	5.8	5.5
1642.8	1670.2	1749.4	2145.2	2797.8	3269.0	4855.3	4831.3

Part II
The Legal, Social, Economic, and Methodological Aspects

Introduction to Part II

To take power over the lives of others on predictions of their future criminality, in particular of the liklihood of future physical injury they may inflict on others, is no light assumption of competence.

Norval Morris and Gordon Hawkins[1]

With the completion of the study, it is important to reexamine some of the basic legal, social, economic, and methodological concerns that were either at the forefront when the study began or became obvious as the study progressed and raised issues that were important to the long-range goals of the project. Can the experiment, on experimental grounds, withstand claims of unconstitutionality? What of the right of privacy, its growing constitutional dimensions, and its significance for predictive sentencing? What are the related issues associated with altering behavior? If all legal questions are satisfactorily resolved, what are the theoretical and practical considerations involved in social action research on sentencing by courts? Are they malleable? What is the significance of the economy in crime and delinquency research and how has it contributed to directing future thinking in the development of predictive sentencing schemes? Finally, what has been learned about methodology in research involving predictive sentencing in particular and sentencing in general? Is the legal and social science community prepared to accept the rigors of large-scale experiments conducted within long time periods to isolate significant variables affecting sentencing? These and related questions all form the substance of Part II.

6 Legal

Predictive Sentencing and Law

Predictive sentencing immediately brings to the forefront pervasive concerns relating to experimentation in sentencing, the right to privacy, and altering behavior to achieve conformity. Without experimentation, without personality and social milieu investigation, without treatment for altering behavior, and without the means to assess the efficacy of that treatment for different types of offenders in relation to the danger to be eliminated with that treatment, predictive sentencing is a hollow shell. Indeed, predictive sentencing may require an ongoing involvement of all four elements if it were ever to constitute a meaningful orientation for improved sentencing.

Unfortunately, the legal path through experimentation, privacy, and altering behavior is either left largely uncharted in the judicial decisions or is a thicket of concept and doctrine that can hardly be separated into manageable components and then synthesized to form meaningful conclusions from which to evaluate the legal implications of the project. Equal protection is most assuredly involved, but what is the standard of review? A new standard of review is said to be evolving,[2] but the Supreme Court has not clearly articulated that standard,[3] nor is there any agreement among constitutional law scholars just what standard of review is emerging.[4] Due process of law is also involved, but it is not clear under what circumstances it will be invoked.[5] The roots of privacy, for example, have been found in various clauses of the Constitution, including due process of law.[6] And, potentially, the legal aspects of the study also involve looking to doctrine enunciated within the context of free speech,[7] involuntary servitude within the 13th Amendment,[8] and cruel and unusual punishment under the 8th Amendment.[9] And these vagaries and varieties of legal doctrine must be weighed in relation to a sentencing program that, beyond general guidelines, has developed and functioned without the benefit of a precise and unified doctrine delineating the rules to be applied in predictive sentencing. At most, the legal concerns of the project must be seen in issue-oriented terms with the legal paths defined broadly in relation to those aspects of predictive sentencing that touch most dearly those values in society that the law seeks to protect.

Experimentation

The use of controlled experiments in the law to measure the application and effect of legal rules and practices has long been advocated.[10] The research in delinquency is overwhelming, beginning, first, with the etiology of delinquent behavior and, later, with studying the effectiveness of various treatments.[11] Yet there have been few, if any, attempts to correlate etiology with treatment in a controlled experimental design in sentencing youthful offenders. Doubtless it is the hesitancy, indeed the fear, that controlled experiments in sentencing will abridge constitutional guarantees of equal protection and due process of law. What are the dimensions of these concerns and how were they resolved within the context of this project?

Potentially, legal limitations on classification for purposes of the research design could arise at four different stages in the collection of the sample: the selection of the target group of 16-18 year-old traffic offenders with three or more violations within a period of 12 months; sequential assignment of the target group in groups of six offenders to each treatment modality; random selection of offenders for fine control or predictive sentencing during the predictive phase; and assignment of the offenders randomly selected for predictive sentencing to one of the four innovative treatment modalities by the use of the regression equations.

The selection of the target group would not appear to pose any constitutional barrier. Classifying 16-18 year-old male offenders committing three or more violations within a 12-month period would seemingly satisfy either the two-tiered system of equal protection review[12] or the other principal models that commentators find the Supreme Court to be applying or developing in the equal protection thicket.[13] Using the two-tiered rubric as the model, the Court will inquire whether the classification impinges upon a fundamental right, *inter alia*, the opportunity to use one's natural endowments and realize personal aspirations. In such cases, the state's interest in moral and societal standards must give way to individual rights, as in the case of a statute authorizing the compulsory sterilization of habitual criminals.[14] This is a suspect class and subject to *strict scrutiny*.[15]

Obviously, classifying 16-18 year-old male habitual traffic offenders would not appear on its face to constitute a suspect class and thus impinge on a fundamental right. If not, second, in the two-tier inquiry, it must be determined whether the classification bears a *rational relationship* to a permissible state objective, for example, remedying bad driving behavior.[16] Classification, for purposes of treatment, by age,[17] sex,[18] and habituality[19] are permitted if there are differences in character, condition, or situation to justify creating a special class composed of these characteristics.[20] In this predictive sentencing project, preliminarily though not exhaustively, statistical studies were made to determine whether the offender of interest did represent a distinct class of offender in which the fine often failed to constitute a deterrent or reformative and thus justify the creation of a class for special treatment. It was found that the members of the class did tend to recidivate at a greater rate, tended to commit other misdemeanor offenses, and were also sometimes involved in the most serious automobile accidents.

Having established the initial class with reference to a permissible state objective, was it then permissible to create subgroups for treatment and to sequentially [randomly] assign offenders to these groups during the descriptive phase. While it is true that sentences do not have to be equal and can be individualized,[21] they must be rationally different.[22] But if nothing is known about which sentences can be rationally individualized, and the offenders are all a part of the same class, they should all be treated similarly. Such was the underlying rationale of the equality in treatment approach during the descriptive phase. With the exception of the $20 fine treatment, each treatment modality in the project involved the same time commitment of one hour per week with the same general type of counseling structure. Only treatment content differed. If this is seen as a possible defect, two further questions with reference to the random subclass of offenders need to be considered. With reference to each subclass, including the fine, were the probationers being exposed to any worse treatment than that already authorized by law? The generally poor recidivism results with the use of the fine in the project's findings over a period of 10 years is certainly suggestive that they were not. When equal protection questions concerning dissimilar treatments of like offenders have arisen, the courts speak of "unequal hands" or "burdensome punishments."[23] If the offenders are not subjected to any greater penalty than that already permitted by law, then the classification should be deemed acceptable. True, it may not be known whether the counseling indeed subjected probationers to any greater penalty. But if it is not ostensibly the case, then the very fact that there is genuine doubt as to the choice between two or more treatments should be sufficient to sustain the classification.[24] The random classification of probationers during the predictive phase between the fine control and predictively sentenced probationers is subject to much the same analysis.

Finally, within the predictively sentenced subgroup during the predictive phase, classification became least suspect, since sentencing was at least based on a priori knowledge of those variables that predicted success on the outcome criteria in the differing treatment modalities. Even here, experimentation was held to a minimum, as evidenced by the policy decision to sentence all offenders in the Little Cities to Group 2 counseling, which, based on descriptive phase results, was demonstrably better than all other treatment modalities, and predictive sentencing in these areas had little chance of succeeding because of small sample size.

In the end, if cross-validation had been achieved, substantial questions relating even to the fining of the probationers in the target population would have been raised. But cross-validation was not achieved. Is further experimentation in sentencing warranted? The modern concern, at least with rehabilitation and social defense, is with individualizing the punishment. Is it not in the public welfare to encourage sentencing practices that will not only rehabilitate or protect society but encourage them by permitting reasonable experimental classes in sentencing with a view to reform?[25]

Twenty years ago Norval Morris wrote that he had to confess that he was troubled by the possible implications of the controlled experiment in sentencing.

> It is only twenty-seven years to 1984, and Orwell and those novelists who have followed him have disturbed all of us. In human affairs the control of the individual for the sake of the statistical many may be seen as benevolent by the controller but never by the controlled. Nevertheless, the possible wastage in our current wide application of the services of probation officers to juvenile delinquents who may not need those services, who may even suffer because of them, and the denial of probation to those delinquents who may benefit from it seem to me such grave harms as to merit some controlled experimentation in an endeavor to find a remedy.[26]

It is now only seven years to 1984. May we venture the thought that these concerns in sentencing are as viable today as they were then? And what of the demonstrable results achieved in this predictive sentencing project? Do they suggest the need for greater understanding than we ever thought we might need? And can we quantify that understanding without further experimentation—experimentation to tell us when to treat and when not to treat?

If anything, this study indicates, albeit in a limited area of sentencing, that society and judges within that society are palpably ignorant of the effects that sentences may have on the behavior of offenders. If society continues to give judges the power over the lives of people that they now have, then experimentation under carefully controlled conditions, with due respect for the fundamental rights of the offenders involved and under strict public scrutiny must not be thwarted by unsubstantiated Orwellian fears of unjustifiable interference with the lives of those who stand convicted for the commission of public offenses. Actions taken through our present ignorance may ultimately be more of an affront to fundamental rights than carefully controlled experimentation in sentencing.

Privacy

Its Dimensions

The right of privacy "flows, as do most of our values, from our concept of the essential dignity and worth of the individual."[27] It has two clear aspects. One is the right of the individual to exercise control over the resources that belongs to him—words, movements, knowledge, states of mind, and material objects acquired through legitimate transactions.[28] The right to control implies retention of something that might otherwise be shared, so in its second aspect, privacy denotes a right to share and to communicate with others.[29] Fundamentally, privacy is:

> . . . the freedom of an individual to pick and choose for himself the time and circumstances under which, and most importantly, the extent to which, his attitudes, beliefs, behavior and opinions are to be shared with or withheld from others.[30]

From this is derived the concept of consent that has become the "essential privacy-respecting ethic" for engaging in behavioral research.[31] And it has been held that there is a constitutional right to informed consent in both the case of adults and minors for the invasion of constitutionally protected rights to privacy.[32] If there is no legally protected right of privacy, then informed consent is not necessary. Such is said to exist, for example, where paramount interests of the government are involved, such as law enforcement, social welfare work, and in the protection of public health.[33] One would also expect that a legally protected right of personality privacy to information concerning the offender and his environment does not generally exist in the case of persons being sentenced for the commission of public offenses.

The Project and Privacy

The goals of the project necessarily required the disclosure of personality information at two stages in the probationary process. First, at the time of intake it was necessary to gather basic personal and social milieu data concerning the offender and his environment, which was conceived as relevant to the needs of the project. Second, at the time of counseling, a perhaps somewhat more intimate disclosure was required, particularly in Group 2 counseling, concerning the offender's feelings, attitudes, and beliefs concerning himself, his family, his peers, law, and conformity. Traditional research methods were employed in gathering the data: self-descriptions by the offenders at intake through interviews, questionnaires, and personality tests; direct observations and recording of individual behavior, particularly in the counseling process; and collection of secondary data consisting of school, police, and court records.

It has been the reasoned belief of project personnel throughout the duration of the project that the data sought for purposes of sentencing the class of offenders studied was not protected by a right of privacy. If the data were so protected, it could be obtained only through informed consent.[34] However, those subject to the program were convicted traffic offenders. They were also habitual traffic offenders whose class did, by investigation, demonstrate a propensity to constitute a threat to the community in increased law enforcement, traffic and nontraffic recidivism and accident involvement, personal injury, and property damage. Moreover, it was not known what effect informed consent might have on the research goals of the project.[35] While this alone would not have been sufficient to justify sentencing without consent, the offenders' status obviated the necessity for an informed consent based upon a full and complete disclosure of the nature and goals of the sentencing project. One would have to consider whether, for example, any such informed consent could realistically be obtained in a sentencing environment. The behavior that brought the offender to court and the authority of the bench in sentencing him are essentially incompatible with informed consent. In short, consent is totally incompatible with the underlying function of criminal law in sentencing.

At the same time, the sentence was thoroughly explained at the time of sentencing by acquainting the offender with the testing process and informing him that he would be fined or placed in probationary counseling at the end of testing, as the case might be. If the offender, either himself or by his parent or guardian, refused to accept the sentence, he was fined and not sentenced for probationary treatment. A similar procedure was followed if, subsequent to sentencing, the offender failed to cooperate, either by refusing to attend the initial intake session or by missing three counseling sessions without an explanation.

Still, sensitivity to the overriding concerns of privacy in the predictive sentencing project led project personnel to develop rules and procedures to guarantee the confidentiality and anonymity of the data, a procedure some have argued constitutes a substitute for consent,[36] though in a strictly research-oriented behavioral study, this may not be adequate if the investigator occupies a position of authority over the person studied.[37]

In this treatment-research sentencing study, for example, in Norman, an ordinance was first enacted to provide that "No person shall release, make public or otherwise disclose any records, reports or any other documents of the Probation Division except as may specifically be authorized by the Rules of the Court."[38] This ordinance secured the confidentiality of the records to all except probationary and other project personnel, and (in implementation) to enable the reporting of project results, the presiding judge of the court issued a rule authorizing only the anonymous disclosure of project results.

Compliance with these policies was implemented in two ways. First, at the first orientation intake session the probation clerk informed the probationer "that everything you say, either in the forms or to your probation officer will be kept strictly anonymous." This was then reinforced at subsequent intake sessions by reminding the probationer that his answers would "be kept strictly anonymous." And, subsequently, each probation officer, in explaining the recording of the counseling sessions, told the probationer that the purpose of the recorders was "to obtained accurate records," but that anytime the probationer wanted "to say something off the record," the recorder would be stopped. Of course, all these procedural safeguards pertaining to the collection and retention of the data would be totally inadequate if legal restraints prevented the personality investigation necessarily involved in any predictive sentencing strategy.

Legal recognition of a right of privacy is not new, either to the private or public sectors of the law.[39] The Supreme Court has recognized, at least as long ago as *Union Pacific R. Co. v. Botsford*, that a right of personal privacy, or a guarantee of zones of privacy, does exist under the United States Constitution, even though it does not explicitly mention any such right.[40] In varying contexts, at least the roots of the right have been found in the 1st Amendment,[41] the 4th and 5th Amendments,[42] in the "penumbras" of the Bill of Rights,[43] in the 9th Amendment,[44] or in the concept of liberty guaranteed by the 14th Amendment.[45] It also seems clear that only personal rights are included in this right of privacy,[46] since only personal rights can be deemed "fundamental" or "implicit in the concept of ordered liberty."[47]

It is not so clear what, or whose, personal rights are protected within the meaning of the Constitution. The Court has made it clear that privacy has some extension to marital activities,[48] procreation,[49] contraception,[50] abortion,[51] child rearing and education,[52] and family relationships.[53] It is also equally clear that these rights are not absolute. Thus while a woman's decision whether to terminate her pregnancy comes within the right of privacy under the 14th Amendment to the Constitution, it is not an absolute right.[54] The right "must be considered against important state interests in regulations."[55]

Is personality, psychological, and social milieu data collection and counseling within the umbrella of privacy under the Constitution? And, if so, is this a right that is protected from state regulation in the case of persons convicted of public offenses? If so, it seems clear that the controlling principles in each instance apply with equal force to both adult and juvenile offenders.[56]

The legal dimensions, much less the constitutional parameters of these issues, have hardly been touched. Presentence psychological and social investigation are widely recognized throughout the country both in federal[57] and state jurisdictions.[58] The Supreme Court has also directed its attention to the sentencing judge's access to information concerning the "character of the man before him" and concluded that it is largely unfettered.[59] However, the decisions all relate to offenses of felony grade and, moreover, deal with whether otherwise inadmissible evidence, or information outside the record, can be considered by the judge,[60] such as illegally obtained evidence,[61] in sentencing the offender. None deal with the more pervasive issue of the circumstances and extent to which a constitutional right of privacy can be invoked to bar personality testing and counseling in the sentencing of offenders.

The Supreme Court has, on one occasion, directed its attention quite obliquely to the issue in ruling that prison censorship of an inmate's mail impinges upon the 1st and 14th Amendment guarantees of free speech.[62] In dealing with this issue, the Court said:

> Whatever the status of a prisoner's claim to uncensored correspondence with an outsider, it is plain that the latter's interest is grounded in the First Amendment's guarantee of freedom of speech. And this does not depend on whether the nonprisoner correspondent is the author or intended recipient of a particular letter, for the addressee as well as the sender of direct personal correspondence derives from the First and Fourteenth Amendments a protection against unjustified governmental interference with the intended communication. . . . We do not deal here with difficult questions of the so-called "right to hear" and third-party standing but with a particular means of communication in which the interests of both parties are inextricably meshed . . . censorship of prison mail works a consequential restriction of the First and Fourteenth Amendments rights of those who are not prisoners.[63]

One may thus speculate that if the "liberties of free citizens [had not been] implicated in censorship of prisoner mail" and only a question of "prisoners rights" had been involved, the course of judicial decision might have been entirely different.

However, in looking to decisions dealing with restrictions on 1st Amendment liberties imposed in the furtherance of legitimate governmental activities to ultimately decide the case, the Court rejected an approach that would have required it to consider "assumptions about the legal status of prisoners"[64] and thus held open questions dealing with the legal dimensions of "prisoners rights." But even without entering this thicket, one may assume that protection against psychological, personal, and social milieu data collection is within the personal rights covered by privacy within the meaning of the Constitution and still conclude, on a basis of the *Procunier Case*, that it is not available to persons convicted of public offense, at least under carefully circumscribed conditions.

The Court was quick to recognize that the censorship case arose "in the context of prisons":

> One of the primary functions of government is the preservation of societal order through enforcement of the criminal law, and the maintenance of penal institutions is an essential part of that task. The identifiable governmental interests at stake in this task are the preservation of internal *order* and discipline, the maintenance of institutional *security* against escape or unauthorized entry, and the *rehabilitation* of the prisoners.[65] (Emphasis supplied.)

Accordingly, to justify censorship, first, the practice involved must further an important or substantial governmental interest unrelated to the suppression of expression. It may not censor simply to eliminate unwelcome opinions or inaccurate statements. Rather it must be shown that ". . . censorship furthers one or more of the substantial governmental interests of *security*, *order*, and *rehabilitation*."[66] (Emphasis supplied.) Second, the limitation on the 1st Amendment freedom must be ". . . no greater than is necessary or essential to the protection of the particular governmental interest involved."[67] In other words, the sweep of the practice must not be unnecessarily broad. One may then conclude that the practice of psychological, personal, and social data collection and counseling may be practiced to rehabilitate persons convicted of public offenses so long as it is no more extensive than necessary to protect the particular governmental interest involved.

If the teachings of the *Procunier Case* can thus be applied to the predictive sentencing and counseling of offenders, then, initially at least, on a basis of current court thinking, there is an adequate Constitutional underpinning for predictive sentencing insofar as the right of privacy is concerned. The data from this predictive sentencing project affords an opportunity to evaluate the legal standards in relation to the practices and objectives sought by predictively sentencing teenage habitual traffic offenders. First, the practice must further a substantial governmental interest unrelated simply to the gathering of information. Did the data collection in this predictive sentencing project further a substantial governmental interest? Certainly, traffic, problems associated with traffic, the risk to person and property through the operation of motor vehicles, and the involvement of youthful offenders in the problem are well-documented facts[68] and ones in which the Supreme Court has indicated a substantial governmental interest.[69] This interest may be collective in terms of reducing traffic and nontraffic recidivism and accident involvement[70] or individual in relation to protecting the rights of offenders involved.[71] Habitual offenders, to which this project applied, have long been recognized as representing a particular class of offender that is subject to special regulation.[72]

Second, was the nature and extent of the data collection limited by the substantial interest to be furthered? Broadly speaking, data were collected relating to the offenders domain and the counseling situation. With reference to the collection of data about the offender, concededly, the data gathering to isolate predictors during the descriptive phase was very broad, but there was very little predictive data available from which an a priori determination could be made as to what kinds of predictors were most significant and what data were important in isolating these predictors. Further, the extent of data collection was substantially reduced during the predictive phase, so that throughout the duration of the project, no more data was collected than necessary to achieve the intended goals of the project.

One may also evaluate the propriety of gathering data from probationers during the counseling processes in relation to furthering a legitimate governmental interest. There is a substantial body of literature suggesting the significance of psychological factors,[73] knowledge of the driving situation,[74] and the consequences of poor driving practices in remedying behavior[75] to justify dealing with these subjects in a counseling environment.

Second, the gathering of data must further an important interest of the administration of the traffic (criminal) laws. In the context of the present project, this interest is seen in reducing traffic and nontraffic recidivism and accident involvement through the rehabilitation, or reorientation, of the offender in the driving situation. And, in this respect, it is not necessary to show with *certainty* that this interest will be furthered by the data gathering but must only reach material that might be thought to encourage rehabilitation and protect society.[76] The essential winowing or narrowing process that is necessarily involved in the project's scheme of predictive sentencing is calculated to meet this standard. The concern is with data relating the offender to a particular type of treatment modality that will optimize a reduction in traffic and nontraffic recidivism and accident involvement. The results of the descriptive phase of the project certainly reinforce compliance with this legal standard insofar as that aspect of privacy dealing with information obtained during counseling is concerned. Looking at Figure 5-5 in Chapter 5, the probationers sentenced to Group 2 counseling during the descriptive phase did consistently better than the fine control probationers in the four-year follow-up period. However, in relation to data gathered during the descriptive phase to determine key probationer characteristics for predictors in model building during the predictive phase, the probe may be less defensible in view of the sequential method of assignment of probationers to treatment groups without relation to the optimal treatment. Again, however, the probe was made only to secure information that might be thought to optimize treatment effect. This, together with the confidentiality and anonymity of the data, would seem to meet the assumed constitutional privacy standards during the descriptive phase. Even stronger arguments can be made against overbreadth for the data gathering in the predictive phase.

The generally poor results disclosed at the end of the predictive phase complicate analysis. One could argue that the now demonstrably poor results foreclose further inquiry; namely, that there is no apparent correlation between offender characteristics and treatment, and thus the interest of the government in rehabilitation is not furthered by the probe and securing of the data. At the same time, it is significant that the Group 2 sentencing equation still had continuing predictability—only the rate of recidivism increased during the predictive phase. This demonstrates a continuing correlation between offender characteristics and treatment such as to justify the data gathering. Indeed, the fact that there is strong evidence of an exogenous variable acting outside the treatment itself, such as the economy, to render treatment ineffective suggests that the personality, psychological, or social milieu probe is not counterproductive over long periods of time insofar as the interests of the offender are concerned. But then, one must consider whether exogenous factors, such as the economy, are so pervasive in influencing behavior that intrusion into personal privacy is not only useless and unnecessary but an immoral affront to human dignity and thus constitutionally indefensible. The status of the offender, the interest of the government in security, order, and rehabilitation, the means selected to further these interests, and the confidentiality and anonymity with which the records resulting from the probe are maintained must all be weighed in determining whether a constitutional right of privacy prohibits the personal, psychological, and social milieu investigation.

Altering Behavior

Ultimately, of course, the critical legal and ethical issue for society, the legislator, and ultimately the sentencing judge and corrections officials is the right or duty to alter the behavior of the offender so that he will conform in a manner that is acceptable to society with only minimal interference with the offender. Can psychological counseling be imposed on offenders who are a risk to society because of a psychological disposition to commit traffic infractions or become involved in accidents? What of a program in driver's education for those offenders who, based on their personality profile, would benefit from driver's education? Can we seek to alter the attitudes of offenders toward the driving situation by sensitizing them to risks inherent in the driving situation? Does the offender have a right not to be treated or rehabilitated? And is it material whether the emphasis is on "social defense" to predict and control offenders dangerous to society as opposed only to treating and rehabilitating the offender?

There are practically no authorities. A few cases dealing with the right of mental patients not to be treated or rehabilitated indirectly support the view that offenders have no right against treatment or rehabilitation, particularly as it relates to preventing danger to society. In *Winters v. Miller*[77] the court said that the failure of physicians to administer a program of treatment and therapy "would have been violation of their obligations to the people of New York to seek to cure mentally ill patients so that they will no longer be dangerous or disruptive to themselves, or to the public, and so they will no longer occupy scarce space in public mental health institutions."[78] At the same time, the treatment or rehabilitative method must not be so devoid of therapeutic purpose that it violates basic constitutional guarantees, such as the prohibition against involuntary servitude under the 13th Amendment,[79] or constitutes cruel and unusual punishment within the meaning of the 8th Amendment,[80] or is a denial of due process of law within the 5th and 14th Amendments.[81]

The treatment modalities employed in this predictive sentencing project would not, in the first instance, appear to run afoul of constitutional limitations. First, traffic safety and accident prevention is a matter of substantial governmental interest. Second, the treatments were all designed to deal with three alternative types of behavior that, on a priori grounds and supported by existing literature, are all significant causal factors in recidivism and accident involvement. Third, by correlating the personality characteristics of the offenders with the type of treatment received, only the minimally essential alteration in behavior was sought. Fourth, the extent and nature of each counseling process was carefully defined and circumscribed to assure, to the extent possible, that only the intended treatment would be delivered. Fifth, none of the treatment modalities, by current standards, were morally offensive or calculated to cause physical harm.

Indeed, apart from compliance with existing legal standards, a paramount concern of project personnel throughout the duration of the project was that the counseling processes have no harmful or unintended consequences. That they did not *in relation to the outcome variable recidivism* is at least supported by the statistical data from the project relative to the Group 2 individual counseling. Of those offenders counseled during the descriptive phase, not only was Group 2 counseling consistently better than the fine control, the recidivism rate declined proportionately to the fine control throughout the four-year follow-up period for which recidivism data was gathered on these probationers. Whatever the explanation for this proportional decline in recidivism may be, it is certainly suggestive that Group 2 counseling was not counterproductive insofar as the intended goals of the project are concerned. See Figure 5-5 in Chapter 5. Inspection of recidivism results in Norman following the predictive phase does, as it has in most other phases of the project, complicate analysis. Here it will be recalled that Group 2 treatment, as measured by the criterion recidivism, was no better than the fine control. See Figure 5-8 in Chapter 5. However, if the economy (or some other exogenous factor) was as influential as it seems to have been, then whatever adverse consequences may have befallen the probationer, it seems unlikely that it was Group 2 counseling.

These poor results during the predictive phase do raise the question of whether now, with the hindsight of the apparent transitory effectiveness of individual counseling, the treatment intervention to alter behavior may still be employed. In other words, quantifiable data bearing on the question of effectiveness of treatment would certainly be a strong legitimizing factor for employing the treatment at any time. If, of course, the ineffectiveness is basically transitory, as is suggested, though without statistical significance, in Figure 5-8 where there was a dramatic drop in the recidivism rate among Group 2 individually counseled probationers from 80 percent in 1973 to 58 percent in 1974, then long-range benefits may vitiate short-term detriments. This is particularly true if something other than the treatment itself was responsible for the increase in recidivism. And finally, what of the fine in comparison? Unlike individual counseling, it was consistently less effective throughout the duration of the project with the exception of the period in the dramatic increase in recidivism in 1973 among individually counseled probationers. How must one weigh the alternative of a consistently demonstrably poor treatment as against at least the much better transitory effects of individual counseling?

Against this backdrop of legal and pragmatic justification for altering behavior to protect society in the achievement of its collectivistic goals, one must ultimately see the issue in an ethical perspective to meaningfully adjust the correlative rights of the individual and those of society. Professor Packard put the ultimate ethical issue of compelled personality change in these terms:

> . . . I am impelled to ask whether a theory of punishment that requires acquiescense in compelled personality change can ever be squared with long cherished ideals of human autonomy.[82]

But if punishments *other* than compelled personality change are to be inflicted, one must still consider actual or potential effects on the offender in terms of his autonomy as a human being. For example, there is some evidence from this predictive sentencing project, though without statistical significance, that in some cases the fine is most effective with those offenders who can least afford to pay that fine, a result that has considerable face validity. Given the pervasive influence that the economy appears to have in the rise and fall of crime and delinquency, fining the offender who can least afford to pay may strike as equally a pervasive affront to human dignity when in comparison to, say the Group 2 counseling during the descriptive phase of the project, long-term beneficial results were obtained without any apparent corresponding detriment to the offender.

In the end, extreme positions either way on the question of right of privacy or altering behavior do not seem productive of meaningful resolution. As at the beginning of the project, resolution is found in the objective of helping the offender "understand his own individuality and express himself as he chooses, but, at the same time, understand his relationship to society and his responsibility to the community in which he lives, so that others might have that same breadth of freedom he seeks without interference from him."

Notes

1. Morris, Norval, and Hawkins, Gordon, *The Honest Politicians Guide to Crime Control* (Chicago: University of Chicago, 1970), p. 188.

2. Nowak, John E., "Realigning the Standards of Review under the Equal Protection Guarantee–Prohibited, Neutral, and Permissive Classifications," *Ga, L. J.* 62: 1071 (1974).

3. Wilkinson, J. Harvie, "The Supreme Court, The Equal Protection Clause, and the Three Faces of Constitutional Equality," *Va. L. Rev.* 61: 945 (1975); Nowak, John E., "Realigning the Standards"; and Gunther, Gerald, "The Supreme Court 1971 Term, Foreword: In Search of Evolving Doctrine on a Changing Court: A Model for a Newer Equal Protection," *Harv. L. Rev.* 86: 1 (1972).

4. See note 3.

5. See the concurring opinion of Chief Justice Stone, who would resort to due process of law rather than to equal protection of the law, as did the majority of the Supreme Court in *Skinner v. Oklahoma*, 316 U.S. 535 (1941) in holding unconstitutional Oklahoma's statute authorizing compulsory sterilization of habitual criminals. *Id.* at 543.

6. *Roe v. Wade*, 410 U.S. 113, 152 (1972).

7. *Procunier v. Martinez*, 416 U.S. 396 (1974).

8. *Jobson v. Henne*, 355 F.2d 129 (2d Cir. 1966).

9. *Knecht v. Gillman*, 488 F.2d 1136 (8th Cir. 1973).

10. The leading exponent is Professor Hans Zeisel. See Zeisel, Hans, "Reflections on Experimental Techniques in the Law," *J. Legal Studies* 2: 107 (1973). See also Zeisel, "Reducing the Hazards of Human Experiments through Modifications in Research Design," Annals N.Y. Acad. Sci. 169: 475 (1970).

11. Norval Morris noted this shift over 20 years ago. See book review, "Juvenile Offenders Before the Courts," *Yale L.J.* 66: 962 (1956). See also, Morris, Norval, and Hawkins, Gordon, *The Honest Politicians Guide*.

12. *Village of Belle Terre v. Boraas*, 416 U.S. 1, 8 (1974), quoting *Reed v. Reed*, 404 U.S. 71, 76 (1971).

13. These are: "that legislative means must substantially further legislative ends." See Gunther, "The Supreme Court 1971 Term"; and "the 'demonstrable basis' standard." See Norvak, "Realigning the Standards"; and "the balancing approach." See Wilkinson, "The Supreme Court."

14. *Skinner v. Oklahoma*, 316 U.S. 535, 541 (1942).

15. Ibid.

16. See note 12.

17. *Cunningham v. United States*, 256 F.2d 467 (5th Cir. 1958).

18. *Hoyt v. Florida*, 368 U.S. 57 (1961).

19. See *Hunter v. State*, 375 P.2d 357 (Okla. 1962), sustaining the constitutionality of Oklahoma's second offender driving under the influence statute. See also, *Moore v. Missouri*, 15 U.S. 673, 678 (1895).

20. See *Skinner v. Oklahoma*, 316 U.S. 535, 541 (1942).

21. *Shepard v. United States*, 257 F.2d 293 (6th Cir. 1958).

22. Rubin, Sol, "Disparity and Equality of Sentences–A Constitutional Challenge," *F.R.D.* 40: 55 (1967).

23. *Slate v. Meyer*, 37 N.W.2d 3 (1949).

24. See Morris, "Juvenile Offenders," p. 969.

25. Ibid p. 971.

26. Ibid. Reprinted by permission of the Yale Law Journal Company and Fred B. Rothman & Company from the Yale Law Journal, Vol. 66, p. 971.

27. Ruebhausen, Oscar M., and Brim, Orville G., Jr., "Privacy and Behavioral Research," *Col. L. Rev.* 65: 1184, 1187 (1965).

28. Shils, Edward, "Privacy: Its Constitution and Vicissitudes," *Law and Contemp. Problems* 281, 284 (1966). See also, *Olmstead v. United States*, 277 U.S. 438, 478 (1927), dissenting opinion of Justice Brandeis; and Warren and Brandeis, "The Right to Privacy," *Harv. L. Rev.* 4: 193 (1890).

29. Shils, Edward, "Privacy: Its Constitution and Vicissitudes."

30. Ruebhausen and Brim, "Privacy and Behavioral Research," p. 1181.

31. Ibid.

32. *Planned Parenthood of Central Missouri v. Sanforth*, CCH U.S. Sup. Ct. Bull., No. 74-1151, July 1, 1976.

33. Ruebhausen and Brim, "Privacy and Behavioral Research," p. 1202.

34. Ibid.

35. Note, "Legal Implication of Psychological Research with Human Subjects," *Duke L.J.* (1960) 265.

36. See Cronbach, Lee J. *Essentials of Psychological Testing*, 2d. ed. (New York, Harper & Row, 1960), pp. 461-462 and compare Ruebhausen and Brim, "Privacy and Behavioral Research," p. 1201.

37. Ibid.

38. *Code of City of Norman*, §14-308.

39. See Prosser, "Privacy," *Calif. L. Rev.* 48: 383 (1960); Pound, "Interests of Personality," *Harv. L. Rev.* 28: 343 (1915).

40. *Union Pacific R. Co. v. Botsford*, 141 U.S. 250, 251 (1891).

41. *Stanley v. Georgia*, 394 U.S. 557, 564 (1969).

42. *Terry v. Ohio*, 392 U.S. 1, 8-9 (1968); *Katz v. United States*, 389 U.S. 347, 350 (1967); and *Boyd v. United States*, 116 U.S. 616 (1886).

43. *Griswold v. Connecticut*, 381 U.S. 479, 484-485 (1965).

44. *Griswold v. Connecticut*, 381 U.S. 479, 486 (1965). Justice Goldberg, concurring.

45. *Meyer v. Nebraska*, 262 U.S. 390, 399 (1923).

46. *Roe v. Wade*, 410 U.S. 113, 152 (1972).

47. *Palko v. Connecticut*, 302 U.S. 319, 325 (1937).

48. *Loving v. Virginia*, 388 U.S. 1, 12 (1967).

49. *Skinner v. Oklahoma*, 316 U.S. 535, 541-542 (1942).

50. *Eisenstadt v. Baird*, 405 U.S. 438, 453-454 (1972).

51. *Roe v. Wade*, 410 U.S. 113, (1972). And, see also, *Planned Parenthood of Central Missouri v. Danforth*, CCH U.S. Sup. Ct. Bull., No. 74-1151, July 1, 1976.

52. *Pierce v. Society of Sisters*, 268 U.S. 510, 535 (1925).

53. *Prince v. Massachusetts*, 321 U.S. 158, 166 (1944).

54. *Roe v. Wade*, 410 U.S. 113, 152 (1972).

55. See *Roe v. Wade*, 410 U.S. 154 (1972).

56. See *In re Gault*, 387 U.S. 1 (1967) and *Planned Parenthood of Central Missouri v. Danforth*, CCH U.S. Sup. Ct. Bull., No. 74-1151.

57. Fed. R. Crim. P., Rule 32 (c).

58. See, for example, 22 Okla. Stat. §982. See further, *People v. Dukett*, 56 Ill.2d 432, 308 N.E.2d 590 (1974), the court, quoting another decision at page 601, said: "... the sentencing court may inquire into the general moral character of the offender, his mentality, his habits, his social environment, his abnormal or subnormal tendencies, his age, his natural inclination or aversion to commit crime, [and] the stimuli which motivate his conduct." Psychological testing is implicit.

59. *Williams v. New York*, 337 U.S. 241 (1949).

60. Ibid.

61. *United States v. Schipani*, 435 F.2d 26 (2d Cir. 1970).

62. *Procunier v. Martinez*, 416 U.S. 397 (1974).

63. Ibid., pp. 408-409.

64. Ibid., p. 409.

65. Ibid., p. 412.

66. Ibid., p. 413.

67. Ibid., p. 413.

68. Accident Facts, National Safety Council, 1921-

69. *Tate v. Short*, 401 U.S. 395 (1971), concurring opinion of Justice Blackmun at 672.

70. Ibid.

71. *Argersinger v. Hamlin*, 407 U.S. 25 (1972), concurring opinion of Justice Powell at 51.

72. See note 19.

73. Laurer, A.R., *The Psychology of Driving* (Springfield, Ill.: Charles C. Thomas, 1972); Parry, Meyer H. *Aggression on the Road* (London: Tavistock Publications, 1968); Pelz, Donald C., and Schuman, Stanley H., *Countermeasures for Young Drivers* (University of Michigan Press, 1972); and Willett, T.C., *Criminal on the Road* (London: Tavistock Publications, 1964).

74. Ibid.

75. Ibid.

76. *Procunier v. Martinez*, 416 U.S. 397 (1974).

77. 306 F. Supp. 1158 (E.D. N.Y. 1969). See also, concerning the right to treatment and rehabilitation, Note, "Conditioning and Other Technologies Used to Treat? Rehabilitate? Demolish? Prisoners and Mental Patients," *Calif. L. Rev.* 45: 616, 641-655 (1972).

78. Ibid., p. 1169. See further, Note, "Conditioning and Other Technologies Used to Treat? Rehabilitate? Demolish? Prisoners and Mental Patients," *Calif. L. Rev.* 45: 616, 655 (1972).

79. *Jobson v. Henne*, 355 F.2d 129 (2d Cir. 1966), involving mandatory prison work programs.

80. *Knecht v. Gillman*, 488 F.2d 1136 (8th Cir. 1973), involving the involuntary administration of apomorphine to induce vomiting as part of an aversion therapy program.

81. *Skinner v. Oklahoma*, 316 U.S. 535 (1942), concurring opinion of Chief Justice Stone at 543.

82. Packer, Herbert L., *The Limits of the Criminal Sanction*, (Stanford: Stanford University Press, 1968) pp. 57-58. Compare: "Free men aren't 'conditioned'! Free men are free because they are ornery and cussed and prefer to arrive at their own prejudices in their own way–not have them spoon fed by a self-appointed mind tinkerer!" Heinlein, Robert A., *Revolt in 2100*, Signet ed., at 118-119 (New York: New American Library, 1954).

7 Social

Social Setting

In retrospect, the social setting for the predictive sentencing project is extremely illuminating. In particular, the social setting permits a critical examination of the varied characteristics of the specific research sites to isolate those factors that may optimize the opportunities for success in a controlled experimental design for sentencing. In looking back, the most significant are: funding stability; sufficient population concentration with political, economic, and social dispersion; community acceptance; commitment of the court to innovative research; coordinated control over related judicial and research functions; coordination between participating units of government; and logistical requirements.

Funding Stability

An obvious, but prime, requisite for successful research is minimum essential funding. Viewing the original research proposal as a whole and its subsequent funding, it is important to observe that the project was conceived out of, at least, the then prevailing rather liberal beliefs centered within the criminal justice system.[1] The "social defense" orientation of the project; with emphasis on rehabilitation, was compatible with these beliefs. Other more traditional, or more radical, approaches to the sentencing study might have been taken with perhaps equally valuable results. But they were not and, it is believed, on reflection, that this was "good" in the long run insofar as the continuation of funding is concerned.

Moreover, not only was the project "compatible" with current assumptions about the posture that should be taken in sentencing and thus deserving of funding, it also offered at one and the same time a nonthreatening solution to a vexing problem of growing public concern. Funding thus stimulated social acceptability of the project in the communities and institutions within the communities affected by offering continuing financial support if the results were favorable, while on the other hand, at least five years without change waiting for the results to come in if they were nil or unfavorable. These kinds of considerations were perhaps instrumental in both the level and duration of the funding.[2] At the same time, it is more than noteworthy that the funding agencies maintained intense interest in the research methodology and outcomes throughout the long duration of the project, including a very thorough site visit when the transition was made from the descriptive to the predictive (cross-validation) phases of the project. Moreover, even at a time when the outcomes produced the four anomolous results, NIMH agreed to extend the project for six months to permit an examination of the effects of external conditions on the effectiveness of individual counseling. Thus, at this point, the ameliorating factor of the importance of the research continued dominant and, what is perhaps more important, permitted the project to be concluded successfully for whatever value the explanation of the anomolous results may have for the future of research in sentencing. In short, while one cannot negate the possible importance of the current social acceptability of the research project in securing funding, experience with this project has demonstrated an essential openmindedness to encouraging good research, independent of outcomes. That this portends good for future court research is a happy note on which to end this particular project.

Funding, however, is only the most obvious prerequisite. There are many other social factors that are also involved. What are these factors and how did they interact to affect the course of this project?

The Research Sites

An Overview

The project was operated in Norman, Oklahoma for over seven years and, during the predictive phase, in the regional areas of Tulsa, Lawton, and the Little City areas of Ardmore-Madill-Durant and Ponca City-Blackwell. The two leading economic factors in Norman are education and public administration, reflecting the presence of one of the state's two largest universities and the largest mental health complex. The per capita income is relatively high, being somewhat over the state average, but because of the economic base, is divided somewhat atypically. There is considerable disparity between a higher-paid professional group and a lower-paid supporting staff.

Tulsa, the second largest city in Oklahoma, is probably the most industrialized and certainly the most cosmopolitan city in the state, and among the highest in per capita income. It offered the greatest ethnic minority concentration, both numerically and proportionally, of any of the research sites. It is also considered by many to be a very progressive city.

Lawton, although the third largest city in the state, has one of the lowest per capita incomes of the research sites. The dominant economic factor, public administration, results largely from being adjacent to an Army training facility that recently boasted a strength of over 40,000 uniformed personnel. This strength, while varying, rarely falls below 15,000 to 20,000 in personnel, and the training facility is therefore always a significant social and economic factor in community life. The original fort was established well before the city existed and therefore has "always been there."

Ardmore-Durant-Madill was made up of three cities, ranging in population from a little over 2000 to somewhat over 25,000, that were pooled to obtain sufficient size to make research viable. While these cities span three counties, it was decided that they were enough alike to represent a specific area of the state. It is commonly stated that they tend toward the southern-conservative both politically and religiously. Economically all three are below the state average in per capita income. They are, however, all roughly adjacent to one of the region's largest lake and recreation areas, and all share a similar type of agricultural surrounding.

Ponca City-Blackwell was made up of two cities with populations of approximately 25,000 and 10,000, respectively, and almost 96 percent Caucasian. While major economic factors within the cities are manufacturing and retail trade, they are both surrounded by miles of wheat and cattle land. Per capita income is among the highest in the states. If characterized politically, the area would be moderately conservative.

Population Dispersion

In selecting research sites for predictive sentencing, it is essential to select sites with an adequate concentration of population with political, economic, and social dispersion to assure as large a representation of personal and social milieu orientations as possible. Of course, the ideal is always balanced against other practical and theoretical considerations that may outweigh this factor in the selection of a site. Norman is a case in point. It is (or has been, until recent light industrial development may have tended to change its character) somewhat atypical of the rest of the state, with the two leading economic factors being education and public administration, creating two more or less disparate income groups with perhaps a somewhat more liberal political and social action orientation than might be true in other communities. Certainly, the other regions, with perhaps the exception of Tulsa, in which the sentencing scheme was tried, represent a far more conservative orientation than that found in Norman. But in the first instance, implementation of the project was limited by the jurisdictional boundaries of the court from which the impetus for the project was derived. Moreover, in the beginning it was believed that the control over the research design factor that the court could exercise in its jurisdiction was more important than initiating the project in a court system with less potential control, even though it would be in a population center more representative in political, economic, and social orientation. Indeed, the subsequent expansion of the project into other areas of Oklahoma was an effort to offset the possibly atypical character of Norman by selecting sites with differing political, economic, and social character.

However, in the trade-off, some of the desirable features of the Norman site, such as control, were in large measure given up. Tulsa is a case in point. Its size, dispersion in political, economic, and social characteristics, and the potential target population obtainable made this community ideally suited for this project. Yet its very size presented logistical problems that were frequently very difficult to manage. Smallness, as in the case of Ardmore-Madill-Durant and Ponca City-Blackwell, ameliorates control problems but may not afford a population base large enough to secure an adequate target population from which interpretable results may be drawn.

With the expansion it is believed that significant diversity in political, economic, and social orientation was achieved with the various participating communities. If anything, achieving good political, economic, and social dispersion came at the expense of sufficient size of the research sites to produce an adequate target population. And in consequence, insofar as any predictive sentencing research scheme is concerned, perhaps first emphasis should be placed on the size of the population from which the target group is drawn. Secondarily, representativeness may be considered; but in the selection of a community of optimal size, representativeness in personal and social milieu factors will, to a degree, be achieved indirectly.

Community Acceptance

Community acceptance of innovative programs, both collectively and individually, can be extremely important in the overall success of community-based social action research. First, the overall receptivity of the community to innovation is important. Second, a minimal level of community acceptance requires the absence of active opposition, a measure of political support, and presumably, confidence in the institutional body conducting the program. And, in the long run, all three of these are directly linked to the degree of support the news media gives such programs and thus influence and shape community attitudes.

In assessing community acceptance of the predictive sentencing program, in the case of Norman, it is believed that the basic educational and mental health orientation of the community provided initially the type of liberal beliefs that were conducive to acceptance of the project throughout its long duration. In fact, of those probationers who were dropped out of the program in Norman for refusal to cooperate, there were only four who could possibly be accounted for hostility to the program: a lawyer's son, a minister's son, and the sons of two local business men. And of these, the only clear case of open hostility toward the program and its goals was that of the lawyer, though it was also claimed the boy did not need counseling, or, if he did, the parents could provide it. In the case of the other three, "they were good boys and counseling for them was really not needed."

In contrast, when the program was expanded into other regions, consideration was given to including a north central Oklahoma community in the study, also the site of a state college. Initially, during the planning phase, the city judge, court clerk, and city manager were contacted and were receptive to the proposal. Local college faculty were seen regarding students who might be used as counselors and seemed enthusiastic. Overall, prospects look good. One faculty member did, however, privately express some pessimism that such a research project could be executed in this conservatively oriented community. When the time came to implement the project, it was greeted with a flat refusal by city officials without explanation.

However, in the long run, refusal at the outset is to be preferred to receptivity and willingness to cooperate, implementation, and then, either for loss of community, political, or institutional support or enforcement practices, failure of the entire effort.[3] The experience in Lawton is a case in point. Lawton's judge, prosecutor, police officials, and city management all seemed quite accepting when the project was proposed. Intake projections were deemed quite reasonable. Hiring and training went smoothly and implementation was completed without incident. Yet it soon became obvious that expected intake was not materializing. In fact, less than 17 percent of expected intake was achieved. Site visits were made and procedures reviewed, but all seemed to be in order. An independent study of the first five months of operation was undertaken, and it was determined that while a number of prospects had been overlooked, the gross intake could never have been over 30 percent of expectations. For some reason, potential probationers, if indeed there were any more, were not coming into contact with the court. A series of interviews were undertaken involving high school and college students, police and court personnel, military administrators, and persons now living outside of Lawton but having previous experience with Lawton. While a variety of explanations were offered, often hearsay, one dominant theme did arise out of these conversations. This was that local law enforcement patterns were abnormally biased against military personnel and thus in favor of local citizens. This seems reasonable since Lawton is the largest social center within over 50 miles, there exists an abnormally high military to civilian ratio, and most of the military are young, unencumbered by family and thus seeking entertainment locally.

Even so, this does not totally explain the low intake rate. Looking back, there was strong central administrative support for the project during the early stages of implementation that was seemingly lost when there was a change in the top level administrative officer of the city. This, together with veiled skepticism concerning the value of the project and confidence in the enforcement system as it existed, may reflect a basic community attitude that is inconsistent with innovation and contributed to the failure in Lawton. Paradoxically, however, Lawton has participated in many funded social action programs that make the Lawton story somewhat of an enigma.[4]

Local political support is essential to community acceptance, and though the initiation of the project in Norman was controversial, it consistently received strong support from the local governing body. The University of Oklahoma in Norman has always been represented on the city council and, indeed, a University faculty member assumed significant leadership in the initial approval of the project for Norman. Views were polarized in the beginning, with one lawyer council member arguing that there was no need in the municipal court for probation since traffic offenses are "... impulse offenses or due to carelessness, rather than being premeditated." Moreover, he argued "I also understand that this system would be intended primarily as a research tool, and I don't believe our citizens should be placed in the position of being guinea pigs for a research project."[5] In the end, however, the generally liberal council led by a mayor who was also the manager of a local radio station at the time, as well as a former probation officer, approved the proposal and consistently participated in its funding.[6] Only in the wake of rising inflation and a budget crises in city government did the program lose its funding at the end of 1975 when the research phase of the project was also in its final stages.

Local political support in the other communities where the project was instituted seemed weaker. The judges of the participating courts were either former students of the principal investigator or associated with him professionally in state judicial conference activities. As such, initial cooperation with these courts was secured and local political dynamics never appeared to be a significant factor. Moreover, at the time of the expansion, the generally favorable results derived from individual counseling during the descriptive phase in Norman certainly made the project much easier to export. Nor did instituting the program in these communities appear to create any controversy from which the level of political support might be assessed. Lawton, as already indicated, is a special case and difficult to assess because, while ostensible local court and community support was present, it is not apparent in the results of the project there.

Turning to public confidence in the institutional body, the Norman court and its judge have been in the forefront of reform efforts in the lower courts in Oklahoma since 1964. Both the court and its judge have been the recipients of both national and state awards for leadership in improving the administration of justice in the lower court system, all of which has been reported by the local news media.[7] The same is largely true of the Tulsa court and its presiding judge. The influence of these types of reported activities in building public confidence and acceptance are difficult to measure. And the reporting of these types of activities may not be as influential as one might like to think. Perhaps public confidence, at least general public confidence, is not nearly so important as a lack of concern or interest in the activity or program so long as it is not significantly threatening to the assumed needs of the community. Indeed, Ross and Blumenthal report that "... defendants' desires to be fined rather than to be placed on any kind of probation were apparently most effective in obtaining a departure from prescriptions of the research when the defendants were represented by counsel."[8] And, in spite of the substantial risk the automobile brings to society, traffic, traffic laws, and habitual traffic offenders do not have a particularly high priority in the scale of public concern with the criminal justice system.[9] Perhaps this is expressed in the other communities where the judges, though competent, were not active in reported judicial reform activities that would engender greater public attention and, presumably, confidence. At the same time, there were no apparent negative community attitudes that would militate against public acceptance of the project in these communities.

Turning to news media support, with only two exceptions,[10] the local news media in the Norman area has given positive support and encouragement to the work of the court and its judge for over 12 years.[11] So far as is known, the same is true in the other regions of Oklahoma. Again, it is difficult to assess the impact of favorable news media support in securing community acceptance. Certainly, this type of praise would not ordinarily be expected to negatively affect community acceptance of innovative social action research.

Innovative Courts

Perhaps one of the most important factors in social action research in the courts is a commitment by the judge to innovation and research. In another experimental study of sentencing traffic offenders, Ross and Blumenthal report that while the presiding judge of the court involved acknowledged the need for the sentencing research, there was no commitment to the research by the trial judges who actually made the sentencing decisions.[12] As a result the research was seriously impaired. Unlike Ross and Blumenthal, with perhaps the exception of Lawton, Durant, and Madill, the judges of the courts involved in this project did commit themselves to the research design, at least based on all indices available to project personnel, such as intake into the program, judicial and clerical confirmation of intake in accordance with the research design, and verification of the administering of the treatment. Certainly, strong commitment existed in Norman where the principal investigator was the presiding judge and, in addition, enjoyed good rapport with the associate judge who participated in the sentencing and was similarly committed to the project.

Interestingly, fidelity to the research design in Tulsa is indicated indirectly by a telephone call by the sentencing judge to the principal investigator to discuss the judge's frustration with one aspect of the research design, namely, the suspension of fines on subsequent convictions while the offender was still undergoing counseling. In effect, he queried: "Isn't it about time I started fining this repeater? Counseling isn't doing him any good!" They talked about the research design, the importance of consistency in sentencing the offenders, and the possible effect of a fine on the offender while still in counseling. The judge felt better and agreed to continue following the sentencing strategy, but it is not at all certain that he was comfortable with his decision. The important thing is that he followed through on his commitment after the desirability of his continuing to do so was reinforced.

Lawton again stands out at the other extreme. In spite of surface indications of commitment to testing the sentencing strategy, it is not at all certain that the judge was genuinely committed to the goals of the project. On several occasions during the initial steps to establish the program in Lawton assertions of satisfaction with the court's existing procedures and current sentencing practices now seem ominous and should have been taken more seriously. However, at the time, they were interpreted as a willingness to cooperate, despite the feeling that predictive sentencing probably would not be a viable alternative to their existing sentencing practices.

The judge of Durant was apparently enticed more by the possibility of clerical assistance from the proposed probation clerk than he was by predictive sentencing, but he did cooperate and, so far as is known, committed himself to the project. The Madill judge was not interested, but the project had the support of several members of the bar association there and he also cooperated, although ultimately no one was sentenced in Madill due to the small population base. With the foregoing, the experience with the predictive sentencing project differs substantially from the experience of Ross and Blumenthal. In all events, without genuine commitment to research and innovation in sentencing, there is no possibility for obtaining measurable results.[13]

Control Over Function

As indicated in Part I, in the end the Norman data were the most reliable data available for evaluating the results of predictive sentencing. It is believed this is due in no small measure to the coordinated control exercised over the related sentencing and research functions of the project in the Norman area. As discussed in Chapter 2, the principal investigator of the research project also served as presiding judge of the Norman court throughout the duration of the study. Accordingly, it was possible for him to exercise the fullest control over the research design as principal investigator by assuring, in his capacity as presiding judge, that sentencing decisions would be made and probationary treatment administered in accordance with the research design. This coordinated control over function must be seen in perspective. Just as it can be an instrument of achieving measurable results in sentencing for the benefit of the criminal justice system, so also it could become an instrument of oppression in the hands of an unscrupulous investigator-judge. Conforming the research design to relevant legal and ethical constraints, careful exposition of the research design, and publicity should provide adequate controls to dissuade the unscrupulous.

Control was more difficult to maintain when the project became regional, stemming, in no small part, from the autonomous role in which courts function. Courts, separated as they are from other functions of government and the rest of the criminal justice system, exercise a large degree of autonomy that can create special problems for the social action researcher. Autonomy, is perhaps not exclusive to courts as institutions, but it tends to be true generally of courts of all jurisdictions. This autonomy intensified by long tradition is most often embodied in the judge of the court and to a lesser extent in those he designates. Thus, any attempt to even partially control the court must come either formally from the legal community, or, as in this project, less formally from cooperation with the judge and his system (if you upset his designates you tend to upset him). Therefore, as often as not this kind of research deals even more with an individual judge to a greater extent than with his institution. In looking back, a probation clerk at one site was hired in spite of reservations concerning her competency because she was a friend of the secretary of the judge of the court and it was feared the project might be jeopardized in that area if the secretary and, possibly the judge, were offended by refusing the preferred applicant.

Given the realities of the structure within which the project had to function during the expansion phase, once a commitment to the research and innovation was secured, it was believed that the organizational structure devised for the expansion provided for minimal interference with the local court but yet maximized the opportunity for coordinating sentencing, and treatment, and research through the office of the probation clerk located at each site. See Figure 2-2.

Coordinating Participating Units

A related problem has to do with control intrinsic to the court itself. In Norman, for example, mandatory court appearances are required for all offenders committing three or more traffic offenses within a period of 12 months.[14] This rule assured proper assignment of all offenders in the project's target group into predictive sentencing.

In contrast, in Tulsa, discretion was vested in the police officer to elect to authorize the payment of an administrative fine in lieu of requiring a court appearance by the offender. The presiding judge sought to deal with this logistical problem by issuing an order requiring that all offenders in the target group be assigned a court appearance by the arresting officer. Unfortunately, the rule was not rigorously followed by the police department, a fact that probably contributed to the loss of a number of potential probationers and thus may partly explain a lower intake rate than was originally projected for Tulsa. When this failure was uncovered, the presiding judge of the court assisted in remedying the problem, at least, during the latter half of the project period in Tulsa.

However, there are still unanswered questions concerning the level of *real* support from the police department, since there is evidence that the program received less than total acceptance. Indeed, it was reported that one police officer who served as a probation officer for the project in Tulsa had significant reservations about the value of the program in remedying poor driving behavior.

As a further example, in Tulsa, probably due to the size of the municipal court operation there, the scope of the judicial process had resulted in a separate court, court clerk's office, and records keeping section. While accountable to some degree to the presiding judge, the clerk's and records functions had gained some degree of autonomy. Although basic accuracy is not questioned, this presented the problem of negotiating with each section separately on issues concerning them.

Logistical Requirements

Among the logistical requirements, in addition to funding, for effective social action research are administrative support for the research, competent research personnel, and adequate records systems. This project spanned seven years and employed from 6 to over 50 paid personnel. The project had the administrative services of the University of Oklahoma Research Institute and later the University's Office of Research Administration. These agencies assumed complete responsibility for managing the grants, supervising and administering the payroll, purchasing equipment, assisting in grant application preparation, and publishing the Interim and Final Reports on the project.

By and large, the people working on the project were competent, hard-working, and committed to its goals. In contrast, personnel problems were encountered in the expansion. One case in point is the probation clerk at one site who proved to be less efficient than necessary for the project. In addition to excessive illness that went unreported until much later, the clerk lacked the required competency and was not, it has been decided, well motivated toward the project. Sometime after the first six months of operation, a study was undertaken to try to explain the disappointing low intake at this site. It was determined that during the first 24 weeks of operation a total of five visits were made to the site by Norman administrative personnel at the rate of one per month for five out of those six months. In the one-week periods following these visits an average of 7.2 people per week were taken into the project as opposed to an average of 3.34 per week during the remaining 19 weeks. Had the intake been constant at the higher rate for the entire period approximately twice as many probationers would have been in the program at that time, and expectations would have almost been met. It was concluded that personal visits tended to motivate the clerk, and perhaps others, for a period of about one week, with rapidly diminishing effects thereafter. Again, however, these insights were gained quite late, and with the research involving a relatively short time period, there was simply not sufficient time to correct the problem after it had been discovered.

Ineptness, or disinterest, on the part of the clerk at another site is also considered to be a factor in the failure there. Again, with sentencing taking place over such a short period as nine months, by the time the problem was uncovered, there was not adequate time to interview, hire, and train a substitute.

In contrast, it is believed that the relative administrative success of the program at another site is directly attributable to the probation clerk for this area. The clerk, as the principal administrative person for the project in this area, was of exceptional intelligence and knowledgable of and committed to the project, as well as a personal friend of the principal investigator. Her competence and confidence were invaluable to the project's operation in this area. The same was also true of the probation clerk at the fourth site.

Another research problem particularly associated with courts of lesser jurisdiction involves record keeping practices. In the sites studied, court and police records, while containing essentially the same data, were kept in a variety of ways ranging from the rudimentary practice of putting more current records in cigar boxes to the sophistication of almost total computer storage. In the end all data for this project were collected and coded but at the expense of substantial human labor that could have been more usefully employed in, for example, supervising personnel. Had these records been either much less accessible or less similar, little analysis could have been done. Investigation of potential research sites should include a thorough examination of record keeping systems. And, even assuming the site is otherwise acceptable, inadequate record keeping should disqualify an otherwise favorable site.

In summary, for Norman, perhaps the factor of greatest importance is control over the implementation and operation of the project in this community. For the entire seven years the same judge presided and exercised direct supervision over the court, the court clerk's office, and the probation division, as well as the project's research division. He was committed to and consistent with the project at all times. Among other things, this resulted in a very clean, easily accessible data base, thus facilitating research. Further, there was direct and ongoing contact between the administrative, operational, and research personnel of the project. It can be said that Norman experienced the highest and most consistent control of all sites. And this, in no small part, may explain the relative operational success of the project in Norman.

Taking everything into consideration, Tulsa seemed ideally suited for the project. Such was not the case. Size, division of function between court, police, clerical, and record keeping, and related problems all contributed to Tulsa's performing far under expectations.

In Lawton, political orientation, commitment, control, personnel, and record keeping all contributed to failure. Lawton may serve as a good case in point of a community where greater study, particularly of records vital to the project, should have been completed before implementation. Had this been done, perhaps the project would have directed its resources to a more viable setting and received greater return. Yet, the presence of its military facility made the community unique among those under consideration. It was found to be unique at least insofar as the results of this project are concerned. In Lawton the frustration of failure is felt most keenly.[15]

In the Little Cities of Ardmore-Madill-Durant, apart from the low intake, which was anticipated, the program functioned well because of the capable administrative support of the probation clerk. The same is largely true of Ponca City-Blackwell. The project received good initial support in this area and cooperation was maintained throughout its duration. Records were well kept and readily available and all personnel were of excellent caliber. Operations were quite smooth throughout, with all factors pointing toward success. In the face of this, achievement of only 58 percent of expected intake into the program is puzzling.

In summary, an adequate research environment is essential to the success of court-related research. A sufficient population base, community acceptance, commitment to innovative research, control, coordination, and minimal logistical support in form of administrative assistance, competent personnel, and good record keeping are all essential. Apart from specific project findings, the project certainly has permitted a thorough examination of the sites to evaluate those conditions that will provide an optimal research environment.

Court Visibility and Research

Courts, as public institutions of general interest, are highly visible in society. And 1st Amendment free press considerations militate against news management of court activities involving the administration of justice, including research involving courts and court functions. The commission of offenses, prosecutions resulting therefrom, and judicial proceedings arising from these prosecutions are events of legitimate concern to the public and consequently fall within the news media's responsibility to report the operations of government.[16]

> A responsible press has always been regarded as the handmaiden of effective judicial administration, especially in the criminal field. Its function in this regard is documented by an impressive record of service over several centuries. The press does not simply publish information about trials but guards against the miscarriage of justice by subjecting the police, prosecutors, and judicial processes to extensive public scrutiny and criticizm.[17]

Moreover, if such research meets legal and ethical constraints, there should be no reason, as such, for screening research projects from public view.

At the same time, it is acknowledged that social action research, often not popularly understood, is subject to possible biases resulting from the extent of public exposure to the population studied of either the existence of the research or the results derived therefrom. Too little exposure, either in quantity or quality, may lead to a public perception of secrecy concerning the research and result in an unfavorable operational environment. On the other hand, too much exposure may lead to undesirable expectations in the population studied. For example, with reference to this project, public claims of the foolproof superiority of Group 2 counseling, if believed by either actual or potential probationers, could cause observed treatment effect, such as no recidivism among Group 2 probationers, to result from the mere *belief* that the treatment was effective rather than the *treatment*. This "Hawthorn effect" has been of concern to project personnel throughout the duration of the study but not to the extreme of attempting to manage the news.[18] The initiation of the project in Norman, the goals sought, and the methodology to achieve these goals were well publicized in the local news media.[19]

Of greater concern to project personnel in their role as researchers was the handling of news releases in Norman at the end of the descriptive phase when the results with Group 2 counseling were clearly superior to any of the other treatments. Reports of the superiority of such counseling might have an effect on the expectations of potential and actual probationers, especially, with the use of a fine control group. But in the end, recognition of the obligation of public disclosure was achieved through cooperation with responsible local news media, resulting in a precisely worded news article that "Counseling May Be Better than Fines" and that the results were "interesting but tentative" and the results "may change substantially after more thorough investigation."[20] This approach of balancing the court's accountability on the one hand and protecting the legitimate interests of the project with precise news reporting on the other was a really important effort for both the press and the project. Of course, as reported in Chapter 5, in the final analysis, the probability of a Hawthorn effect in project findings now seems highly unlikely. Without the benefit of hindsight, it was of substantial concern at the time, but all recognized that the public's right to know was paramount. Happily, the news media in Norman recognized the importance of the research to an understanding of the concept of predictive sentencing.

Notes

1. See Bennett, Stephen A., "Rehabilitation in Check," *12 Trial 12* (Cambridge, Mass.: Association of Trial Lawyers of America, 1976), suggesting that the mood toward sentencing may be shifting away from rehabilitation and toward retribution.

2. A growing body of literature lends credence to this speculation. See, for example, Galliher, John F., and James L. McCartney, "The Influence of Funding Agencies on Juvenile Delinquency Research," *Social Problems* 21:1, (Summer 1973).

3. For the impairment of a research design due to the failure of judges to cooperate, see Ross, H. Lawrence, and Blumenthal, Murray, "Some Problems in Experimentation in a Legal Setting," *The American Sociologist* 10:150-155, (August 1975).

4. "H.U.D. Management Assistance Program—Survey and Analysis Findings and Recommendations," Prepared for Model Cities Department, City of Lawton, Lawton, Oklahoma by CONSAD Research Corporation, December 1971.

5. *The Norman Transcript*, Wednesday, September 29, 1965, p. 3.

6. *The Norman Transcript*, Wednesday, October 27, 1965, p. 1.

7. See, for example, *The Norman Transcript*, Thursday, November 3, 1966, p. 1 and *The Norman Transcript* March 4, 1971, p. 1.

8. See Ross and Blumenthal, "Some Problems in Experimentation," p. 154.

9. Ross, H. Lawrence, "Traffic Law Violation: A Folk Crime," *Social Problems* 8 (Winter 1960-1961), pp. 231-241.

10. See the editorial, "Watch That Tongue," *The Oklahoma Daily*, Wednesday, November 12, 1969, p. 12, criticizing the court for its interpretation of a city ordinance involving interference with official process, and the editorial, "New City Policy on Filing DWI Cases Aid to Safety," *The Norman Transcript*, Monday, February 17, 1969, p. 6, implying the court had been entirely too lenient in punishment assessed on convictions for driving while intoxicated.

11. See, for example, the editorial, "His Concern Aids Justice," *The Norman Transcript*, Wednesday, March 10, 1971, p. 6, and the editorial, "Comments in Brief: On Young Offenders," *The Norman Transcript*, Wednesday, September 15, 1971, p. 6.

12. See Ross and Blumenthal, "Some Problems in Experimentation."

13. See the interesting study of Long, Lucinda, "Innovation in Urban Criminal Courts," in Jacob, H. (ed.) *The Potential for Reform of Criminal Justice* (Beverly Hills, Ca: Sage Publications, 1974).

14. *Code of City of Norman,* § 14-310(b).

15. There is evidence of a total breakdown in city government that may account for the failure there. See "Lawton Citizens Request Probe of Local Government," *The Sunday Oklahoma*, October 6, 1974, p. 6.

16. *Cox Broadcasting Corp. v. Cohn*, 420 U.S. 469 (1975).

17. *Sheppard v. Maxwell*, 384 U.S. 333, 350 (1966). And, see further, *Nebraska Press Association v. Hugh Stuart*, Judge, U.S. Sup. Ct. Bull., CCH, B-4248, June 30, 1976.

18. Roethlisberger, Fritz, J., and Dickson, William J., *Management and the Worker* (Cambridge, Mass.: Harvard University Press, 1939), p. 193.

19. See the news story, "City, OU Combine on Juvenile Program," *The Norman Transcript*, Thursday, September 26, 1968, p. 1.

20. See "Counseling May Be Better than Fines," *The Norman Transcript*, Sunday, September 12, 1971 and "Unique Study Offers Clues to 'Repeaters,'" *The Oklahoma Daily*, Tuesday, September 14, 1971. Compare the news release in an Oklahoma City, Oklahoma newspaper "Counseling Found Best Penalty," *The Sunday Oklahoma*, September 12, 1971.

8 Economic

When Experiments Fail

It was under the pressure of unresolved anomalous findings that the project personnel finally departed from their own familiar disciplines and the conventional delinquency paradigm to venture into economics as a possible explanation for these unresolved anomalies. On the positive side, by stepping out of the paradigm in which the experiment was conducted and by testing the resulting hypothesis to the limits of available data, it was at least possible to deal creatively with the four anomalous outcomes. In the process lessons have been learned about delinquency research that merit sharing with others and that also point to the importance of the cross-fertilization of two streams of work that have not heretofore significantly influenced each other.

On the negative side, there are still some residual fears that the results may have been over-interpreted and, at worst, forced order upon extremely unlikely, but nevertheless, random outcomes. It is acknowledged that the economic aspect of this work constitutes secondary analysis of the data. In contrast with the predictive sentencing experiment itself, the strictly correlational sorts of analyses conducted to test the adequacy of the economic explanation of the anomalies could not be conclusive—only suggestive.

This chapter records the venture into economics in chronological sequence in order to share the intense debate, exhilaration, and frustration that ensued among project personnel and to convey the conclusions finally reached. The benchmarks of the path of the unexpected expedition consisted of: (1) Roszak: "Honest experiments may fail . . . when they do . . ."; (2) Brenner: "Mental Illness and the Economy"; (3) Fleisher: "The Effect of Unemployment on Juvenile Delinquency"; (4) NIMH grant extended to examine external conditions; (5) traffic offenses are different from other crimes; (6) manpower studies on offenders and defendants; and (7) final assessment of the impact of the economy.

None were prepared for the results obtained. Several likely outcomes had been sketched, but the printouts resembled none of these. Project optimists, middle-grounders, and nay-sayers were all wrong. After ruling out coding, keypunch, and format statement aberations, Roszak's advice was followed: ". . . if the scientific spirit has taught us anything of value, it *is* that honest experiments may well fail. When they do, there must be a radical reconsideration. . . ."[1] The experiment had failed to produce a method that consistently, year in and year out, reduced traffic recidivism. To start our reconsideration, we asked: How had other delinquency prevention programs fared?

Krisberg and Takagi contended:

> We know that the history of delinquency prevention has been grossly disappointing. From the Glueck's 1926 study of Judge Baker's Child Guidance Clinic to the highly sophisticated and elaborate study of Empey and Lubeck in the Silverlake Experiment, not one single delinquency project has been able to demonstrate the achievement of programmatic goals.[2]

Why have these projects failed? Krisberg and Takagi argue that they all erred by accepting the false assumption of Healy and Aichhorn, made at the turn of the century, that delinquents are defective persons needing education and treatment using individual-oriented approaches. The projects have failed because poverty and racism contribute more to delinquency than do the supposed shortcomings of the delinquent. The delinquency projects deal with the personal deficits while ignoring the social milieu's deficits.[3]

The racial and economic roots of delinquency and their relation to reduction of delinquency have been similarly linked by Wolfgang, Figlio, and Sellin:

> We know that boys who commit many offenses, some of them very serious, are very likely to be nonwhite members of the low socioeconomic group. We also know that only 35 percent of these particular boys desist from further delinquency after their first contact with the law. With this knowledge in mind, as unsurprising as it may be, it seems appropriate to suggest that community action programs which have as their goals the alleviation or modification of the above mentioned conditions may also influence the course of juvenile delinquency within the subject areas.[4]

Certainly, this predictive sentencing project had shared what Galliher and McCartney had identified as the most striking trend in government-funded delinquency research, namely, the assumption that the offender's behavior was the problem (as opposed to that of the offender's society).[5] And although this line of attack might handle the project's failure to reach its program goal, it does not address the anomalies, particularly the striking success for individually counseled probationers from the early, descriptive phase of the project and the persistence over a four-year period of the success of the offenders counseled during this period on traffic recidivism, nontraffic offenses, and accidents relative to the control group.

Mental Illness and Economy

For several weeks, a plausible and testable answer was not discovered to the question: What could have extinguished a once powerful treatment and frustrated the protection of the randomized control group design? Also, what mechanism could account for all four of the anomalies? It was evident from the start that separate explanations for each anomaly would be no more than empty ad hoc explanations. For a while, the best candidate was the dramatic drop in confidence in the government resulting from the Watergate crimes and their subsequent coverup. But without adequate indices of this variable and without a body of literature relating this to crime and delinquency, the political disaffection notion was reluctantly put aside. Having been sensitized to the possible role of economics with delinquency from the survey of the literature and, helped along by whatever benign fate deposited a copy of Brenner's *Mental Illness and the Economy* in Moe's Used Books of Berkeley, California, a plausible, testable hypothesis tumbled into our laps.

Using sophisticated econometric techniques, Brenner has marshalled formidable evidence to support the notion that, "instabilities in the national economy have been the single most important source of fluctuation in mental hospital admissions or admission rates." Further, in his preface Brenner asserted:

> The major theoretical implication is that, despite our philosophic orientation, the destiny of the individual is to a great extent subject to large-scale changes in the social and economic structure that are in no way under his control. . . . These findings raise questions about the utility of therapies that do not take into account disturbances in the patients' social environment.[6]

Were Brenner's claims about the potency of unemployment (or, generally, economic disturbances) for undermining treatment effectiveness correct? Even if he were right, could this notion of the effect of unemployment be tested as a credible explanation for the failure of the continued effectiveness of individual counseling? One point in the favor of the unemployment argument was that unemployment had been generally low during the descriptive phase of the project and generally high during the predictive phase. In grossest terms, the failure of treatment effectiveness occurred during economically bad times and the treatment was effective during economically good times. Not surprisingly, the staunchest advocate of Brenner's unemployment hypothesis was the 50 percent unemployed project member stationed in the economically depressed-recessed San Francisco Bay area who had chanced upon Brenner's book. The other project staff supported further inquiry into the unemployment hypothesis while retaining active skepticism. They demanded a more immediate and convincing argument than hospitalization-employment data on New York state from the previous 127 years reported by Brenner.

Unemployment and Juvenile Delinquency

Brenner's arguments and facts seemed powerful but remote from the project, but they did stimulate pursuit of the relationship between economics and delinquency. Belton Fleisher's "Effect of Unemployment on Juvenile Delinquency" was then examined as either a transition point of these foreign economic notions into our work or as "the ugly facts" that would slay this appealing, but still far fetched, explanation for the project anomalies.[7] First, it was necessary to determine whether Fleisher's findings were persuasive in tying delinquency to economic variables. Also, it was necessary to determine whether the project's data were consistent with those of Fleisher.

Fleisher investigated the relationship between juvenile delinquency and labor market conditions, specifically unemployment, to determine whether policies that reduced unemployment would also reasonably be expected to reduce delinquency.[8] He felt that a relationship between these two variables would be expected on a priori grounds, "since acts of delinquency may be viewed as alternatives to legitimate allocations of time, one expects to find the frequency of such acts negatively correlated with opportunities for legitimate activity among young people." And, "when unemployment rates are high not only is it especially difficult for new entrants into the labor force to find legitimate means for satisfying the desire to acquire market goods and to secure a foothold in a trade or occupation, but it is also more difficult for families to provide market goods and services for their young." Fleisher concluded that,

> An examination of delinquency rates and other variables by age and through time suggest that the effect of unemployment on juvenile delinquency is positive and significant . . . a plausible estimate of the elasticity of the arrest rate for property crimes with respect to the unemployment rate is probably between 0.10 and 0.25, depending in part on which age group is in question.[9]

Further, he observed:

> Evidence from examination of a sample of arrests of individuals age 15 to 24 for property crimes in eleven large United States cities in 1961 further indicates that unemployment is positively correlated with delinquency rates; the estimated elasticity of the effect of unemployment on delinquency is 0.46.[10]

The term *elasticity* indicated the percentage change in one variable due to a 1 percent change in the other variable. For example, the last indicated elasticity of 0.46 implies that 100 percent increase in the unemployment rate would be associated with a 46 percent increase in the delinquency rate.

As an immediate check of the pertinence of Fleisher's findings to the predictive sentencing project, a scatter diagram between the recidivism rate for individual counseling for all the years in which data in Norman were available and the unemployment rate, lagged one year, was constructed. That is, the unemployment rate of one year was paired with the recidivism rate for probationers who completed individual counseling in the following year, because the econometric literature contends that the effect of unemployment on variables such as crime are most evident after a lapse of one year.

The scatter diagram produced using this procedure appeared random, but faith was revived on discovering that the unemployment rate had not been lagged behind the recidivism rate. On making the correction, the scatter diagram lost much of its random appearance. The traffic recidivism rate, the unemployment rate, and the school drop-out rate (another explanatory variable suggested by Fleisher) was then graphed to parallel the three similar graphs in Fleisher's article. See Figure 5-7. Like Fleisher's graphs, Figure 5-7 discloses roughly parallel relationships. The data were persuasive because they came out at least roughly similar to that of Fleisher's data and more study was warranted, but now the practical barrier of funding became significant with the approaching termination date for the project.

NIMH approved a six-month extension of the research grant to permit an examination of the effects of external conditions on the effectiveness of individual counseling. The results and conclusions of this effort are reported in Chapter 5. These can be summarized by noting that the analyses gave support to our hunch about unemployment undermining individual counseling, but the results were suggestive rather than conclusive. Nor could it have been otherwise, because of the very gross, highly intercorrelated economic data and the few number of years of outcome available (actually very many years for an experimental study, but very few when compared with econometric, naturalistic studies). The literature relating economic variables to crime was then consulted to determine if the hunches concerning the attenuation of treatment could be given further support. Fleisher's pioneering work on the relation between unemployment and delinquency has already been mentioned. More recently, increasing numbers of economists have filled in detail on this relationship and are also determining the strength of this phenomena relative to the influence of law enforcement activities. Votey and Phillips performed a series of statistical analyses that supported Fleisher's earlier finding of a positive correlation between the unemployment rate and the crime rate for young males.[11] However, they went further by refining the relationship between crimes committed by youth and the economic opportunities of these youths, showing "the important distinction probably is not simply between working and not working, but between working or temporarily unemployed, and long-term unemployment that would cause an individual to stop seeking employment."[12] They concluded by asserting that *both* reform of social and economic conditions to reduce the economic incentive for crime and more effective law enforcement would reduce felony crime rates by youths.

Using index crime data from across the United States, Ehrlich reported "the existence of a deterrent effect of law enforcement activity on all crimes and a strong positive correlation between income inequality and crimes against property."[13] He interpreted the relationship between the employment-linked variable, extent of community income inequality, and crime as suggesting "a social incentive for equalizing training and earnings opportunities across persons, which is independent of ethical considerations. . . ."

Also, Danziger and Wheeler found levels of criminal activity responsive to both level of sentences given by judges and by such employment-related variables as changes in the distribution of income and personal comparisons between the gains from legal versus illegal money generating activities.[14] These economists, additionally, discovered that a 1 percent reduction of financial inequality reduced the crime rate more than a 1 percent increase in deterrence.

Really sophisticated work to delineate the fine structure of all of these relationships continues, as indicated by the report of the 1974 Frascati Workshop of the United Nations Social Defense Research Institute on "Economic Crisis and Crime," which brought together an international panel of economists, systems analysts, political scientists, scientists, psychologists, sociologists, lawyers, and criminologists.[15] Both the findings and speculations are beginning to reach public awareness, albeit often with headlines that contradict the more balanced perspective of the articles themselves.[16] While some of the literature on crime and economic factors, particularly employment and employment-linked variables, has been mentioned, it still remains to point out differences between traffic recidivisms and other crimes.

Traffic Offenses Are Different

It is important to reiterate that it is not contended that there is a direct relationship between unemployment (or employment-linked phenomena) and traffic recidivism rates of individually counseled probationers. A test of that direct relationship would have involved correlating the base rate in traffic offenses with employment data; but on the other hand, the anomalies sought to be explained with the employment data were confined to fluctuations in the effectiveness of individually counseled probationers rather than fluctuations in the traffic recidivism rates of the fine controls. The anomalies regarding this particular treatment were of higher priority than shifts in the fine control base rate. Also the early work of Ross[17] shows traffic offenses to be very peculiar relative to other offenses, and Skogan[18] has presented data indicating that the critical determinant of traffic arrest rate is "the size of the scoop (number of police performing traffic enforcement) and the enthusiasm with which it is wielded."

In any event, unlike the employment rate that we hypothesized interacted with the individual counseling treatment itself, changes in the extent and enthusiasm of traffic enforcement should, by the logic of the randomized groups design, have had similar effects on all groups.

How could economic pressures, as measured by employment, act to attenuate individual counseling and thereby affect driving behavior? A review of the literature on the effects of economic pressures on the effectiveness of therapy, such as individual counseling of a habitual traffic offender, would have been to the point and of material assistance. Unfortunately, such literature does not yet exist. In the absence of such studies, let us turn to a different source that does have a literature: the manpower, or job-oriented, offender studies.

The studies just cited relied upon existing crime data and economic data as well as court and police data to determine the nature and extent of relationships among these three sectors. In the absence of experimental intervention, these studies had to employ correlation approaches. However, starting in the 1960s, the Department of Labor began funding so-called manpower programs which consisted of various counseling and training services designed to help offenders and accused persons diverted into such programs to acquire and hold jobs. Ideally these activities would have constituted a test for both the relation between jobs and crime and the relation between counseling effectiveness and times of increasing unemployment. Joan Mullen and her associates have assessed the Manhattan Crossroads Projects as well as nine second-round projects that grew from the first two.[19] Unfortunately, and in spite of claims of the effectiveness of the projects as measured by rearrest, due to the absence of truly comparable control groups, Mullen and her associates do not attach a great deal of confidence to the findings. In his assessment of manpower services for offenders (as opposed to the accused persons diverted from prosecution), Taggert reached the conclusion that "... nothing is known about the number and successes of exoffenders in existing manpower programs. Despite several investigations, there is little comprehensive knowledge about the effectiveness of prison institutions or training."[20]

Impact of Economy

Seemingly inexplicable results became interpretable after examination of the affects of the economy on the dramatic change in the outcome of individual counseling on traffic recidivism. The economy's impact on this study and future research in sentencing has at least three dimensions. First, the economic variable of unemployment became the triggering mechanism that forced a reexamination of the paradigm in which the traffic offender had been conceptualized at the inception of the study. This, in turn, led to reevaluation of the traditional approach of either explaining and remediating antisocial behavior on an individually based or socially based approach, each to the exclusion of the other. Both the individual's world and his social milieu have seemingly been placed in greater perspective in the effort to explain the anomalous findings through resort to the economic indicator of unemployment.

Second, having found a close association between the economic variable of unemployment and recidivism, one is then forced to ask whether there aren't other social milieu variables acting alone, or in combination with others, such as loss of confidence in government,[21] that may be important in explaining and remediating behavior. The controlled research design of this project has thus prompted further reflection on the importance of social milieu variables in crime and delinquency, albeit within the narrower frame of reference of traffic law enforcement.

Third, this study, together with the work of others, suggests poignantly the pervasive influence of the economy on behavior and behavior modification in crime and delinquency. Accordingly, the study's controlled experimental design should underline the importance of carefully measuring the influence of the economy in any future experimentation involving sentencing, including sentencing for the violation of the traffic laws.

Notes

1. Rosak, Theodore, *Where the Wasteland Ends. Politics and Transcendence in Postindustrial Society* (Garden City, New York: Doubleday and Co., Inc. 1972).

2. Krisberg, B., and Takagi, P., "Ethical Issues in Evaluating Criminal Justice Demonstration Projects." Paper read at American Criminology Society, New York, November 1973.

3. Ibid.

4. Wolfgang, M.E., Figlio, R.M., and Sellin, T., *Delinquency in a Birth Cohort* (Chicago: The University of Chicago Press, 1972).

5. Galliher, John F., and McCartney, James L., "The Influence of Funding Agencies on Juvenile Delinquency Research," *Social Problems* 21, no. 1, (Summer 1973).

6. Brenner, M. Harvey, *Mental Illness and the Economy* (Cambridge, Mass.: Harvard University Press, 1973).

7. Fleisher, Belton, M., "The Effect of Unemployment on Juvenile Delinquency," *Journal of Political Economy* 71, no. 6, (December 1963), pp. 543-55.

8. Ibid.

9. Ibid, pp. 553-554. Reprinted with permission.

10. Ibid, footnote 15, p. 554. Reprinted with permission.

11. Fleisher, Belton, M., *The Economics of Delinquency* (Chicago: Quadrangel Books, Inc., 1966).

12. Votey, Harold L., and Phillips, Llad, "The Control of Criminal Activity: An Economic Analysis," in, Glaser, D. (ed.), *Handbook of Criminology* (Chicago: Rand McNally, 1974).

13. Ehrlich, Isaac, "Participation in Illegitimate Activities: A Theoretical and Empirical Investigation," *Journal of Political Economy* 81, no. 3, (1973), pp. 521-565.

14. Danziger, Sheldon, and Wheeler, David, "The Economics of Crime: Punishment or Income Redistribution," *Review of Social Economy* 33, no. 2, (October 1975), pp. 113-131.

15. United Nations Social Defense Research Institute. *Economic Crisis and Crime* (Rome, Italy: UNSDRI, Publication no. 9, 1974). The new work lends support to the arguments advanced in this chapter. For example, Brenner (1976) has just published a 40-page summary of the relation among crime, the criminal justice system, and the state of the economy in the United States and four other English-speaking countries from 1900 to 1970. (UNSDRI, Publication no. 15, 1976). He concludes:

> The two outstanding findings of the present study are that both absolute economic loss and comparative decline in socio-economic status (as a result of greater gain in such status by the majority of the population) are the pre-eminent causes of variations in criminal statistical trends.

(See Brenner, M. Harvey, "Time-Series Analysis-Effects of the Economy on Criminal Behavior and the Administration of Criminal Justice," in *Economic Crises and Crime*, ibid., p. 57.) Furthermore, Brenner points out that trends in crime can be "forecasted" to greater than 90 percent accuracy for several major populations using only three variables: the economic indicators of unemployment, inflation, and per capita personal income; the under-30 years of age population; and extent of urbanization. He concludes trends in crime thus proceed under known measurable conditions regardless of criminal justice system activity. (Ibid., p. 61.)

16. Anonymous, "Crime: A Case for More Punishment." *Business Week* (September 15, 1976), pp. 92-97. Malloy, Michael T., "Punishment Is a Deterrent to Crime." *National Observer* (June 19, 1976), p. 1 and p. 13.

17. Ross, H. Lawrence, "Traffic Law Violation: A Folk Crime." *Social Problems* 8 (Winter, 1960-61), pp. 231-241.

18. Skogan, W., "Traffic and the Crime: Social Change and Organizational Response," in Jacob, H., (ed.), *The Potential for Reform of Criminal Justice* (Beverly Hills, Ca.: Sage Publication, 1974).

19. Mullen, Joan, et al., *Pretrial Services: An Evaluation of Policy Related Research* (Cambridge, Mass.: Abt Associates Inc., 1974).

20. Taggart, Robert, *The Prison of Unemployment: Manpower Programs for Offenders* (Baltimore, Md.: Johns Hopkins University Press, 1972).

21. *ISR Newsletter*, Institute for Social Research, The University of Michigan (Summer 1975).

9 Methodology

Large-Scale Experiments

Any experiment stands or falls on the strength or weakness of the methods employed. Part I reported the methodology utilized, the data collected, and the results disclosed in this project. This chapter is an attempt to stand back from the activities of the seven years duration of the project and highlight those particular methods that may prove beneficial to other large-scale social action research efforts.

In relatively small laboratory experiments the problem probed is usually sharply defined. In contrast, social action research usually focuses on a more global diffused area.[1] This lack in the greater particularity of the problem delimitation makes designing a large-scale project more difficult. Criterion measures are typically ill-defined and usually consist of a plethora of factors. While this project was not as complex as projects such as Head-Start, National Follow-Through, or the New Jersey Negative Income Tax Project, the experiences of this project suggest some possible solutions.

Given a problem area, such as the predictive sentencing of youthful habitual traffic offenders, it is necessary to translate this broader, overall objective into manageable units consisting of major research questions. The predictive sentencing study was guided by the following major research questions:

1. What are the characteristics of the offenders treated in the program?
2. How many offenders in the sample recidivate within one year after termination of treatment?
3. Are there significant differences in the rates of recidivism among the five treatment modalities?
4. Are the differences among offenders who recidivate and those who do not recidivate the same across all treatment modalities?
5. What differences are there among the offenders in each treatment modality who do recidivate and those who do not recidivate; that is, which of the variables discriminate among those who do and those who do not recidivate in each treatment modality?

Consider the first question. In characterizing any sample, one wants to use the minimal number of variables that convey the maximum amount of information about the sample. If there is no literature to guide the researcher in choosing these defining variables, as many variables as resources allow must be collected, and from this set, those variables that contain the most nonredundant information can be identified. Thus, at the start of this project over 365 variables per offender were collected and these variables were then reduced by first eliminating those with negligible variance and those having over 50 percent missing values. The remaining variables were then grouped into similar domains, such as the personality domain, and these were subjected to principal component analyses. The resulting factors were rotated to the varimax criterion. This procedure identified the minimally redundant key variables later used in the typology studies and model building.

Consider question two. The interest in recidivism raised a number of related questions. In keeping with the project's social defense orientation, what dangers to society ought to be minimized by predictive sentencing? What offenses committed after the intervention constituted recidivism? How long was the recidivism period? Did accident involvement, with no offense charged, constitute recidivism? Deciding these questions was a prerequisite to meaningful assessment of the recidivism rate. Eventually, three criteria were established; nontraffic recidivism, traffic recidivism, and accident involvement. The recidivism period was defined as the first year following treatment termination, with the refinement of determining the actual amount of time, in half-months, that the probationer spent in the project area. This half-month data provided the means for weighing the probationer's recidivism score, assuring that recidivism was not merely a reflection of the amount of his absence from the project area. The half-month recidivism data were used to calculate these weighted recidivism scores.

Thus, division of the overall objective of the project into specific research questions resulted in a more coherent research project whose activity was guided by the need to answer these research questions. In the process other questions arose. Two such questions were:

1. Were probationers significantly different from nonprobationers?
2. Was entry into the program dependent on illegal driving behavior?

If probationers were not significantly different from nonprobationers and entry into the program was not dependent on illegal driving behavior, then a major rationale of the project would have been demonstrated to be false. The high school study noted in Chapter 3 was undertaken to answer those questions, and as reported in Chapter 3, probationers were significantly different from nonprobationers. Entry into the program was found to be unrelated to such incidental factors as amount of time of driving or car characteristics. On the other hand, entry into the program was directly related to self-reported illegal driving behavior.

During the course of any study, society changes and as a consequence the researcher is constantly forced to balance political requirements against the scientific requirement of maintaining the integrity of the experimental design. During the course of this study, there occurred in Norman a strong rise in the woman's movement. Thus, when the law student assistant probation officer resigned, the usual procedure was followed. Announcements were placed around the law school at the University of Oklahoma announcing the vacancy of this position. This announcement, however, specified that only male law students were acceptable because the original design of the study focused on male habitual traffic offenders and the introduction of women into the treatment process midway in the project would have jeopardized the integrity of the research design. Needless to say, this caused an outburst of protest by the women students. This dispute was, fortunately, settled after lengthy discussions with the women students where the research design was explained and the importance of maintaining the integrity of the design was emphasized.

In retrospect, the study might have been able to permit women to fill 50 percent of the APO positions. Indeed, this might have allowed an assessment of the effect of sex on the treatment process. In any case, this confrontation between a growing political force and the research design underscores the necessity that a researcher weigh the political repercussions of a change against the threat that a change poses to the integrity of the research design.

The operation of a large-scale project can be made more flexible, manageable, and productive by dividing the project into a series of objectives that are consecutively processed. Indeed, it is this flexibility in being able to examine related issues that primarily distinguishes the large-scale research project from the classical, laboratory-conducted experiment.[2] Moreover, if a project is broken down into multiple hypotheses that are the nodes of the logical tree representing a project, then the evaluation is sharpened and the inferences drawn from the project are greatly strengthened.[3]

Within this approach to methodological problems, most issues were solved as they arose. However, one methodological problem that was never adequately resolved was treatment modality assessment.

Treatment Modality Assessment

It has already been observed in Chapter 4 that an issue of major concern throughout the duration of the project was the degree of adherence to the prescribed treatment. Were the treatments delivered according to the prescribed treatment formats? If not, one could not validly conclude that treatment content rather than some other process was responsible for the differences in results on the criterion variables. Ultimately, treatment modality assessment proved the most vexing methodological problem of the project. Treatment modality assessment was guided by four questions. First, to what extent were the treatment contents in adherence to the prescribed curricula? Second, in the case of Groups 2 and 3, to what extent were the treatments in adherence to Reality Therapy? Third, to what extent was the degree of adherence to the prescribed curricula and/or Reality Therapy positively related to nonrecidivism? Fourth, was there some other process, not included in the prescribed curricula or in Reality Therapy that was more strongly related to nonrecidivism? There have been continuous efforts for several decades to devise reliable human monitoring techniques. Unfortunately, none of these techniques were judged adequate or appropriate for treatment modality assessment.

The first decision made concerning technique was to tape record all treatment sessions with the knowledge and consent of both the assistant probation officer and the probationer. This decision limited the assessment to an evaluation of only verbal content. While it was recognized that other, nonverbal content may have also been important in the assessment, it was not possible to include these contents. First, given several physical problems, particularly the lack of space, visual observation was not feasible. Also, if an observer were present, it was feared that his presence might confound the entire process. Second, given the poor fidelity of the tape recordings, analysis of tone variables was also not feasible. Thus in designing a human monitoring technique to meet the requirements of treatment modality assessment, only the verbal communication between the assistant probation officer and the probationer could be content analyzed.

Content analysis is any process whereby communication is coded or mapped into more meaningful categories.[4] To do this an attempt was made to develop a set of categories that would accurately capture or describe the content of the treatment sessions. This set of categories and the rules used in applying them had to possess three characteristics. First, the categories and rules had to be definite enough that different monitors would obtain the same results after monitoring the same tape. The categories employed had to be reliable. Second, the categories had to be flexible. That is, they had to describe as many aspects of the treatment sessions as possible, since it was not possible to predict which aspects would prove important. Third, the categories had to be *practical.* There had to be as few categories as possible, so that the person monitoring the tape recordings of the treatment sessions could keep up with the tapes so that the number of sessions evaluated would not be severely limited.

Because the questions of what was significant and what should be measured had to be answered before categories could be constructed, it was possible, indeed almost certain, that important or meaningful categories might have been missed. Therefore, because the characteristics of flexibility and practicality could not simultaneously be obtained, the alternative of human monitoring of treatment sessions was abandoned.

General Inquirer

The abandonment of human monitoring led to the exploration of the utility of computer-based content analysis, which had been reported to be efficient, reliable, flexible, and valid in many social science applications.[5] Specifically, the most current version of the *General Inquirer* system of content analysis was adapted to the monitoring requirements of treatment modality assessment. *General Inquirer* is a complex system of computer programs that analyzes a statement into various thematic categories. At the heart of this system is a dictionary that contains the categories (tags) and the rules for applying these tags to a sentence.

The dictionary used for the treatment modality assessment was the *Harvard Fourth Psychosociological Dictionary (Harvard IV)*. Writing about an earlier version of this dictionary Stone stated, "We have termed this dictionary 'psychosociological' dictionary because it was designed primarily for those investigators with psychological and sociological objectives and themes."[6]

Pilot Study

To gain an initial estimate of the adequacy of computer-assisted monitoring, a pilot study was conducted. The first step in this study was to enumerate the expected rank-order of treatment groups on selected categories. That is, each category was examined to determine which treatment group could be expected to show the greatest frequency of occurrence for each category. As an example, for the category, DRIVER, Group 4 was expected to show the highest frequency of occurrence, since it was a drivers education treatment group. Likewise, Groups 2 and 3 were expected to show highest frequency on the category, KIN, since family relations was a major topic of discussion in these treatment groups. To determine the extent to which the observed rank-order corresponded to the expected rank-order, the data output by *General Inquirer* were analyzed as follows: first, category indices were formed by dividing the frequency of occurrence of each category by the total number of words spoken in the session. This step was taken to produce a common metric, since the total number of words spoken in each session varied across the sessions. Second, these category indices were then analyzed using the program BMD-07D, which calculated the distribution by groups on each category together with means, standard deviations, and a one-way analysis of variance.[7] Three conclusions were derived from this study. First, based on mean values, the special purpose categories clearly differentiated treatment Groups 4 and 5 from each other and also from treatment Groups 2 and 3. Second, 95 percent of the 151,000 words comprising the 30 analyzed sessions were classified or "tagged," suggesting that even in its present form the dictionary would be able to accommodate this particular set of words. Third, the observed rank-order of the treatment groups on individual *Harvard IV* categories often (but by no means always) corresponded with the expected rank order. Thus the pilot study resulted in a mixed situation in which it was necessary to investigate in detail reversals in the expected rank ordering of means across treatment groups. These analyses of reversals suggested that the problems encountered were tractable and that the dictionary could be accommodated for treatment modality assessment.

The Sampling Study

How many minutes of the treatment sessions from the different treatment modalities should be monitored? Since it was anticipated that the number of words spoken in the treatment groups during the course of the predictive phase of the program would be in excess of 5 million, it was essential to devise a sampling plan. An empirical study was conducted to examine the effects of different sample sizes on computer-assisted monitoring. Specifically, various intradocument sampling techniques were tested, using the same treatment sessions as were used in the Pilot Study. First, population values of 33 critical categories were taken from the full hour-long transcriptions. Next, 16, 12, 8, and 6 minute samples from these 30 transcriptions were taken. Then the values on these same 33 critical categories were obtained for each of the four samples of varying temporal length.

This scheme permitted identification of an optimum sample size in terms of a maximum correlation combined with minimal sample duration. The 16, 12, and 8 minute samples correlated highly with the entire document in contrast with the 6-minute samples. The ranges and medians of the correlations for the different-sized samples and the 30 sessions were:

16-minute sample: 0.703 to 0.959, median = 0.887
12-minute sample: 0.635 to 0.949, median = 0.875
8-minute sample: 0.530 to 0.922, median = 0.815
6-minute sample: –0.206 to 0.104, median = –0.053

Because the difference, between 16, 12, and 8 minute samples was small, it was concluded that the 8-minute sample was optimal for this particular type of data. Using the above 8 minute sampling scheme, 103 treatment sessions were sampled, transcribed, keypunched, and analyzed using *General Inquirer.*

Validation Study of General Inquirer Categories

Determination of the validity and reliability of the *General Inquirer-Harvard IV* categories, without the added expense of duplicating *General Inquirer*, had been an important consideration in monitoring the treatment modalities. To make these determinations, human monitors were employed to analyze the appropriateness of *Harvard IV* categories by examining retrievals keyed to *Harvard IV* categories.[a] Because many of these categories were not useful, and to avoid making conclusions based on chance occurrences, only 23 tags were selected for the validation study. Again, these tags appeared to be the most useful in monitoring the adherence to curricula and Reality Therapy.

Three graduate and undergraduate women students evaluated the appropriateness of these 23 tags. None of the three women had a working knowledge of *General Inquirer*, although one was familiar with its outputs and their applications.

Retrievals on all 23 tags were obtained from transcriptions of 73 individual counseling sessions. Each monitor was instructed to read those retrievals, judge the appropriateness of the tag assigned to the retrieval, and count the number of inappropriate taggings.[b]

The frequencies of inappropriateness for each tag across each monitor were first analyzed to measure the degree to which a tag had been incorrectly applied. This was done for each tag by dividing the number of inappropriate taggings for each document by the total number of taggings for that document. The means of these indices were then computed for each tag.

The relative frequency of inappropriate taggings ranged from 6 percent (DRIVER) to 76 percent (POLITICAL MARKER). Obviously, this represented a rather complex phenomenon. Normally, any tag that has been incorrectly applied in more than 50 percent of the cases would have to be rejected as invalid. However, upon closer examination of the retrievals it appeared that incorrect taggings occurred on specific tags, while within classes of categories the correct tag has been applied. This finding was not surprising because *General Inquirer's* content categories are neither factorially pure nor mutually exclusive. Consider: "And the cops don't hassle people?" This passage was retrieved on the tag LEGAL, but this tagging was deemed inappropriate by at least one monitor, although all monitors agreed that the tag POWER was accurate. Indeed, *General Inquirer* applied both LEGAL and POWER to this passage.

Thus while the validity of individual tags appeared rather low, the validity of classes of tags seemed to be much higher. Admittedly collapsing categories into classes of categories raised the problem of how to manipulate these classes without adding unwanted redundancy.

By viewing the correlation coefficients between each monitor as reliability

[a]Retrievals are those sentences that have been isolated because a word in the sentence has been marked as belonging to a particular category of the *Harvard IV Dictionary*, e.g., if one was interested in those sentences with legal examples, only the sentences with this exemplar would be isolated or retrieved.

[b]*Tagging* simply refers to how a particular word was classified into a particular *Harvard IV Dictionary* category. Thus, an inappropriate tagging means that a word was categorized incorrectly.

indices, the complexity of *General Inquirer's* categories was further revealed. The correlations ranged from a low 0.18 (VICE, rater 1 and 2) to a high of 0.92 (INJURY, rater 2 and 3). Certainly the reliability of a tag is suspect when the correlation between two monitors is lower than 0.60. Scatter plots between each monitor were obtained for all tags. While there was never complete agreement between any two monitors, the scatter plots indicated that the reliability was generally higher than was suggested by the correlation coefficients, because a few extreme values drastically decreased the magnitude of the correlations.

Summary

While the computer-assisted monitoring study was undertaken with great optimism, it soon became apparent that severe problems existed with the *General Inquirer* approach. The costs, in terms of both money and time, of transcribing the sessions sampled were extremely high. Also, as the validation study pointed out, there were formidable problems with the categories of the *Harvard IV Dictionary*, problems that did not appear in the pilot study. Besides being neither factorially pure nor mutually exclusive, the categories were poorly defined. That is, evidently despite the claims of its developers, no systematic approach was used for defining exemplars for any particular category. The more abstract these categories, the greater the ambiguity. Indeed, as was pointed out, the relative frequency of inappropriate taggings ranged from 6 percent (DRIVER) to 75 percent (POLITICAL MARKER). This situation made the assessment of adherence to curriculum and Reality Therapy impossible. Also, this lack of well-defined categories invited gross misinterpretation. A regression analysis to determine the relationship of counseling content, as mapped by *General Inquirer*, to traffic recidivism produced results exactly opposite of those expected. Unfortunately, an interpretation of this outcome was not feasible, given the ambiguity of the *Harvard IV Dictionary* categories.

In conclusion, the results of the pilot study disclosed a significant relationship between the expected and observed rank orderings for treatment Groups 2, 3, 4, and 5, though Groups 4 and 5 were best on the special purpose categories as expected. However, when the treatment modality assessment on Groups 2 and 3 was submitted to comprehensive human validation, there was little indication that computer-assisted monitoring measured the degree of adherence to curricular or to Reality Therapy. This failure, while less attributable to the *General Inquirer* computer programs, is in a large measure due to the inadequacy of the *Harvard Fourth Psychosociological Dictionary* in describing real, ongoing, counseling processes. This inadequacy reflects two primary defects. First, from a theoretical viewpoint, very little is known about what takes place within a one-to-one counseling situation. (If it works, why? What should distinguish a successful counseling encounter from an unsuccessful encounter?) This lack of a theoretical framework greatly handicapped a systematic classification of the *Harvard IV* categories as they were applied to a counseling process. Second, and more fundamentally, despite the author's claim of devising categories on the perspectives of Parsons and Freud, close examination of the dictionary revealed instance upon instance of words assigned to categories without rhyme or reason. Further, again without rhyme or reason, the same words were assigned to many categories. So extreme was the arbitrariness and redundancy that efforts to tap abstract themes ended in a morass of ambiguity.

The failure of treatment modality assessment was obviously disappointing, particularly in light of the need to explain the anomalous results arising out of the study. More generally, the failure of the treatment modality assessment pointed to a flaw common in many experimental endeavors. Typically, the assessment of treatment is confined to an analysis of the criterion measure. Thus, if the subjects of a treatment do well on the criterion, then the treatment is called a success. Likewise, if the subjects of a treatment do poorly on the criterion, then the treatment is called a failure. Unless a treatment is very straightforward, such as administering a drug to a patient in a drug study, this summative procedure fails to provide any substantive knowledge about what it was that contributed to the success or failure of the treatment. Indeed, when one uses human subjects to change their attitudes or behaviors, the intervention process is usually quite complex, and the lack of the assessment of the treatment process, formative evaluation, weakens any inference about the treatment, particularly when the outcomes are not straightforward.

A possible remedy of these flaws would be the institution of "criterion-referenced" treatments. Like a criterion-referenced test, a subject in this type of treatment would continue in the treatment until he reaches some a priori criterion, perhaps based on social indicator studies of requisites of effective functioning and social health.[7] While this kind of intervention could easily raise serious ethical and legal questions, an equitable solution should be feasible, possibly along the lines of a probationary period for new employees or work samples.[8] In any case, much more attention must be given to the formative evaluation of the treatment process. Again, the results of the formative treatment modality assessment of Groups 2 and 3 were disappointing. Nevertheless, the process used for treatment modality assessment (five steps: problem formulation to pilot study to sampling study to validation study to regression study) generally appeared valid. In retrospect it was rather obvious that the results of the pilot study were misleading. However, the conclusion is not to refrain from pilot studies, but rather to conduct them much more vigorously.

So again the advantages of conducting a large-scale study by a series of steps is evident. Further, as each step approaches the ideal of rendering implausible all but one of the several competing hypotheses, the inferences are strengthened and the project reaches its goal by the shortest path. That is, the project progresses by removing plausible, rival hypotheses and thus inferences are stronger.[9] It is perhaps obvious, however, that simply dividing a project into a series of subgoals does not guarantee strong inference. Indeed more is needed. The anomalous results of predictive sentencing underscore the importance of adequate time duration for the study as well as the use of random control groups.

Adequate Time Duration

Certainly most researchers believe that time is the best ally one can have in studying any problem. As our experience indicates, if an assessment is to be made, then enough time must be allotted so that the effects of all the various independent factors can be seen. Figure 5-10 discloses that had the recidivism data on the fine groups for the 10 years shown not been collected, erroneous conclusions might have been reached about the effectiveness of the fine with youthful, male habitual traffic offenders. A much more poignant example of the importance of adequate time duration is provided by the four-year follow-up of the descriptive phase Groups 1 and 2 reported in Figure 5-5. Without this data it would have been far more difficult to explain the decline in treatment effectiveness of Group 2 from the descriptive to the predictive phase. Indeed, had this study not spanned several years, the outcome of the descriptive phase might have been falsely attributed to Hawthorn effects. But, in fact the year-by-year recidivism rates rendered this interpretation implausible. It must be recognized, however, that if large-scale social action research is permitted adequate time duration and this research is conducted as rigorously as possible with the use of random control groups, and the progressive assessment of the guiding research questions, these sorts of experiments become high-risk endeavors. Clearly, it is dangerous to tell the truth. Few administrators or agencies are willing to undergo constant evaluation, particularly when the outcomes might very possibly jeopardize their jobs or their programs. But this is the position that experimentation will find itself in as it is conducted more rigorously. A useful approach to this problem is to redirect the attention from the cure of a social ill to concentrating on the problematic nature of the illness. Campbell outlined this position when he wrote:

> One simple shift in political posture which would reduce the problem is the shift from advocacy of a specific reform to the advocacy of the seriousness of the problem, and hence to the advocacy of persistence in alternative reform efforts should the first one fail. The political stance would become: 'This is a serious problem. We propose to initiate Policy A on an experimental basis. If after five years there has been no significant improvement, we shall shift to Policy B.'[9]

Random Control Groups

Despite an extensive statistical literature asserting the importance of randomization, there are surprisingly few case study enumerations. Usually it is simply taken for granted that randomization is the ideal, and very little attention is given to the real-life benefits of this experimental design. Certainly randomization eliminates bias in the assignment of subjects to interventions and thus ensures the comparability of the different treatment groups. Clearly, the most important contribution that the use of random control groups can make is the reduction in the plausibility of alternative explanations for differences in outcome.

A useful way to conceptualize this discussion of random control groups is to list those extraneous variables that threaten the internal validity of the experiment. Campbell and Stanley delineated eight classes of extraneous variables that threaten the internal validity (did the treatment make a difference) of an experiment. These were: (1) history; (2) maturation; (3) testing; (4) instrumentation; (5) statistical regression; (6) selection; (7) experimental mortality; and (8) selection-maturation interaction.[10] These eight factors can, if not controlled in the experimental design, produce effects that might be mistaken for the treatment or experiment effects.

Of these eight factors, history, maturation, and selection stand out as being particularly troublesome in social action research. History refers to those events other than treatment that occur between measurements. If history is not accounted for, then the effects of those intervening events may mistakenly be attributed to experimental effect. Maturation refers to those changes that are solely functions of the passage of time; and if these changes are not controlled for in the experimental design, they too may mistakenly be taken as experimental effect.

Selection refers to the biases arising from the differential assignment of subjects to the interventions. Thus, in this case, the putative experimental effect may be no more than a reflection of the preexisting differences in the groups.

Certainly in many experimental situations, the use of random control groups is not necessary to render implausible the effects of these extraneous factors. If the interval between measurements is sufficiently short, history, as well as maturation, may be implausible as a rival explanation of the observed effects. However, in social action research, which deals with human subjects and operates over considerable lengths of time, such is not the case. In criminology research, identification of treatments, short of incapacitation, that reduce recidivism almost invariably require random control groups.

Precisely because the outcomes of this project were so unexpected, nothing less than abandoning the paradigm currently directing most criminology research and examining economic factors was needed to explain these outcomes. But, as is the case with any correlational, secondary data analysis, the results are only suggestive. Despite this limitation, why is the economic explanation offered? In large measure, the use of random control groups rendered whole classes of other sorts of explanations implausible.

Preserving the Data Base

A final issue that arose in this study was less a methodological issue and more a legal, ethical issue. As the study drew to a close, it was important that the probationer's data records be destroyed to preserve the probationer's anonymity; yet, at the same time, it was important to save those records for future secondary data analyses. As pointed out by a committee of the Social Science Research Council, the problem is how to sufficiently aggregate the data to preserve an individual's privacy, and likewise preserve sufficient disaggregation to permit experimental assessment.[11] In this study this problem was resolved by substituting a random number for each probationer into the indentification fields of all his records stored on computer cards. After this process, all the probationer's original records, including questionnaires, police/court records, and other testing results were destroyed by shredding. Hence the data is available, thus permitting reanalysis, and the anonymity of the probationers is also maintained, thus protecting their privacy.

Notes

1. Baker, Frank B., "Experimental Design Considerations Associated with Large-Scale Research Projects" in Julian C. Stanley (ed.), *Improving Experimental Design and Statistical Analysis*. Seventh Annual Phi Delta Kappa Symposium on Education Research (Chicago, Ill.: Rand McNally & Co.), pp. 206-256.

2. Ibid.

3. Platt, John R., "Strong Inference," *Science* 146:3642, (October 16, 1964), pp. 347-353.

4. Holsti, Ole R. *Content Analysis*, in Lindzey, Gardner, and Aronson, (eds.), *The Handbook of Social Psychology* (Reading, Mass.: Addison-Wesley, 1968).

5. Stone, Philip J., Dexter C. Dunphy, Marshall S. Smith, and Daniel M. Ogilire. *The General Inquirer: A Computer Approach to Content Analysis* (Cambridge, Mass.: The M.I.T. Press, 1971).

6. Ibid.

7. Dixon, W.J., (ed.), *BMD: Biomedical Computer Programs* (Berkeley: University of California Press, 1972).

8. Platt, John R., "Strong Inference."

9. Campbell, Donald T., "Legal Reforms as Experiments." *Journal of Legal Education* 23:1, (1970), pp. 217-239. Reprinted with permission.

10. Campbell, Donald T., and Julian C. Stanley. *Experimental and Quasi-experimental Designs for Research* (Chicago, Ill.: Rand McNally & Co., 1963).

11. Boruch, Robert, and Henry W. Riecken, (eds.), *Social Experimentation: A Method for Planning and Evaluating Social Intervention* (New York: Academic Press, 1974), pp. 245-261.

Part III
The Implications

Introduction to Part III

The implications of this study are complex and diverse. They range all the way from the immediate theoretical and practical utility of predictive sentencing as a viable alternative in the remediation of the habitual traffic offender, to the utility of the particular regression equations employed in this study, to the conceptualization of alternative approaches to predictive sentencing, not only to explain the anomalous results of the study but to suggest a more effective use of regression, or prediction, techniques in sentencing within the criminal justice system. The implications of this study also suggest alternative approaches to predictive sentencing but do not deal with these alternatives in any significant way, since they are beyond the confines of this work. Finally, if this research effort, the anomalous results that it produced, and the attempts of the investigators to explain these results are persuasive, then further research is clearly indicated. Such research might explore not only the range of intrapersonal and social milieu factors, it might broaden its research base by looking at target populations that encompass not only the traffic offender, but those committing high misdemeanors and felonies as well and in as many diverse courts and communities as possible to make any future findings as generalizable as possible.

10 Looking Back

The Judge, the Sentence, and Prediction

Prediction and prediction techniques are appealing concepts in their theoretical application to the sentencing process. The rationale of predictive sentencing is particularly appealing to the judge concerned with fashioning a sentence that provides him with some assurance that the objective of the sentence will be achieved. However, there was, and still is, very little reliable predictive data available to guide the judge in any sentencing scheme.

Moreover, while considerable attention has been given to the theoretical application and desirability of predictive sentencing in the crime and delinquency literature, there have been few, if any, rigorous and systematic evaluations of prediction techniques in sentencing. In point of fact, this study probably represents the only effort to empirically evaluate rigorously prediction techniques in sentencing, albeit in the limited area of traffic law enforcement. Unfortunately, as appealing as the concept may be, if the study has accomplished nothing else, it has demonstrated severe practical limitations on the implementation of any predictive scheme as presently conceptualized. It has also demonstrated the need for a more sophisticated understanding of the factors affecting the sentencing process in any prediction scheme, irrespective of the type of offender involved.

Prediction and Habitual Traffic Offenders

Prior to considering these more general implications, there are certain specific conclusions that can be drawn concerning the utility of the sentencing scheme employed in this project, its general utility, and its generalizability for the class of offender studied. However, these conclusions must be confined to the Norman experiment, where there was greatest administrative control and strictest adherence to the research design. Further, the Norman experiment generated data over a period of 10 years in contrast to the 2 years of available data elsewhere. Finally, except for Tulsa, the Norman experimental results are based upon larger sample sizes than in any other region.

There are four perspectives from which to evaluate the predictive sentencing model employed in the Norman experiment. These are the statistical power of the model, that is, its capacity to predict outcome; the gain to be derived from employing a particular sentencing equation as opposed to simple assignment to the most effective treatment observed; the number of probationers within the population of interest predicted to benefit is of sufficient size to warrant the use of the particular regression equation; and treatment effectiveness.

Within these perspectives, the Group 2 individual counseling equation is clearly superior to the other four equations, except on the dimension of treatment effectiveness during the predictive phase. With the possible exception of the Group 5 sentencing equation, the Groups 1, 3 and 4 equations do not appear particularly useful as treatment alternatives to fining the 16-18 year-old male habitual traffic offender. The Group 3 sentencing equation predicted everyone to recidivate in the group psychological counseling treatment modality.

Much the same conclusions are drawn for the Group 4 drivers education treatment modality. There were simply not enough offenders testing favorably on the dimensions of the Group 4 predictors to assign anyone to a program of driver's education. This suggests that a program of driver's education of the type employed in this project is not a viable treatment alternative for a 16-18 year-old male habitual traffic offender from either a prophylactic or practical point of view. Additionally, these conclusions are supported by the ineffectiveness of drivers education during the descriptive phase. Further, the gain on the drivers education examination before and after treatment did not discriminate recidivators from nonrecidivators. As a result, the project hypothesis that habitualness in poor driving practices stems from a lack of knowledge of the driving situation is not supported by this study.

The Group 5 sentencing equation predicted more subjects to do well in the Group 5 treatment than in any of the other groups except Group 2. This is consistent with the fact that Group 5 was second only to Group 2 in reducing recidivism among habitual teenage traffic offenders during the descriptive phase. Treatment failure prevented a testing of the Group 5 equation, but even assuming treatment effectiveness, the relative efficiency of this type of model in reducing traffic recidivism is low because few habitual teenage offenders were predicted to do well in this treatment. Finally, given the overall results, it is not surprising that the Group 1 sentencing equation produced no better results than the fine control during the predictive phase.

Except for these global assessments of the predictive sentencing scheme, the unexpected and even counter-intuitive findings of continuing predictability, juxtaposed with treatment failure, and the remarkable persistence of the strong treatment effectiveness of individual counseling for probationers counseled during the descriptive phase complicates evaluation of the predictive sentencing scheme. If the hypothesis that some external event, such as unemployment, attentuated treatment during the predictive phase is accurate, then any predictive sentencing scheme must monitor and compensate for those external factors that affect treatment.

Assuming one can overcome the vexing difficulty of isolating predictors of treatment outcome and the associated criterion variables, predictive sentencing must still cope with at least five major problems. These are: adequate administrative control and supervision over the sentencing and treatment processes; a region of sufficient population to produce enough offenders required by the variability of the equations to permit prediction; sufficient research capability to measure observed results accurately; social conditions that are conducive to unattenuated treatment; and research extending over a sufficiently long period of time to measure treatment effects over time to account for the dynamic change in societal structure.

Adequate administrative control and supervision is absolutely essential in coping with the complexities inherent in predictive sentencing. This is perhaps best illustrated by the application of the Norman sentencing scheme to the large metropolitan municipal court of Tulsa. The sheer size of the court's caseload presented problems in identifying, sentencing, testing, and administering the treatment processes. There also existed the possibility that the court's administrative order requiring the accused teenagers to appear in court for adjudication was not being followed by all arresting officers in the wake of a prior long-standing practice giving them the discretion to permit alleged traffic violators either to pay a fine administratively or to appear in court. Further, evidence that the rate of intake varied with the recency of site visits to Tulsa by Norman project personnel strongly suggests the inadequacy of ongoing local judicial administrative control and clerical supervision. This is highlighted in Lawton where the court's caseload was approximately the size of Norman's, but at the same time, the intake was a paucity of the rate projected on the basis of population. This can only be explained by inadequate control and supervision.

Even if administrative control is adequate, the jurisdiction must still have within it sufficient offenders in the population of interest, varying across the critical variables and associated treatments, to make predictive sentencing feasible and, at the same time, practical. This is illustrated to a large extent by the experience in the Little Cities. There was adequate administrative control but not sufficient numbers of teenage habitual traffic offenders to cross-validate the sentencing model there. Accordingly, the less rigorous test of the model employed was simply assigning the offenders to Group 2, the group that the Norman descriptive phase of the project demonstrated was most successful in reducing traffic recidivism, accident involvement, and nontraffic recidivism.

A prerequisite of predictive sentencing is that the results of the sentence be monitored systematically. Yet without the necessary legal, psychological, sociological, and statistical (experimental) expertise to develop methodology and monitor and assess the sentencing scheme, prediction is neither possible nor worthwhile. Moreover, this presupposes the existence and maintenance of adequate police and court records to assure the reliability of the assessment of the sentencing process. Unfortunately, the quality of record keeping was found to vary from jurisdiction to jurisdiction, which often made quantification difficult.

The Intrapersonal and Social Milieu Paradigms

Prediction in this study consisted of associating characteristics of, and within, the offender to compensatory psychological, educational, or psychosociological treatment modalities. In keeping with the prevailing paradigm, no social milieu, exogenous factors, or other external events were considered in the design and implementation of this study. Only in the face of the anomalous results and their refusal to yield to conventional explanations were external factors then considered.

Typically there are two dominant schemes for dealing with the rehabilitation of offenders. By far the more common approach is to look exclusively at the intra-psychic characteristics of the offender in fashioning a sentence. Judges and behavioral scientists frequently ignore the social milieu in which the offender interacts. On the other hand, economists have paid far greater attention to the social milieu but restricted themselves to economic considerations in explaining crime, its causes, and correction to the exclusion of the intrapersonal characteristics of the offender. Moreover, for the most part, no one has dealt in a rational sentencing process with noneconomic social milieu factors that may be relevant to criminal behavior. These prevailing disjunctive or mutually exclusive paradigms are diagrammed in Figure 10-1. With reference to Figure 10-1, little additional explication is needed concerning the intrapersonal paradigm and its relation to the sentencing process. Turning to the social milieu paradigm, despite the fact that much recent work has demonstrated the pervasive association between the state of the economy and crime, and furthermore, despite the fact that this relationship is acknowledged by some public officials, most of the attention in sentencing has been confined only to a consideration of intrapersonal factors and the remedying devices of either punitive or therapeutic sanctions, as opposed to, for example, job training and job placement. Does it then follow that any effective predictive sentencing scheme must account not only for intrapersonal variables but also those social milieu factors, both of which are significant in predicting whether a person should be institutionalized, given therapy, placed in job, or given some combination of these categories? The double lines separating the two paradigms in Figure 10-1 emphasize the fact that one paradigm views crime as solely caused and remedied in terms of the intrapersonal orientation of the offender; while the social milieu paradigm locates the cause and remedy of crime solely in factors external to the offender. Recognizing that this study was conceived and executed within the constructs of the intrapersonal paradigm, ultimately it only became possible to understand the anomalous results by bringing into focus the constructs of the social milieu paradigm, in this instance, the economy and unemployment. Do the findings of the study then suggest the desirability of an integration of both? The rationale of this study is based on the premise that rational sentencing is best justified

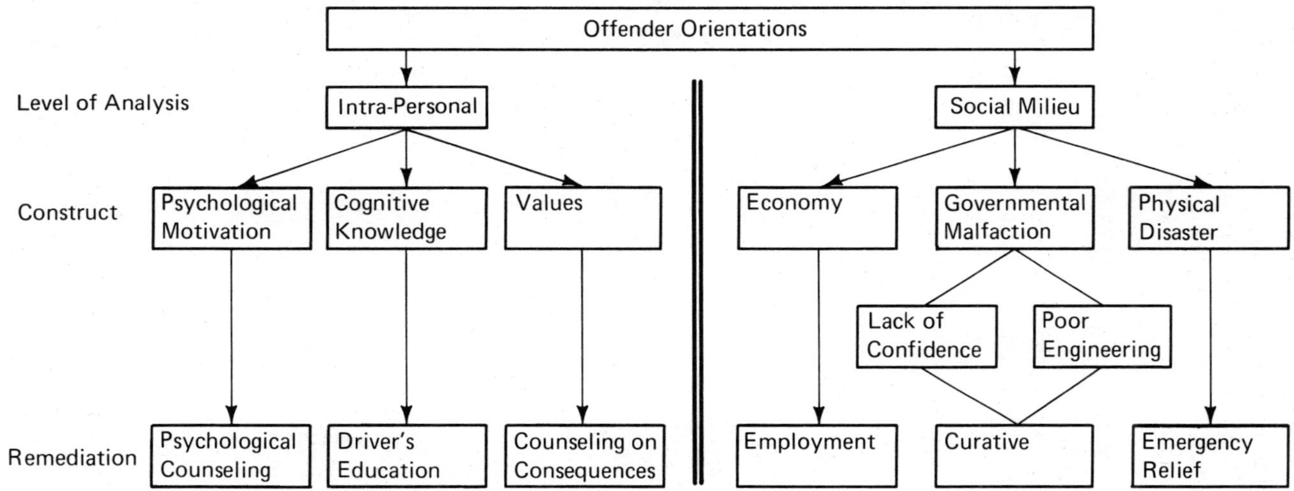

Figure 10-1. Current Mutually Exclusive Intrapersonal and Social Milieu Paradigms.

through the theory of social defense and employing the mechanism of prediction to diminish the risk, or danger, to society. If indeed, prediction is to have both theoretical and practical utility, then this study suggests that simply associating intrapersonal offender characteristics with associated treatments does not fully allow for the range of variables that are significant in successfully predicting desirable outcomes from varying treatment modalities. Rather, not only must those variables relating to intrapersonal characteristics be considered in prediction techniques, so also must the variables of the social milieu paradigm be considered. See Figure 10-2.

Obviously, there are some social milieu factors that typically do not lend themselves to direct judicial intervention. (Even here, however, the judge may, through nonsentencing intervention, engage in indirect remediation through cooperation with other governmental agencies, such as calling upon the traffic department to relocate a poorly placed traffic control device.)

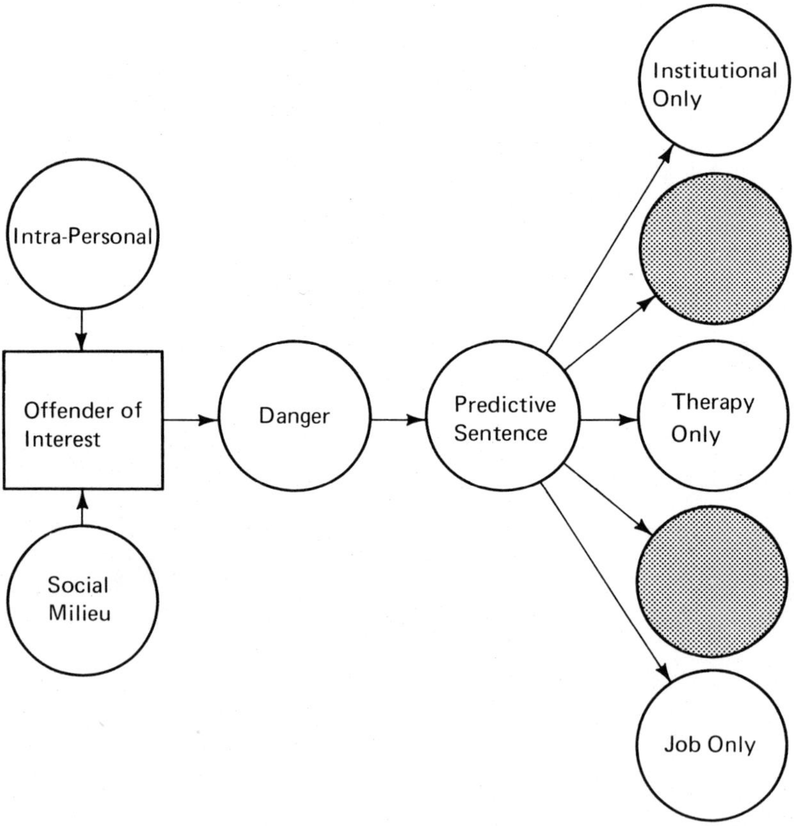

Figure 10-2. Proposed Integrated Intrapersonal and Social Milieu Paradigms.

Of course, our concern here with social milieu factors are with those that the judge can more directly effect through predictive sentencing techniques. However, to take the economy, as measured by the variable, unemployment, as an example, one may argue that the sentencing judge has no control over and cannot alter the economy to improve offender behavior. But as in the case of the intrapersonal paradigm and the use of "psychological counseling" to neutralize the antisocial behavior of the offender, isn't it just as reasonable to suggest that a sentencing judge might engage in prediction techniques that will isolate those types of offenders where remediation is likely to occur through employment?

The Changing Times

Perhaps the most significant, if not startling, outcome of this project is the finding that the effectiveness of social intervention varies over time. Specifically, the effectiveness of individual counseling appears to vary inversely, for example, with the level of employment. Certainly this suggests that in any predictive sentencing scheme attention must be given to the social conditions in which the predictive sentencing takes place. Quite independent of this project, Cronbach suggests that this state of affairs is as it should be:

> A decade from now, with changes in the economy, in social morale, in the family structure, and in aspirations, community attitudes will be different. The rules tested in 1970 might compare very differently if tested again in 1985. We tend to speak of a scientific conclusion as if it were eternal, but in every field empirical relations change.[1]

Of course one may argue that the outcomes observed in this project are nothing more than random fluctuations. The anomalies that were observed may be nothing more than the result of a total lack of treatment effect and the relationships posited between unemployment and treatment effectiveness may simply be spurious associations. Even if this is true, given the overall costs of any predictive sentencing endeavor, the additional time and expense involved in monitoring the treatment effectiveness and associated changes over time in the income and employment levels (or other social conditions) of the offenders sentenced is really quite modest. Consequently, future research might confirm or refute the hunch that the effectiveness of social intervention programs fluctuate over time.

Note

1. Cronbach, Lee J., "Beyond the Two Disciplines of Scientific Psychology," *American Psychologist* 30:2 (February 1975).

11 Looking Ahead

There are at least five research insights that have emerged from this study that should be of assistance to future investigators of prediction and prediction techniques in sentencing. First, the research should extend over a sufficient period of time to allow for and measure fluctuations in social conditions that may influence behavior. Otherwise there is grave risk that results will be clouded with inconsistent findings that will not be supported by sufficient data for reanalysis to even hint at the causes of the inconsistencies.

Second, the investigation should be sufficiently broad in scope to secure as wide a dispersion as possible in the potential target population to include representation in different ethnic, social, and economic strata offenders who differ in the types and seriousness of the crimes committed and courts of varying jurisdictions.

Third, rather than dividing studies between "individually-based" and "job-based" studies, future research should minimally measure explicitly both the offender's world and his social milieu. And, ideally, such experiments would make provision for alteration of crime-linked conditions, such as unemployment.

Fourth, such experimentation might also be stratified to include, say, five periods: typology studies; hypothesizing treatment alternatives for various offender types; sentencing according to the offender–treatment-type hypotheses; evaluating results on danger criteria; and cross-validation to a new population. Such a procedure would have the advantage of separating hypothesis development from hypothesis testing that was a confounding problem with which to deal in this project. Moreover, such a procedure might be less suspect on experimental grounds, since the initial sentencing would begin with an empirically oriented justification for the sentence based upon typology-treatment hypotheses.

Fifth, the features of treatments that work need to be delineated experimentally, and the allocation of treatment(s) needs to be tested experimentally. These proposals are extremely ambitious relative to the typical types of research that are funded. Not only would the first suggestion multiply the time span of research projects, but the other four would multiply the cost per year of such research. The justification for such a time-consuming and expensive path for those who would undertake such an effort is that it would permit the sort of multifactor verification/falsification that Platt maintains separates the branches of science (law) that progress from those that vegetate.[1]

Nor, as is surely obvious, would such an approach lessen the burden placed on sentencing judges who would be willing to function within such a program. Rather, it highlights the complexities inherent in trying to deal with any social problem. Social intervention, generally, and predictive sentencing, particularly, must seemingly cope with individual characteristics, intervention charactertistics, and the interactions between these and the prevailing social conditions if it is to be effective accordingly to current mores over long time periods. If the judicial process is unwilling to deal systematically with these complexities or society is unwilling to find viable alternatives to the current approach to sentencing, we can hardly demand that the sentence of the judge be anything more than a reflection of society's condemnation of the conduct in which the offender has engaged.

Note

1. Platt, J., "Strong Inference," *Science* 146 (October 16, 1964).

Bibliography

Bibliography

Constitutions

Oklahoma Constitution, Article VII, Section I.

United States Constitution, Amendments I, V, VIII, IX, and XIV.

Statutes

Oklahoma, Title 10, §1101(a).

Oklahoma, Title 10, §1111.

Oklahoma, Title 11, §794.

Oklahoma, Title 22, §982.

Ordinances

Code of City of Norman, Oklahoma, §13-504.

Ibid., §14-308.

Ibid., §14-310(b).

Ibid., §20-214.

Court Rules

Federal Rules of Criminal Procedure, Rule 32(c).

Judicial Decisions

Argersinger v. Hamlin, 407 U.S. 25 (1972).

Boyd v. United States, 116 U.S. 626 (1886).

Cox Broadcasting Corp. v. Cohn, 420 U.S. 469 (1975).

Cunningham v. United States, 256 F.2d 467 (5th Cir. 1958).

Eisenstadt v. Baird, 405 U.S. 438 (1972).

Griswold v. Connecticut, 381 U.S. 479 (1965).

Hoyt v. Florida, 368 U.S. 57 (1961).

Hunter v. Slate, 375 P.2d 357 (Okla. 1962).

In re Gault, 387 U.S. 1 (1967).

Jobson v. Henne, 355 F.2d 129 (2d Cir. 1966).

Katz v. United States, 389 U.S. 347 (1967).

Knecht v. Gillman, 488 F.2d 1136 (8th Cir. 1973).

Loving v. Virginia, 388 U.S. 1 (1967).

Meyer v. Nebraska, 262 U.S. 390 (1923).

Moore v. Missouri, 15 U.S. 673 (1895).

Nebraska Press Association v. Hugh Stuart, Judge, U.S. Sup. Ct. Bull., CCH, B-4248, June 30, 1976.

Olmstead v. United States, 277 U.S. 438 (1927).

Palko v. Connecticut, 302 U.S. 319 (1937).

People v. Dukett, 56 Ill. 2d. 432, 308 N.E.2d 590 (1974).

Pierce v. Society of Sisters, 268 U.S. 510 (1925).

Planned Parenthood of Central Missouri v. Danforth, CCH, U.S. Sup. Ct. Bull., no. 74-1151, July 1, 1976.

Prince v. Massachusetts, 321 U.S. 158 (1944).

Procunier v. Martinez, 416 U.S. 397 (1974).

Reed v. Reed, 404 U.S. 71 (1971).

Roe v. Wade, 410 U.S. 113 (1972).

Shepard v. United States, 257 F.2d 293 (6th Cir. 1958).

Sheppard v. Maxwell, 384 U.S. 333 (1966).

Skinner v. Oklahoma, 316 U.S. 535, 541 (1942).

Stanley v. Georgia, 394 U.S. 557 (1969).

Slate v. Meyer, 37 N.W.2d 3 (1949).

Tate v. Short, 401 U.S. 395 (1971).

Terry v. Ohio, 392 U.S. 1 (1968).

Union Pacific R.R. Co. v. Botsford, 141 U.S. 250 (1891).

United States v. Schipani, 435 F.2d 26 (2d Cir. 1970).

Village of Belle Terre v. Boraas, 416 U.S. 1 (1974).

Williams v. New York, 337 U.S. 241 (1949).

Winters v. Miller, 306 F.Supp. 1158 (E.D. N.Y. 1969).

Books

Accident Facts, National Safety Council, 1921-

Ancel, Marc, *Social Defense: A Modern Approach to Criminal Problems* (New York: Schocken Books, 1965).

Baker, Frank B., "Experimental Design Considerations Associated with Large-Scale Research Projects" in Julian C. Stanley (ed.), *Improving Experimental*

Design and Statistical Analysis. Seventh Annual Phi Delta Kappa Symposium on Education Research (Chicago: Ill.: Rand McNally & Co.).

Boruch, Robert, and Henry W. Riecken (eds.), *Social Experimentation: A Method for Planning and Evaluating Social Intervention* (New York: Academic Press, 1974).

Brenner, M. Harvey, *Mental Illness and the Economy* (Cambridge, Mass.: Harvard University Press, 1973).

Campbell, Donald T., and Julian C. Stanley, *Experimental and Quasiexperimental Designs for Research* (Chicago, Ill.: Rand McNally & Co., 1963).

Cronbach, Lee. *Essentials of Psychological Testing*, 2d. ed. (New York: Harper & Row, 1960).

Dixon, W.J., (ed.), *BMD: Biomedical Computer Programs* (Berkeley: University of California Press, 1972).

Fleisher, Belton, M., *The Economics of Delinquency* (Chicago: Quadrangle Books, Inc., 1966).

Frankel, Marvin E., *Criminal Sentences: Law without Order* (New York: Hill and Wang, 1973).

Gerber, Rudolph J., and McAnany, Patrick D., *Contemporary Punishment: Views, Explanations and Justifications*, University of Notre Dame Press, (1972).

Glasser, William, *Reality Therapy* (New York: Harper and Row, 1965).

Gottfredson, Don M., "Prosecution and Sentencing Decisions" in *Decision Making in the Criminal Justice System.* Reviews and Essays, National Institute of Mental Health, Center for Studies of Crime and Delinquency, (1975).

Heinlein, Robert A., *Revolt in 2100*, Signet ed. (New York: New American Library, 1954).

Holsti, Ole R., *Content Analysis*, in Lindzey, Gardner, and Bronson, (eds.), *The Handbook of Social Psychology* (Reading, Mass.: Addison-Wesley, 1968).

H.U.D. Management Assistance Program, *Survey and Analysis Findings and Recommendations*, Prepared for Model Cities Department, City of Lawton, Lawton, Oklahoma by CONSAD Research Corporation (December 1971).

Laurer, A.R., *The Psychology of Driving* (Springfield, Ill.: Charles C. Thomas, 1972).

Long, Lucinda, "Innovation in Urban Criminal Courts," in Jacob, H., (ed.), *The Potential for Reform of Criminal Justice* (Beverly Hills, CA.: Sage Publications 1974).

Michael, Jerome, and Wechsler, Herbert, *Criminal Law and Its Administration* (Chicago: The Foundation Press, 1940).

Middendorff, Wold, *The Effectiveness of Punishment (Especially in Relation to Traffic Offenses)* (South Hackensack, N.J.: Fred B. Rothman & Co., 1968).

Morris, Norval, and Hawkins, Gordon, *The Honest Politicians Guide to Crime Control*, University of Chicago, 1970.

Mullen, Joan, et al., *Pretrial Services: An Evaluation of Policy Related Research* (Cambridge, Mass.: Abt Associates Inc., 1974).

Packer, H., *The Limits of the Criminal Sanction* (Stanford: Stanford University Press, 1968).

Parry, *Aggression on the Road* (London: Tavistock Publications, 1968).

Pelz, Donald C., and Schuman, Stanley H., *Countermeasures for Young Drivers*, University of Michigan Press, (1972).

Roethlisberger, F.S., and Dickson, W.J., *Management and the Worker* (Cambridge, Mass.: Harvard University Press, 1939).

Roszak, Theodore, *Where the Wasteland Ends. Politics and Transcendence in Postindustrial Society* (Garden City, New York: Doubleday and Co., Inc., 1972).

Skogan, W., "Traffic and Crime: Social Change and Organizational Response," in Jacob, H., (ed.), *The Potential for Reform of Criminal Justice* (Beverly Hills, Ca.: Sage Publication, 1974).

Stone, Philip J., Dunphy, Dexter C., Smith, Marshall S., and Ogilvie, Daniel M., *The General Inquirer: A Computer Approach to Content Analysis* (Cambridge, Mass.: The M.I.T. Press, 1966).

Taggart, Robert, III, *The Prison of Unemployment: Manpower Programs for Offenders* (Baltimore, Md.: Johns Hopkins University Press, 1972).

United Nations Social Defense Research Institute. *Economic Crisis and Crime* (Rome, Italy: UNSDRI publication no. 9, 1974; Publication no. 15, 1976).

Veldman, D.J., *Fortran Programming for the Behavioral Sciences* (New York: Holt, Reinhart and Winston, 1967).

Votey, Harold L., and Phillips, Llad, "The Control of Criminal Activity: An Economic Analysis," in Glaser, D., (ed.), *Handbook of Crimonology* (Chicago: Rand McNally, 1974).

Whinery, et al., *Predictive Sentencing of 16-18 Year-Old Male Habitual Traffic Offenders*, Final Report, University of Oklahoma Office of Research Administration (1976).

Willett, T.C., *Criminal on the Road*, (London: Tavistock Publications, 1964).

Wolfgang, M.E., Figlio, R.M., and Sellin, T., *Delinquency in a Birth Cohort* (Chicago: The University of Chicago Press, 1972).

Articles

Bennett, Stephen A., "Rehabilitation in Check," *12 Trial 12*, Cambridge, Mass.: Association of Trial Lawyers of America (1976).

Campbell, Donald T., "Legal Reforms as Experiments." *Journal of Legal Education* 23:1, 1970, pp. 217-239.

Cronbach, Lee J., "Beyond the Two Disciplines of Scientific Psychology," *American Psychologist* 30:2, (February 1975).

Danziger, Sheldon, and Wheeler, David, "The Economics of Crime: Punishment or Income Redistribution," *Review of Social Economy* 33, no. 2, (October 1975), pp. 113-131.

Ehrlich, Isaac, "Participation in Illegitimate Activities: A Theoretical and Empirical Investigation," *Journal of Political Economy* 81, no. 3, (1973), pp. 521-565.

Fleisher, Belton M., "The Effect of Unemployment on Juvenile Delinquency," *Journal of Political Economy* 71:6, (December 1963).

Galliher, John F., and McCartney, James L., "The Influence of Funding Agencies on Juvenile Delinquency Research," *Social Problems* 21:1, (Summer 1973).

Gunther, Gerald, "The Supreme Court 1971 Term, Foreword: In Search of Evolving Doctrine on a Changing Court: A Model for a Newer Equal Protection," *Harv. L. Rev.* 86:1, (1972).

Heussenstamm, F.K., "Bumper Stickers and the Cops," *Trans-Action* (February 1971), pp. 32-35.

"IRS Newsletter," Institute for Social Research, The University of Michigan, (Summer 1975).

Nowak, John E., "Realigning the Standards of Review under the Equal Protection Guarantee–Prohibited, Neutral, and Permissive Classifications, *Ga. L.J.* 62:1071, (1974).

Note, "Conditioning and Other Technologies Used to Treat? Rehabilitate? Demolish? Prisoners and Mental Patients," *Calif. L. Rev.* 45:616, 641-655, (1972).

Note, "Legal Implication of Psychological Research with Human Subjects," *Duke L.J.* 1960:265.

Pepinsky, Harold E., "Police Decision-Making," in Don M. Gottfredson, (ed.), *Decision-Making in the Criminal Justice System: Reviews and Essays* (Rockville, Md.: National Institute of Mental Health, Center for Studies of Crime and Delinquency, 1975), pp. 40-43.

Platt, John R., "Strong Inference," *Science* 146:3642, (October 16, 1964), pp. 347-353.

Prosser, "Privacy," *Calif. L. Rev.* 48:383 (1960).

Pound, "Interests of Personality," *Harv. L. Rev.* 28:343, (1915).

Rachin, Richard L., "Reality Therapy: Helping People Help Themselves," *Crime and Delinquency* 20:1974, p. 45.

Ross, H. Lawrence, and Blumenthal, Murray, "Some Problems in Experimentation in a Legal Setting," *The American Sociologist* 10:150-155, (August 1975).

Ross, H. Lawrence, "Traffic Law Violation: A Folk Crime," *Social Problems* 8 (Winter 1960-1961), pp. 231-241.

Rubin, Sol, "Disparity and Equality of Sentences—A Constitutional Challenge," *F.R.D.* 40:55 (1967).

Ruebhausen, Oscar M., and Brim, Orville G., Jr., "Privacy and Behavioral Research," *Col. L. Rev.* 65:1184, 1187 (1965).

Shils, Edward, "Privacy: Its Constitution and Vicissitudes," *Law and Contemp. Prob.* 1966:281, 284 (1966).

Warren and Brandeis, "The Right to Privacy," *Harv. L. Rev.* 4:193, (1890).

Whinery, "Policy, Legislation and Organization of Municipal Courts in Oklahoma," *Okl. L. Rev.* 18:1, (1965).

Whinery, "Organizing Municipal Courts in Oklahoma under the New Judicial Article, *O.B.A.J.* 39:2511, (1968).

Wilkinson III, J. Harvie, "The Supreme Court, The Equal Protection Clause, and the Three Faces of Constitutional Equality," *Va. L. Rev.* 61:945, (1975).

Zeisel, Hans, "Reflections on Experimental Techniques in the Law, *J. Legal Studies* 2:107, (1973).

Zeisel, Hans, "Reducing the Hazards of Human Experiments through Modifications in Research Design, *Annals N.Y. Acad. Sci.* 169:475, (1970).

Book Reviews

Morris, Norval, "Juvenile Offenders before the Courts," *Yale L.J.* 66:962, (1956).

News Articles

Anonymous, "Crime: A Case for More Punishment," *Business Week* (September 15, 1976), pp. 92-97.

Malloy, Michael T., "Punishment is a Deterrent to Crime," *National Observer* (June 19, 1976), p. 1 and p. 13.

The Norman Transcript, September 29, 1965.

Ibid., October 27, 1965.

Ibid., November 3, 1966.

Ibid., September 26, 1968.

Ibid., February 17, 1969.

Ibid., March 10, 1971.

Ibid., September 12, 1971.

Ibid., September 14, 1971.

Ibid., September 15, 1971.

The Oklahoma Daily, November 12, 1969.

The Sunday Oklahoma, September 12, 1971.

Miscellaneous

Krisberg, B., and Takagi, P., "Ethical Issues in Evaluating Criminal Justice Demonstration Projects." Paper read at American Criminology Society, New York (November 1973).

Tarver, Don, Personal Communication, 1972.

Index

Index

About the Authors

Leo H. Whinery is a professor of law at the University of Oklahoma, Presiding Judge of the Municipal Criminal Court of Norman, Oklahoma, and a member of the Oklahoma and American Bar Associations. Judge Whinery also serves as a member of the Faculty of the National College of the State Judiciary and lectures for the American Academy of Judicial Education. He has written extensively in the fields of Federal Taxation, Evidence and Juvenile Delinquency, and is a co-author of *Final Report, Predictive Sentencing of 16-18 Year Old Male Habitual Traffic Offenders* (University of Oklahoma Office of Research Administration, 1976) and *Cases and Materials on Tax Practice and Procedure* (University of Oklahoma Law Center, 1975), and is the author of *Manual of Evidence* (National Highway Traffic Safety Administration, 1973), and *Readings on Problems of the Juvenile Offender* (University of Oklahoma College of Law, 1972). He has held fellowships from Columbia University and the Ford Foundation and is the recipient of numerous awards for excellence in teaching, research, and judicial improvement. Judge Whinery lectures extensively throughout the United States on evidence and the sentencing of misdemeanants.

Thomas J. Nagy is a research fellow at the Center for the Study of Law and Society of the University of California, Berkeley. Dr. Nagy serves as research director for the Law Enforcement Assistance Administration funded Empirical Investigation of the Effects of Omnibus Hearing on Measures of Efficiency and Justice Project of the American Bar Association's Section of Criminal Justice. He held research fellowships and assistantships from the Office of Education and National Aeronautics and Space Administration during graduate studies at the University of Texas at Austin. While coauthoring *Final Report, Predictive Sentencing of 16-18 Year Old Male Habitual Traffic Offenders* (University of Oklahoma Office of Research Administration, 1976), he held appointments at the University of Oklahoma College of Law, and the Department of Human Relations. He has published in research methods, statistics, content analysis and psychopharmacology.

Gregory A. Sather is a Research Associate for the Southwest Center for Human Relations Studies, Oklahoma Center for Continuing Education, University of Oklahoma. He received the B.S. in Physics from the University of Oklahoma and served as Research Associate for the Predictive Sentencing Project. He is coauthor of *Final Report, Predictive Sentencing of 16-18 Year Old Male Habitual Traffic Offenders* (University of Oklahoma Office of Research Administration, 1976) and is a participant in various educational and psychological conferences.

Kaye Donald Fisher served as Chief Probation Officer, City of Norman, Oklahoma from 1968-1975. He received the B.S. in Business Administration from the University of Oklahoma. He is a coauthor of *Final Report, Predictive Sentencing of 16-18 Year Old Male Habitual Traffic Offenders* (University of Oklahoma Office of Research Administration, 1976), and has served as an active counselor in the Boy Scouts of America and the Community Mental Health Center in Norman. Mr. Fisher is also the author of procedures manuals and technical reports relating to the Predictive Sentencing Project.